LEADERING VISUALS ONE

LEADERING VISUALS ONE

Paradigm Shift to Peak Legacy

Lauren Holmes

Naturality.Net

Toronto

Copyright © 2010 by Lauren Holmes.

All rights reserved.

This publication may not be reproduced, stored in a retrieval system, or transmitted in whole or in part, in any form or by any means, electronic, mechanical, photocopying, recording, or otherwise, without the prior written permission of the copyright owner. For private use only.
Reproduction or translation of any part of this work beyond that permitted by Section 107 or 108 of the 1976 United States Copyright Act without the permission of the copyright owner is unlawful. Brief quotations embodied in critical articles and reviews are permitted.
LEADERING and FRONTIERING are trademarks owned by Lauren Holmes. All rights reserved.
Requests for permission or further information should be addressed to Permissions, Leadering, 123 Queen Street West, Box 164, Toronto, ON, Canada or emailed to info@leadering.com.
Leadering Education:
    Leadering.com   Leadering™ Expertise Development
Leadering Application:
    Frontiering.com   Leadering™ Legacy-Making Services and Products

FIRST EDITION

Cover Image © iLexx

Library of Congress in Publication Data

Holmes, Lauren
    Leadering Visuals One

1. Success 2. Personal Development 3. Professional Development 4. Leadership
5. Performance 6. Entrepreneurial Development 7. Self-Help I. Holmes, Lauren II. Title

ISBN: 978-0-9711981-4-2

Manufactured in the United States of America by Naturality.Net, LLC

Dedicated to those who commit their unique creative expression to advancing our world

Many persons have a wrong idea of what constitutes true happiness. It is not attained through self-gratification but through fidelity to a worthy purpose.
Helen Keller

Only the consciousness of a purpose that is mightier than any man and worthy of all men can fortify and inspirit and compose the souls of men
Walter Lippmann

There were moments of epiphany in Leadering™ that brought tears to my eyes and left me forever changed, forever elevated by a more expansive vision, a greater truth that, once experienced, can never be forgotten or reversed.
EVP, a global financial institution

LEADERING VISUALS ONE
Paradigm Shift to Peak Legacy

LEADERING SUPPORT

info@leadering.com

EDUCATION: **Leadering.com** Leadering™ Expertise Development

Educational support for such things as speeding and integrating the paradigm shift, Leadering's paradigm personalization exercises, identifying client strategies for peak legacy, growth, and re-centring to core strength, action-learning experimentation, and breaking through frontiering and adaptivity challenges.

APPLICATION: **Frontiering.com** Leadering Legacy-Making Services and Products

On your behalf, multi-disciplinary experts will design, launch, and accelerate companies, philanthropic organizations, careers, and fields of study or invention personalized in Leadering terms for your peak legacy until you feel you comfortable taking over. Alternatively, we can support you in launching your own structure(s) through which to achieve your peak legacy.

RECRUITMENT: Become a Leadering Support Services Provider

If you wish to provide products and services through either Leadering.com or Frontiering.com you are invited to email the following to info@leadering.com: your proposed offerings, your credentials, and a brief summary of your personal peak legacy findings from Leadering's flow maximization exercises (*Leadering Visuals Two*, recordings 10-18).

Leadering™ instills an integrated system of meta-skills, dynamics, drives, reflexes, instincts, identities, ways of operating, and evolved states of being and consciousness shared by adept leaders, entrepreneurs, innovators, and achievers. This system has been formulated into a powerful paradigm so that it can be assimilated through a single paradigm shift. The shift spans 25 recordings and a multitude of original visuals and exercises. The magnitude and speed of transformation is unprecedented.

Nature has a plethora of mechanisms and forces dedicated to *maximizing* and *synchronizing human systems* that are already advancing our world. Leadering™ empowers one to adapt to and harness these existing powers and processes inside and outside of us to achieve one's greatest legacy, one's greatest contribution to that advance.

As such, leaving your most impactful lifetime footprint - your peak legacy - requires *frontiering*™ *to* penetrate new territory, and *creation* to bring 'the new' into existence. All of these elements define the essence and dynamics of leadership, even if leading is not your goal. Hence the name, '*Leadering*™'.

LEADERING™ CULTIVATES NEW FUNCTIONALITY IN HUMAN SYSTEMS:
individuals - companies - countries - civilizations

- **Mental agility and thinking modes** such as systems, conceptual, abstract, deductive, inductive, relational, and big-picture thinking
  (expanded and unity consciousness)

- **Frontiering™ new territory**: leading, entrepreneuring, pioneering, innovating, creating, adapting, resolving ambiguity, learning agility, model development / application, pattern / trend recognition, environmental scanning, problem reframing, and a propensity for unfounded knowing, AHA! experiences, creative inspirations, and coincidences

- **Collaboration and cooperativeness:**
  - multi-system mode of operation
  - mass maximization, mass transformation, mass synchronization
  - co-evolving, co-creating, integrating, adapting, synergizing, partnering, and clustering
  - the thinking modes listed above, especially systems, relational, conceptual, and big-picture thinking
  - contributions to humanity's evolution goals as a byproduct of meeting one's own goals.

- **Performance:** as a result of the above. As well, Leadering™ maximizes us in our peak-performing, peak-growth, talent-based, *flow* state

LEADERING VISUALS ONE
Paradigm Shift to Peak Legacy

LEADERING BOOK INDEX

1. GETTING STARTED

2. PRE- AND POST-PROGRAM ASSESSMENT

3. THE PROGRAM

4. THE PARADIGM

5. THE PARADIGM SHIFT PROCESS

6. FIFTEEN PARADIGM LEADER DRIVES
   to maximize human systems for goal achievement

7. PERSONALIZING THE PARADIGM - EXERCISES I
   I FLOW maximization exercises   (Leadering *Visuals Two*)

8. PERSONALIZING THE PARADIGM - EXERCISES II
   II BELIEF maximization exercises

9. COMPLETING THE PARADIGM SHIFT

10. OPERATIONALIZING THE PARADIGM

11. LEADERING: A POWER TOOL FOR
    LEADERS or SYSTEM MAXIMIZERS

12. THE USER'S GUIDE

13. THE DEVELOPMENT OF LEADERING

LEADING VISUALS INDEX

LEADERING VISUALS INDEX

LEADERING RECORDING TITLE and DESCRIPTION	MINUTES	FIGURES	PAGE NO.
1 GETTING STARTED			
2 PRE- AND POST-PROGRAM ASSESSMENT			
3 THE LEADERING™ PROGRAM			1
1. Leadering™ Program Overview	17	3	1
THE MULTI-HOUR PARADIGM SHIFT NOW BEGINS			
4 THE LEADERING™ PARADIGM			
2. Leadering™ Paradigm Overview	43	1	5
3. *Leadering frequency workout gym™*	5		7
4. Leadering™ Paradigm Components	38	6	7
5 THE PARADIGM SHIFT PROCESS			
5. Leadering™ Paradigm Shift	19	1	17
6. Leadering™ Quantum Leap Overview	16	4	19
7. Leadering™ Quantum Leap Process	50	10	25
8. The Quantum Leap to Quantum Leap Expert	74	6	37
6 FIFTEEN PARADIGM LEADER DRIVES			45
to maximize human systems for goal achievement Adept leaders and system maximizers operate as extensions of nature's system's maximization process. The 15 dynamics of the Leadering™ systems maximization toolkit are presented in 1 presentation that has been broken into 8 parts. The same 21 recordings are shared by each of these 8 recordings.			
9. 15 Leader Drives			45
9.1 Introduction	23	Same 21	46
9.2 Systems mindset: congruence, systems-based expanded consciousness	22	Same 21	47
9.3 Advancement mechanics: quantum leap templating, self-organizing, emergence	22	Same 21	47
9.4 Advancement directions: knowledge-pursuit	16	Same 21	47
9.5 Advancement directions: adaptation, evolution	17	Same 21	48
9.6 Leader drives quantum leap preparation and initiation, plus the part that the frontier-pursuit drive, creation / creativity-pursuit drives play in all the dynamics	22	Same 21	48
9.7 Co-evolution, talent-based flow, flow-to-flow plus additional information for the frontier-pursuit drive and the creation / creativity-pursuit drives	55	Same 21	49
9.8 Quantum leap to operating with the 15 leader drives as a way of life. Repeated post-paradigm-shift as recording 24: Driving a Multi-System Paradigm	57	Same 21	50

LEADING VISUALS INDEX

LEADERING RECORDING TITLE and DESCRIPTION	MINUTES	FIGURES	PAGE NO.

7 PERSONALIZING THE LEADERING™ PARADIGM
INSTRUCTIONS:
I FLOW MAXIMIZATION EXERCISES
II BELIEF MAXIMIZATION EXERCISES
    Completing the Paradigm Shift
    Operationalizing the Paradigm

I FLOW MAXIMIZATION EXERCISES: Transferred to *Leadering Visuals Two*

These exercises may be started any time after the Paradigm Shift Launch but cannot be completed before completing 6. The *Fifteen Paradigm Leader Drives*.

Take advantage of your altered state of more expanded functionality resulting from each audio to aerial view your system and your life as a system to more accurately complete the *Paradigm Personalization Exercises* (Sections 7 and 8).

(a) This will increase your precision and power when driving the Leadering™ paradigm.
(b) Improving your accuracy with these core determination exercises for your own system will train you to more accurately apply the same insights to other human systems such as individuals, organizations, families, communities, countries, and all of human civilization in order to maximize them for goal achievement.

10. Big-Picture positioning for developing your 5 maximizing formulas	22	15	Visuals Two
ADVANCING YOUR SYSTEM			
Formula 1: Talent-based lifetime development formula			
Formula 2: Greatest lifetime level of talent-based operation as an individual			Visuals Two
ADVANCING YOUR SYSTEM BY ADVANCING OTHER HUMAN SYSTEMS			
Formula 3: Talent-based leadership formula			Visuals Two
Formula 4: Talent-based leadership development formula			
Formula 5: Greatest life-time level of talent-based operation as a leader or *systems maximizer*			
11. Introduction to the 5 Leadering™ Maximizing formulas	18	12	
12. Advice for the core determination exercises for identifying one's 5 maximizing formulas for the Leadering™ paradigm	11	4	Visuals Two
13. Life Themes Exercises	48	5	
14. Key-Talent System-Application Exercise	36	28	
15. Growth built into the Leadering™ paradigm	23	19	
16. Key Talents Exercises	21	17	
17. 5-Formula Exercise Preparation	51	18	

LEADERING VISUALS INDEX

LEADERING RECORDING TITLE and DESCRIPTION	MINUTES	FIGURES	PAGE NO.
18. Determining your 5 Formulas for maximizing in the Leadering™ paradigm	34	18	Visuals Two
Exercises, notes, and questions to assist you in determining each of your 5 formulas for maximizing within the Leadering™ paradigm			Visuals Two
Formula 1: 14 figures	0	14	
Formula 2: 8 figures	0	8	
Formula 3: 17 figures	0	17	Visuals Two
Formula 4: 18 figures	0	18	
Formula 5: 13 figures	0	13	
8 PERSONALIZING THE PARADIGM			74
II BELIEF MAXIMIZATION EXERCISES to support Flow Maximization			
These exercises may be started any time after the Paradigm Shift Launch but cannot be completed before completing the Paradigm-Based Leadership segment			
19. Belief Maximization Introduction: Identity Quantum leaps:	108	41	74
9 COMPLETING THE PARADIGM SHIFT			113
20. Natural Identity quantum leaps (immutable beliefs):	50	39	113
Subset: Growth or expansion identity quantum leaps			
Completing the Paradigm Shift: Natural identity quantum leaps (immutable beliefs)			
Operationalizing the Paradigm: Growth or expansion identity quantum leaps			
The transition from completing the paradigm shift to operating in the paradigm is made within this recording			
10 OPERATIONALIZING THE PARADIGM			155
21. Goal-driven Identity quantum leaps (changeable beliefs):	35	20	155
Subset: Flow-driven identity quantum leaps			
Subset: Corporate identity quantum Leaps			
22. Belief Clearing with Identity quantum leaps	18	9	177
23. Multi-System Identity quantum leaps	41	23	189
Leadering™ toolkit identity quantum leaps			
Subset: Leadering™ meta-competency identity quantum leaps			
Quantum leaps to goal 'states of being' rather than goal 'states':			
Subset: Assimilated Expert Identity quantum leaps			
Subset: Projected Expert Identity quantum leaps			

LEADERING VISUALS INDEX

LEADERING RECORDING TITLE and DESCRIPTION	MINUTES	FIGURES	PAGE NO.
24. Driving a Multi-System Paradigm (Repeat of 9h post-shift)	57	1	213
OPERATING THE LEADERING™ PARADIGM: **Action-Learning Experimentation** Action-learning experimentation with the Leadering™ paradigm is encouraged for the rest of your life to accelerate the advancement of your functionality and achievement.			215
11 Leadering - A POWER TOOL FOR LEADERS or SYSTEMS MAXIMIZERS			
25. Capitalizing on human systems for goal achievement	24	10	215
12 THE LEADERING™ USERS GUIDE			225
1. Powering your paradigm shift	14	0	
2. Only need to be a paradigm driver not a mechanic	8	0	
3. Timing for progressing through the program	5	0	
4. Overwhelm is a Leadering™ tool for stretching you to new meta-competencies	3	0	
5. Falling asleep during the recordings: What is really going on?	4	0	
6. Visuals: their importance	3	0	
7. Personalization Exercises Tips	1	0	
8. Leadering™ Program Support	4	0	
9. Arguments for beliefs create reality concept	8	0	
10. Examples of cascading quantum leaps incited by a quantum leap to a belief-created reality. The strengthening of the beliefs and belief engineering capabilities to create and develop leaders.	13	0	
11. How Leadering™ Works	5	0	
12. The Leadering™ frequency workout gym	5	0	

We would value your feedback

Send comments, experiences, or suggestions to info@leadering.com

Leadering - Merging man's machinery with nature's	**1 GETTING STARTED**	Leadering - Capitalizing on a Man-Nature synergy

The Leadering™ paradigm shift program is not a course. It is not about learning the content of these recordings. Rather, Leadering™ is about being transformed by listening to them. Leadering™ is experiential learning. As you stretch to understand the expansive content of these recordings, you will emerge with new functionality and a compelling new modus operandi based on them.

Each recording is similar to a trip to the gym for a workout. Each recording allows you to experience an upgraded way of operating. Each installs an integrated system of drives, reflexes, meta-skills, beliefs, information, identities, and expansions of consciousness normally inherent in adept leaders, entrepreneurs, innovators and achievers. The 'new muscles' resulting from the workout lock the upgraded way of operating into your system. Leadering™ rewires individuals for maximum growth, functionality, and achievement. Entrepreneurship, leadership, and innovation are obviously byproducts whether they are your goals or not.

Every 'workout' recording activates natural growth mechanisms inside of you. The concept parallels how holistic medicine stimulates the body's natural healing mechanisms. Levers are triggered by the Leadering™ recordings which will launch self-compelling, addictive growth continuums which will advance your system for the rest of your life. Continuous and accelerating increases in functionality and performance maximums will become routine once Leadering™ initiates the process.

The program includes almost 20 hours of recordings plus transforming exercises which will take from 1 to 10 hours depending on how centred you already are on the natural core of your system. We recommend that you complete the paradigm shift with its personalization exercises within 1 month at most.

Each recording builds on the previous one to accumulate transformative pressures within your system. Therefore, for each time you choose to repeat the paradigm shift over your lifetime, listen to the recordings in the order prescribed in a concentrated time period. This will build the intensity required to fuel your quantum leap into the Leadering™ paradigm. Work at the ideal transformative pace for you while trying to honour these timing and order guidelines.

Most recordings need only be reviewed once. To return to them before you have completed your current paradigm shift would undo the progress of that paradigm shift. Repeating others such as those below will accelerate and enhance your transformative experience.
- Audio 8: the quantum leap to quantum leap expert
- Audio 9h and 24: driving a multi-system paradigm
- Audios 10 to 19: the paradigm personalization exercises

There are Users Guide recordings listed at the end of the program to assist with your successful paradigm shift. You can listen to these as often as you want. To pick up any information you missed or to upgrade your functionality further, repeat the paradigm shift in its entirely as many times as you would like over your lifetime. You will hear and absorb different information at each level of your advancement.

So much excess capacity is built into the Leadering™ program that it is equally suited to individuals and world players, and whole human systems spanning from individuals to families to companies and even to countries. Excess capacity has been built in by design to stretch participants beyond previous capabilities. Leadering™ is universally transformative no matter who you are or how many times you repeat the paradigm shift over your lifetime. You will experience comparable magnitudes of transformation no matter what your level of functionality is when you start.

Become comfortable with the necessary overwhelm. If Leadering's excess capacity becomes too overwhelming, listen to recording 4 in the Users Guide. Give yourself permission to absorb only what is comfortable for you with each repeat of the program and leave the rest for a future iteration of the paradigm shift. A cup can only be filled to its brim. When you have integrated what is in the first cup into your system, you will have an empty cup to be filled again with your next repeat of the paradigm shift. You will come to value the comprehensivenss and complexity that is behind Leadering's ability to continuously advance your system to new levels of functionality, achievement, and understanding over your lifetime, no matter how advanced you become.

Penetrating exercises in sections 7 and 8 provide extreme self-knowledge. They personalize the Leadering™ paradigm to maximize your system and performance. You can begin the exercises anytime after completing the *Quantum Leap to Quantum Leap Expert* at the end of the section entitled: 5. *The Paradigm Shift Process*. However, you will need to incorporate the information from Section 6 about the 15 leader dynamics and drives inherent in the paradigm before finalizing your exercise results.

Enjoy your paradigm shift to the extraordinary. Leadering equips you to achieve your most profound, most impactful, and most meaningful lifetime legacy and to significantly advance our world. **Leadering**™ **creates and arms world changers.** Imagine the impact of a massive number of maximized people. *Join the global paradigm shift to evolved states of being and contributing.*

LEADERING SUPPORT   info@leadering.com

EDUCATION: Leadering.com   Leadering™ Expertise Development

APPLICATION: Frontiering.com   Leadering™ Legacy-Making Support Services

RECRUITMENT: Become a Leadering™ Support Services Provider

2   PRE- AND POST-PROGRAM ASSESSMENT

PRE-PROGRAM ASSESSMENT TEST
Operating in the Leadering paradigm is continuously transformative. If you would like to track your increase in functionality, take one or more recognized assessment tests to establish a baseline for comparison. Assess cognitive skills such as abstract thinking, conceptual-thinking, big-picture thinking, system thinking, mastering unknown territory, self-knowledge, strength that comes from being centred on one's natural core, creativity, innovation, leadership, entrepreneurship, and the other meta-skills identified in the program.

POST-PROGRAM ASSESSMENT TEST
Six months or more after your paradigm shift and periodically over your lifetime, take the same recognized assessment test to determine the magnitude of the improvement in your relevant meta-skills, cognitive skills, self-awareness, understanding, and ability to achieve goals.

3 THE LEADERING™ PROGRAM

1. **Leadering™ Program Overview** 17 minutes 3 figures
   The Leadering™ intervention incites a shift to a new paradigm in which the dynamics underpinning leaders, entrepreneurs, innovators, and high achievers have been embedded as a logically integrated system.

   This presentation provides an introduction and orientation to the Leadering™ program: Leadering™ does not simply impart useful information as so many other education programs do. Nor is it a skill development course. Rather, Leadering™ installs dynamics. Leadering™ is a transformative intervention. It is a transforming experience.

   Leadering™ cultivates an integrated system of the meta-competencies, dynamics, drives, reflexes, instincts, identities and consciousness underpinning natural leaders, entrepreneurs, innovators and high achievers. This system is engrained into a powerful logically integrated paradigm so that it can be assimilated through a simple paradigm shift. This differs from traditional leadership and personal development courses which tend to teach skills or address learning topics serially.

   Because this paradigm is logically interconnected, parts of the paradigm can be deduced by knowing other parts of the paradigm. Eventually you will have a critical mass of knowledge which catalyzes the paradigm shift.

   Each recording feeds you more systems of information, beliefs, and ways of operating until you have internalized a critical mass of knowledge about the paradigm. You basically reach a point of no return whereby the paradigm makes too much sense not to govern your behaviour. You emerge operating with the dynamics, drives, reflexes, and meta-competencies that we associate with natural leaders, entrepreneurs, innovators and top performers. Your ability to lead, pioneer, innovate and achieve are launched on an ever-advancing continuum.

   This paradigm is not simply a generic paradigm whereby one size fits all. Rather, the Leadering™ machinery needs to be personalized to each individual wanting to drive it. As a result, your natural talents and their associated drives, beliefs, and passions are incorporated into the system of dynamics comprising the paradigm. This not only customizes the paradigm to your system, but launches you along a series of natural growth paths built into both your system and the paradigm.

   The more you use your natural talent-based drives, the more you will want to use them. They are self-addicting. The paradigm couples these addictive drives with the installation of a series of conditioned reflexes to accelerate you along evolving pathways that your system would pursue anyway if given total freedom and resources.

Paradigm Shift to Peak Legacy

The result is life-long personal development, leadership development, entrepreneurial development, innovation development, and performance enhancement. It never ends. This Leadering™ program merely launches a series of automatic natural growth continuums. For the rest of your life, your functionality and the baseline potential of your system will continuously increase. Progress along these continuums is prompted by internal and external events triggering conditioned reflexes and igniting your natural drives.

Leadering™ is about operating and advancing naturally. If somehow over the course of your life, you have moved away from the natural modus operandi of your system, Leadering™ puts you right back into the centre of your being so you can operate continuously to the maximum capacity of your system, expressing the meaningful creativity your system has evolved to do, and achieving the level of greatness that has always been latent within your system.

Learning about the Leadering™ paradigm is used as the means to prepare participants to drive the Leadering™ machinery for goal achievement which is the goal of the paradigm shift. This recording introduces a new, more powerful way of achieving given the advantages of this paradigm. This process is repeated with each recording until all parts of the logically integrated paradigm have been introduced and assimilated.

KEY ELEMENTS OF LEADERING™

Paradigm

Paradigm Shift Process

Systems Maximization Toolkit
(for all human systems)

Driving the Paradigm Machinery

THE LEADERING™ PARADIGM:
Nature's systems maximization process is the metaphor defining the paradigm

THE LEADERING™ PARADIGM is a logically integrated system composed of the following subsystems:

systems of beliefs	beliefs systems are installed through: • quantum leaps • metaphors or comparison to existing shared systems of beliefs • identities • models • the compelling logic of how the paradigm operates
systems of drives	new drives include reactivating drives which have been culturally repressed
systems of natural dynamics, forces, and growth mechanisms acting on all human systems from inside and outside	scientifically based
systems of conditioned reflexes	reflexes are triggered by internal and external events
systems of meta-competencies	especially those found in successful leaders, entrepreneurs, innovators and high performers
systems of information	audios, visuals, metaphors, models
your system	especially your core system of key talents and the addictive drives which draw you to use and improve them. This is how natural forces are trying to maximize your system.

© 2006 Lauren Holmes

THE LEADERING™ PARADIGM SHIFT:
A Worldview Replacement

THE LEADERING™ PARADIGM SHIFT uses the following to dramatically augment your performance and functionality and to launch mechanisms for accelerated growth over your lifetime.

Almost 20 hours of audios explaining how the paradigm works	<ul><li>to provide compelling logic for the shift</li><li>to define the target modus operandi and dynamics</li><li>to prepare one to drive the machinery</li><li>to stretch one's capabilities to increase functionality (like a workout at the gym)</li><li>to expand consciousness, perspective and conceptual skills</li><li>to cultivate systems thinking</li></ul>
Visuals	<ul><li>to clarify</li><li>to provide more information more quickly than can be achieved verbally</li><li>to compensate for less developed cognitive skills and stimulate their development</li><li>to change perspective – see the world differently</li><li>to push natural growth levers</li><li>to coalesce individuals around natural vortexes within their systems</li><li>to build a visual of all of the dimensions of the paradigm</li></ul>
Iterations of explaining the component and then reintegration of component(s) into the total dynamic paradigm	moving up and down a continuum from fragmentation to unity consciousness
Paradigm personalization exercises	<ul><li>learning about one's system and the paradigm from historical themes from one's past</li><li>capitalizing on those themes and dynamics over one's lifetime</li><li>maximizing one's performance in the paradigm</li><li>action learning experimentation</li><li>the exercises prove the paradigm</li></ul>
Quantum leap process	a rapid-fire nonlinear process of exchanging one systems of beliefs for another
Conditioned reflexes	to launch event-driven life-long growth continuums and processes.
Innate natural levers and growth mechanisms	
Metaphors and models	to improve the speed and magnitude of the communication of beliefs and information

Leadering™ may be the most life-changing and world-changing program in existence today. Courses add new information to one's "existing machinery". Leadering™ adds new information to a more powerful "replacement machinery". A single paradigm shift installs the replacement.

THE MULTI-HOUR PARADIGM SHIFT NOW BEGINS

4   THE LEADERING™ PARADIGM

    2.   Leadering™ Paradigm Overview   43 minutes   1 figure
    3.   *Leadering frequency workout gym*™   5 minutes
    4.   Leadering™ Paradigm Components   38 minutes   6 figures

2.   **Leadering™ Paradigm Overview**   43 minutes   1 figure

The Leadering™ process incites a paradigm shift to a new paradigm in which the dynamics underpinning leaders, entrepreneurs, innovators, and high achievers have been embedded as a logically integrated system.

This presentation introduces the logically integrated Leadering™ paradigm so the target dynamic state of this transformative intervention is understood. The components, forces, and operation of the paradigm are introduced.

Nature's system maximization process is introduced as a metaphor for how the Leadering™ paradigm operates and how natural leaders, entrepreneurs, innovators, and high achievers operate. Metaphors based on shared beliefs are frequently used in Leadering™ to speed the absorption of the systems of beliefs and information required to facilitate the paradigm shift.

Participants experience the first of many "workouts" in *Leadering's expanded consciousness gym or frequency* workout *gym** by stretching to hold nature's perspective and mindset and consciousness and how nature operates the interconnectedness of all human systems.

The paradigm shift process is launched during this presentation as is a new way of thinking about how leaders operate and what they actually do given this new paradigm. The essence of leadership is the maximization of human systems for goal achievement which is a universally advantageous capability.

This redefinition of leadership is instructive for how entrepreneurs, innovators and high achievers operate? Why the meta-competencies and dynamics are shared by these 4 groups is explained along with how they will emerge during the Leadering™ paradigm shift process.

> ## Leadering™ Reactivates Leader Drives
>
> ### We are all born with the drives
> ### that energize natural leaders

Drives for creativity, innovation, frontiering™, advancement, learning, achievement, adaptation, self-expression, and talent-based flow

Our drives hook us to nature's endless evolutionary flow
with all the other successful living systems.

All are drives for penetrating the unknown
or bringing the unknown into existence
— the essence of leadership —

A NASA test for hiring innovative engineers and scientists
was given to 1,600 children as they aged:
Leader drives at age   5:   98%
Leader drives at age 10:   30%
Leader drives at age 15:   12%
Leader drives of 280,000 adults: 2%

Leader drives are culturally deterred.

The Leadering™ paradigm shift *reactivates*
the drives underlying natural leadership

© copyright 2003 Lauren Holmes

© 2003 Lauren Holmes

RECORDING 3-4

Leadering™ maximizes human systems . . . . whether those systems are individuals, companies, countries or families. Once you learn how to maximize your own system you can use the same process to maximize any human system that can help you to achieve your goals.

4   THE LEADERING™ PARADIGM continued

3. **Leadering™ frequency workout gym**　　　　　5 minutes
   This is a brief introduction to Leadering's expanded consciousness or frequency workout gym. Each recording is designed to be a workout to stretch the perspective of your consciousness and cognitive capabilities in addition to advancing the paradigm shift process. The goal is to have you experience more of the dimensions of the natural levers being pushed in each Leadering™ recording, beginning with the one which immediately follows.

4. **Leadering™ Paradigm Components**　　　　38 minutes　　6 figures
   - Participants learn about all of the components of the target paradigm and how they fit together as a means to facilitate the pending paradigm shift.
   - Participants experience a workout in the Leadering's expanded consciousness or frequency gym* by stretching to holds the interconnectedness of the components of the Leadering™ paradigm. This session is the first experiential learning event.
   - Describing how the paradigm operates is used as the means to push levers within participants to advance their functionality so as to enable them to drive the Leadering™ machinery. It is this ability to drive, the new functionality, the launch of life-long growth continuums, and the new modus operandi that are the real goals of the shift to the Leadering™ paradigm.
   - While the paradigm is very complex, participants are only asked to learn to drive it as they would learn to drive a car. Just as with driving a car, they do not need to become mechanics or engineers who know everything about how a car operates. People are able to drive a car without that knowledge. The same is true of the Leadering™ paradigm or machinery.

Leadering™ Paradigm Components

I FORCES, DRIVES, DYNAMICS maximizing human systems

15 Dynamics or Leader drives: Nature's process of maximizing human systems is a metaphor and blueprint for systems-based, core-based leadership.

Systems Mindset: systems-based dynamic, expanding consciousness

Advancement Mechanics: quantum leap dynamic, templating dynamic, self-organizing dynamic, emergence dynamic

Advancement Directions: knowledge-pursuit drive, adaptation drive, evolution drive, co-evolution drive, talent-based flow drive, flow-within-flow drive, congruence drive

Drives for the Unknown: frontier-pursuit drive, creation/creativity-pursuit drive

Addictive talent-focused drives cultivated and capitalized upon by Leadering™ (the more you use them, the more you want to use them):

Drives to: learning, pioneering, creativity, innovation, meaning, positive emotions, adaptivity, creativity, learning knowledge, achievement, flow, (the optimal experience), self-expression, self-knowledge, advancement, unity, growth

Drives to using and improving your key talents - a must for operating at your full potential

Built-in talent-based growth continuums to advanced functionality and performance

A participant's talent-based life themes:

unpaid work theme, knowledge-pursuit theme, frontier-pursuit theme, creativity-pursuit theme, learning-pursuit theme, meaning-pursuit theme, talent-based flow state events theme, naturality expansion theme resonance events theme, positive emotion events theme, spontaneous knowledge events theme, creative invention events theme, spontaneous creativity events theme, theme of talent-based projects which had many coincidences and flow events.

II YOUR TALENT-BASED CORE

III STRATEGIES - 5 Talent-based Operating Formulas:

Advance your system: 1. lifetime development 2. greatest lifetime performance

Advance other systems to advance your system:
3. leadership 4. leadership development 5. greatest leader lifetime performance

IV TECHNOLOGIES

System-based operation, core-driven operation, belief engineering, emotional engineering, reality creation technology, quantum leap technology: *nature-initiated, self-initiated, and identity quantum leaps*, paradigm shifts, capitalizing on naturally occurring quantum leaps such as: *coincidences; sudden knowledge; sudden creativity; emergence (nature's preferred method of achieving creative solutions to performance and survival challenges); flow state (a quantum leap to peak performance and/or re-optimization); facilitating events; positive emotions.*

V BELIEF UPGRADE TOOLS

Quantum leaps, paradigm shifts, reality partnering, action-learning experimentation, the Leadering™ systems maximization toolkit and machinery.

VI PARADIGM PERSONALIZATION EXERCISES

Core Determination Exercises for: a) Flow Maximization   b) Belief Maximization:
Leadering's expanded consciousness workout gym

© 2006 Lauren Holmes

Leadering™ Paradigm Components - continued

VII SYSTEM UPGRADES
(a) Conditioned reflexes, (b) enhanced functionality, (c) beliefs
(d) Meta-competencies of leaders, entrepreneurs, innovators, and high achievers:

Systems-Based and Core-Based Operation
systems thinking, relational thinking, big-picture thinking, conceptual skills, belief system management, model development and application, system co-evolution and co-adaptation, leadership (advancing human systems in opportunistic synergy for goal achievement; multi-system driving)

Accelerating and Continuous Development
- conditioned reflexes installed to trigger multi-front, life-long advancement and leadership development.
- addictive drives installed to pull one to growth.
- learning to learn, mental agility, adaptivity, expanding self-expression and self-awareness, belief engineering, expanding consciousness

Improved and Improving Cognitive Capabilities
- thinking: conceptual, inductive, deductive, abstract, big-picture, relational
- learning to learn, mental agility, pattern recognition, internally referenced, emotional intelligence, use of models, theories, and inferences

Expertise with Ambiguity and the Unknown
- pioneering: penetrating the unknown
- creativity/innovation: bringing the unknown into being

systems thinking, informationless decision-making, abstract thinking, conceptual skills, pattern recognition, trend perception, change detection, environmental scanning, problem reframing, ambiguity resolution

Improved Performance
flow (our peak performance state), enhanced functionality, systems-based operation, accelerated implementation through quantum leap change management

VIII A BELIEF-CREATED REALITY: Reality is a self-correcting feedback system

IX PARADIGM HIGHLIGHTS:

Advancing by wholes: Promotes: systems-based thinking and operation; a quantum leap process; template-based change management; coincidences; spontaneous knowledge; spontaneous creativity; spontaneous self-organization. Used to adapt and enhance human systems such as a leader, a follower, an organizational system, a market system, or leadership development.

Maximization, adaptation, co-evolution: All paradigm dynamics and drives serve these never-ending goals synergistically and opportunistically.

Flow-within-flow: Paradigm is powered by the flow of systems to congruence internally and externally.

Talent-based flow: The peak-performing/peak-evolving goal state of being which capitalizes on natural forces attempting to maximize a human system's core: talents, drives, beliefs, dynamics

Advancement direction: Human systems intensify around their natural core through an endless series of expansion quantum leaps rather than advance linearly.

Belief Engineering: Each human system and its reality are a single system defined by a single belief template. Change beliefs to change both the system and its reality. Beliefs can thus be known from reality event patterns. Leadering™ conditioned reflexes triggered by problem events internally and externally activate an automatic belief template upgrade process. Reality is used as a self-correcting feedback system to increase system functionality and achievement.

© 2006 Lauren Holmes

COMPONENTS OF THE INTEGRATED TARGET PARADIGM - 1

DYNAMICS Maximizing actions	DRIVES links to maximization	META-COMPETENCIES capabilities from dynamics/drives

System Organization:
a congruence dynamic
a self-organizing dynamic
a systems-based dynamic
a templating dynamic
an emergence dynamic
 	
Multi-System Organization:
an adaptation dynamic
a co-evolution dynamic
an expanding consciousness dynamic
a flow-within-flow dynamic
  (subsystems achieve congruence with their contextual system
 	
Improved Performance and Functionality:
a quantum leap dynamic
a frontier-pursuit dynamic
a creation/creativity dynamic
a flow dynamic
an evolution dynamic
a knowledge-pursuit dynamic
	Drives to
	  internal congruence
	  external congruence
	
	flow state
	  (our peak-performance / peak-evolution state of int/ext congruence)
	naturality
	  (internal congruence)
	expanded natural core
	  (growth congruence)
	resonance
	  (frequency congruence)
	meaning
	positive emotions
	adapt
	learn
	new knowledge
	emergence
	co-evolve
	frontiering
	creativity/creation
	achievement
	self-expression
		Systems-Based Approach
		systems thinking, systems-based operation, systems-based emotional intelligence, belief system management, quantum leaping, expanded consciousness, conceptual skills, templating
		
		Continuous Development
		accelerating growth, co-evolution, re-optimization, agility, fluidity, expanding self-expression, learning/adaptation agility, belief upgrading, expanding consciousness
		
		Cognitive Capabilities
		learning agility, knowing, conceptual skills, abstract thinking, expanding consciousness, internally referenced, expanding self-expression and self-awareness, emotional intelligence, deductive reasoning, pattern recognition
		
		Mastering the Unknown
		frontiering, creating, innovating, systems thinking, informationless decision-making, abstract thinking, conceptual skills, expanded consciousness
		
		Performance Improvement
		talent-based flow and other peak performance states, accelerated implementation, advancement by nonlinear quantum leaps, systems thinking, systems-based operation, expanding self-expression, learning/adaptation agility

© 2006 Lauren Holmes

COMPONENTS OF THE INTEGRATED TARGET PARADIGM - 2

KEY THEMES TRACKED FOR HARNESSING THE FLOW OF SYSTEMS TO CONGRUENCE
unpaid work theme, knowledge-pursuit theme, frontier-pursuit theme, creativity-pursuit theme, learning-pursuit theme, meaning-pursuit theme, talent-based flow state events theme, resonance events theme, positive emotion events theme, spontaneous knowledge events theme, creative invention events theme, spontaneous creativity events theme, theme of talent-based projects which had many coincidences and flow events.

HIGHLIGHTS OF THE TARGET PARADIGM

Advancing by wholes: Promotes: systems-based thinking and operation; a quantum leap process; template-based change management; coincidences; spontaneous knowledge; spontaneous creativity; spontaneous self-organization. Used to adapt and enhance human systems such as a leader, a follower, an organizational system, a market system, or leadership development.

Re-optimization, adaptation, co-evolution: All paradigm dynamics and drives serve these never-ending goals synergistically and opportunistically.

Flow-within-flow: Paradigm is powered by the flow of systems to congruence internally and externally.

Talent-based flow: The peak-performing/peak-evolving goal state of being which capitalizes on natural mechanisms built in to support a system's natural talents and passions.

Evolution direction: Human systems intensify around their natural core through an endless series of expansion quantum leaps rather than advance linearly.

Belief Engineering: Each human system and its reality are a single system defined by a single belief template. Change beliefs to change both the system and its reality. Beliefs can be known from reality patterns. Leadering conditioned reflexes triggered by problem events internally and externally activate an automatic belief template upgrade process. Reality is used as a self-correcting feedback system.

Leadering™ Reactivates Leader Drives

We are all born with the drives that energize natural leaders

Drives for creativity, innovation, frontiering™, advancement, learning, achievement, adaptation, self-expression, and talent-based flow

Our drives hook us to nature's endless evolutionary flow
with all the other successful living systems.

All are drives for penetrating the unknown or bringing the unknown into existence
— the essence of leadership —

A NASA test for hiring innovative engineers and scientists
was given to 1,600 children as they aged:
- Leader drives at age 5: 98%
- Leader drives at age 10: 30%
- Leader drives at age 15: 12%
- Leader drives of 280,000 adults: 2%

Leader drives are culturally deterred.

The Leadering™ paradigm shift *reactivates* the drives underlying natural leadership

EVENT PATTERNS TRACKED FOR THEMES
These patterns are indicative of the flow to internal and external congruence or the flow to flow

In the target paradigm, the life-long patterns of the following 'talent-based' or 'work' events are analyzed for themes indicating the flow to generative congruence or flow internally or externally:

- **an unpaid work theme** based on patterns of events in which you freely give away "work" that others would charge for or that you are so passionate about that you would pay for the opportunity to do.
- **a knowledge-pursuit theme** based on patterns of events of seeking knowledge passionately and willingly for the application of key talents (learning-pursuit theme)
- **a spontaneous knowledge theme** based on patterns of events in which spontaneous knowledge emerged to support the application of key talents
- **a frontier-pursuit theme** based on patterns of events of new territories of growth, learning and achievement the system was drawn to pursue for the application of key talents
- **a creativity-pursuit theme** based on patterns of events of preferred creative expression or creative expression which you or system was drawn to pursue for the application of key talents along with events in which creativity or creative invention or innovation spontaneously emerged for the application of key talents
- **a talent-based creative expression theme** based on patterns of events of creative expression in which your passion and enthusiasm were inflamed
- **a meaning-pursuit theme** based on patterns of events of work or achievements or contributions considered a meaningful application of key talents
- **the theme(s) of talent-based flow states** indicated by patterns of events whereby you went into flow state during the application of key talents
- **a naturality expansion theme** indicated by patterns of expansions or intensifications of your system around its core to greater impact on reality - the key direction of growth and advancement of any system in the Leadering™ paradigm.
- **a flow-to-flow theme, theme(s) of projects** requiring the application of key talents which were supported by lots of coincidences, flows, spontaneous knowledge / creativity
- **a resonance theme** based on patterns of subjects or activities for the application of key talents with which you resonated
- **a positive emotion theme** based on patterns of events in which passion, excitement, and enthusiasm emerged during the application of key talents

All of the above themes indicate when a system is integrated into the flow to congruence.

FIVE PERSONAL FORMULAS
for operating in the target Leadering™ paradigm

Based on the themes of the event patterns tracked in the paradigm, the following 5 formulas will emerge to help participants determine how to capitalize on the flow to flow of all human systems.

Your key talents are a system of your strongest capabilities which you are passionate about using and improving which advance reality in some way. This system is what is being acted upon by the flow to flow and your addictive drives.

ADVANCING YOUR SYSTEM

1. **Talent-based lifetime development formula** or personal evolution formula

2. **Greatest lifetime level of talent-based operation**: the culmination of living one's lifetime development formula.

ADVANCING OTHER SYSTEMS TO ADVANCE YOUR SYSTEM

3. **Talent-based leadership formula**: leadership as an expression of one's lifetime development formula

4. **Talent-based leadership development formula**: merging one's lifetime development formula with one's talent-based leadership formula.

5. **Greatest lifetime talent-based operating level as a leader**: based on the previous 4 formulas.

© 2006 Lauren Holmes

Recording4: Leading Paradigm Components   14

ANATOMY OF A COINCIDENCE IN THE PARADIGM

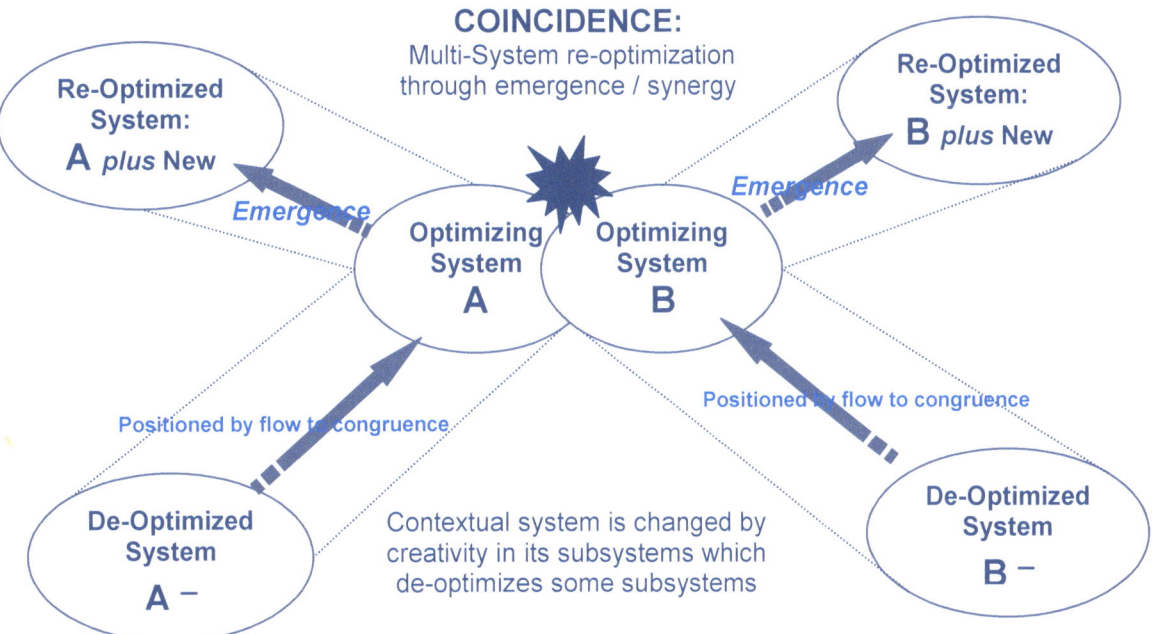

Coincidences: multi-system re-optimizations

To create coincidences: Subsystems have to all be moving with the flow to congruence of their shared contextual system to be orchestrated to collide with the best available subsystems for emergence to merge their information to advantage for multi-system re-optimization.

Corollary: Coincidences are ideal indicators of the flow to congruence – the force which is harnessed in the paradigm.

Emergence: Nature's tendency to organize unpredictable and complex things out of simple components whereby the whole is greater than the sum of its parts.

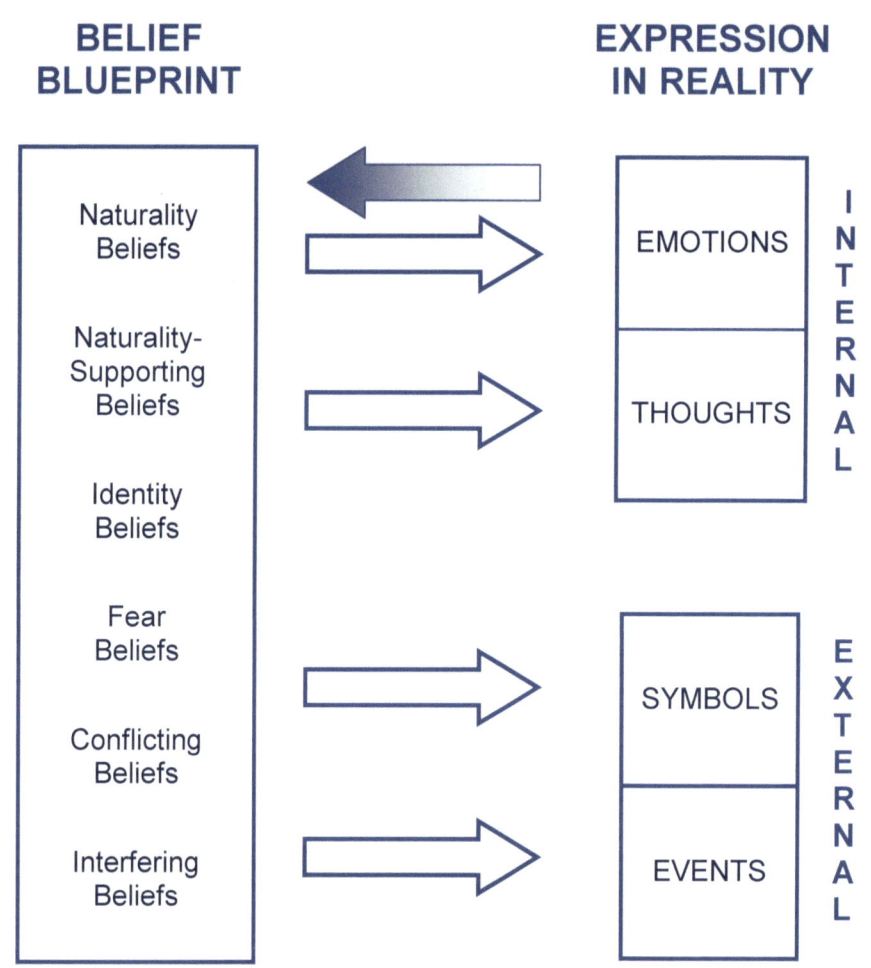

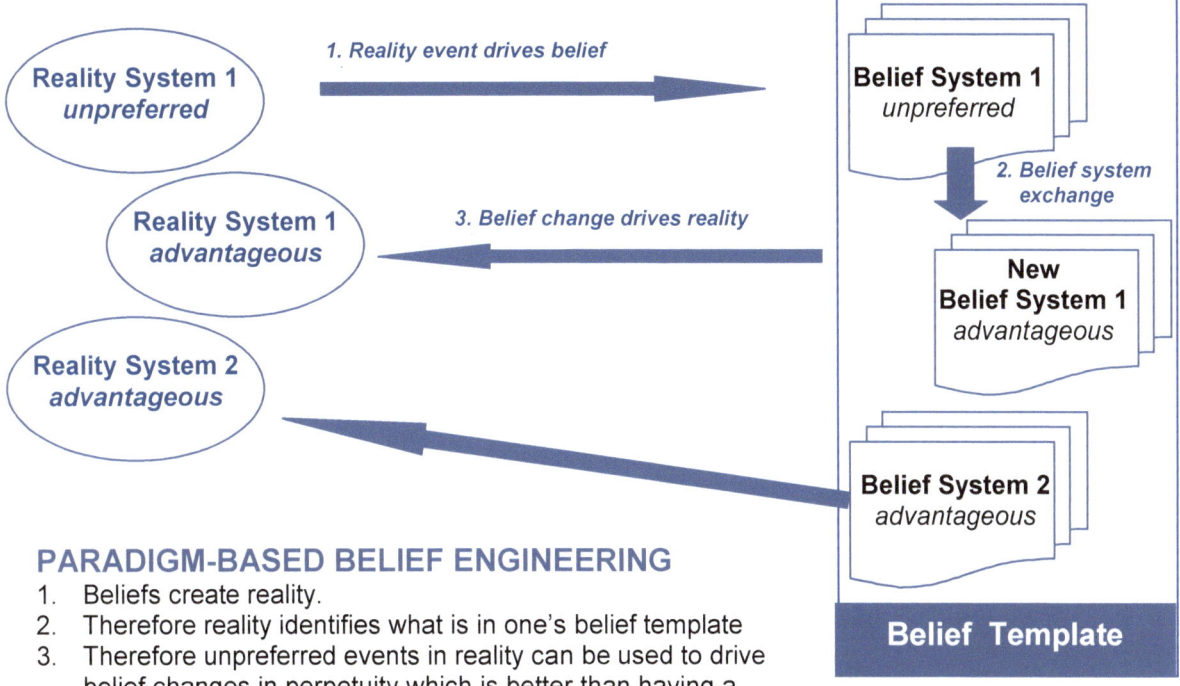

PARADIGM-BASED BELIEF ENGINEERING
1. Beliefs create reality.
2. Therefore reality identifies what is in one's belief template
3. Therefore unpreferred events in reality can be used to drive belief changes in perpetuity which is better than having a coach.

Benefits of the Belief Template Upgrade Process
1. for leadership strength, clarity and consistency
2. to enable the belief and emotion engineering required for leadership consistency required for proficient change execution
3. to operate at full-power without dilution from interfering beliefs
4. for precise personal reality creation
5. for precise imprinting of culture and thus precise reality creation for organizational systems
6. for template-based change management of individual and organizational systems
7. to enable rapid-fire template rewrites in order to use the quantum leap or template exchange processes of the paradigm shift and paradigm modus operandi of this invention
8. to enable the quantum leap or template exchange from externally referenced to internally referenced that is critical in the creation and amplification of leaders.

Leadering™ normalizes you to your core system of strengths, passions, and drives – the only foundation for peak performance and achievement.

5 THE PARADIGM SHIFT PROCESS

5. Leadering™ Paradigm Shift — 19 minutes — 1 figure
6. Leadering™ Quantum Leap Overview — 16 minutes — 4 figures
7. Leadering™ Quantum Leap Process — 50 minutes — 10 figures
8. The Quantum Leap to Quantum Leap Expert — 74 minutes — 6 figures

The **Paradigm Personalization Exercises** may be started at this point but cannot be completed before completing the 15 paradigm-based Leader Drives segment

5. The Leadering™ Paradigm Shift — 19 minutes — 1 figure
- An overview of what is coming up in the Leadering™ program is provided so that you not only feel comfortable with the paradigm shift but you are in a position to assist the process. The goal of Leadering™ is a paradigm shift to be able to drive the Leadering™ machinery for creation.
- An overview of the Leadering™ paradigm shift process to facilitate your personal paradigm shift.
- How the paradigm shift has already started in the previous session
- Leadering™ paradigm shift process
- Leadering™ quantum leap process
- An introduction to Leadering's single systems maximization toolkit: the same systems-based process is applied to your system and any human systems you wish to advance for goals
- How Leadering™ utilizes natural levers and dynamics to facilitate the paradigm shift or quantum leap
- A Leadering™ frequency workout gym experience

THE LEADERING™ PARADIGM SHIFT

Quantum leaps to internalize subsets of an integrated paradigm belief system result in an integrated system of leader drives, reflexes and meta-competencies

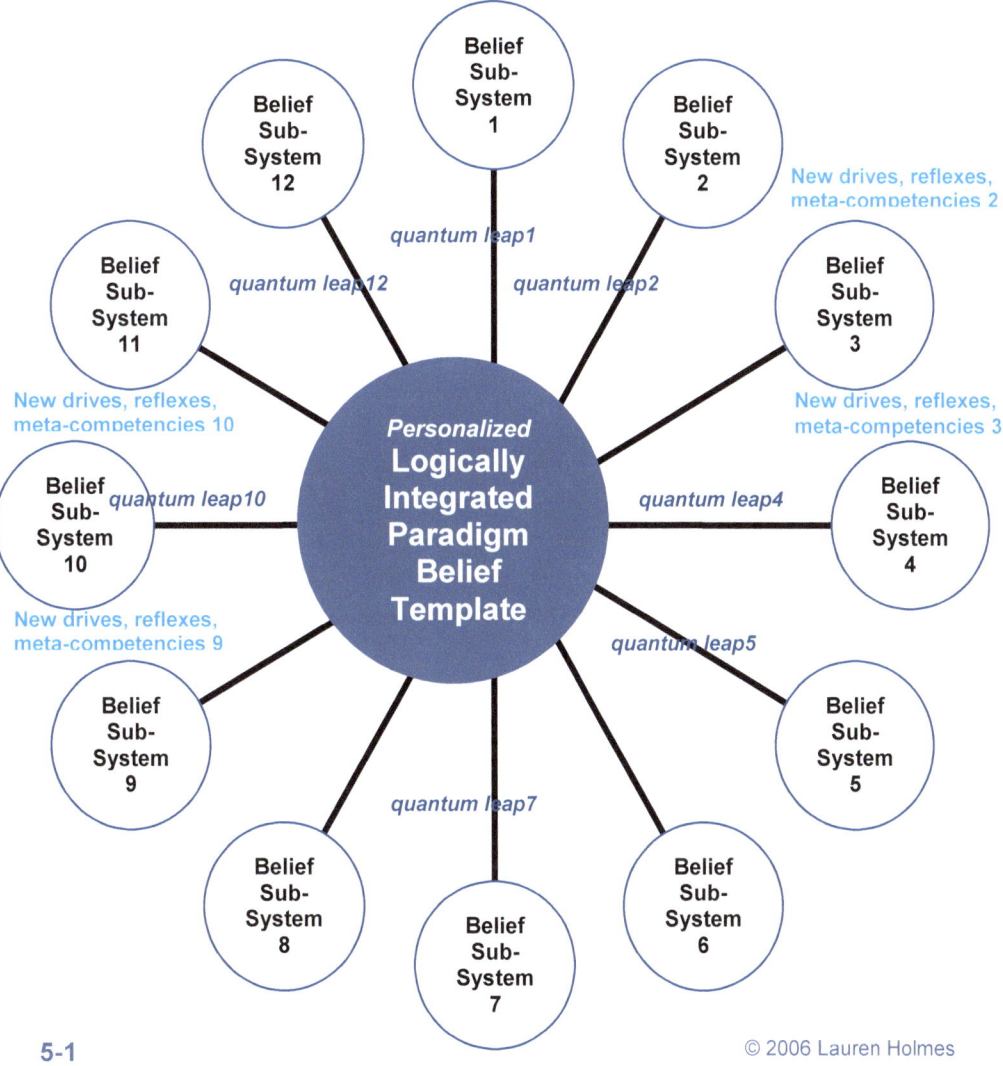

5-1 © 2006 Lauren Holmes

> Leadering's ability to normalize your system to its natural core stimulates natural growth processes otherwise inaccessible. *Extraordinary functionality results.*

5   THE PARADIGM SHIFT PROCESS continued

6. **The Leadering™ Quantum Leap Process Introduction**   16 minutes   4 figures   This recording addresses:
   - A definition of quantum leaps: a sudden nonlinear advancement that bypasses intermediate linear steps. Metaphor: rebooting a computer system with new software.
   - How Leadering's paradigm-based quantum leap method is used for both (a) the paradigm shift and (b) operating in the Leadering™ paradigm.
   - Why nature uses quantum leaps?
   - How nature uses them?
   - What are naturally-occurring quantum leaps and how can we capitalize on them: *coincidences; sudden knowledge; sudden creativity; emergence (nature's preferred method of achieving creative solutions to performance and survival challenges); flow state (a quantum leap to peak performance and/or re-optimization); facilitating events; positive emotions.*
   - How to capitalize on nature's quantum leaping process and mechanisms rather than simply duplicating them.
   - A quantum leap operating style as your new modus operandi in the Leadering™ paradigm for both leadership development and leading: based on installed conditioned reflexes, fluidity for belief and identity exchanges, and nonlinearity.
   - Using several quantum leaps to internalize the Leadering™ paradigm
   - A Leadering™ frequency workout gym experience

ANATOMY OF A COINCIDENCE IN THE PARADIGM

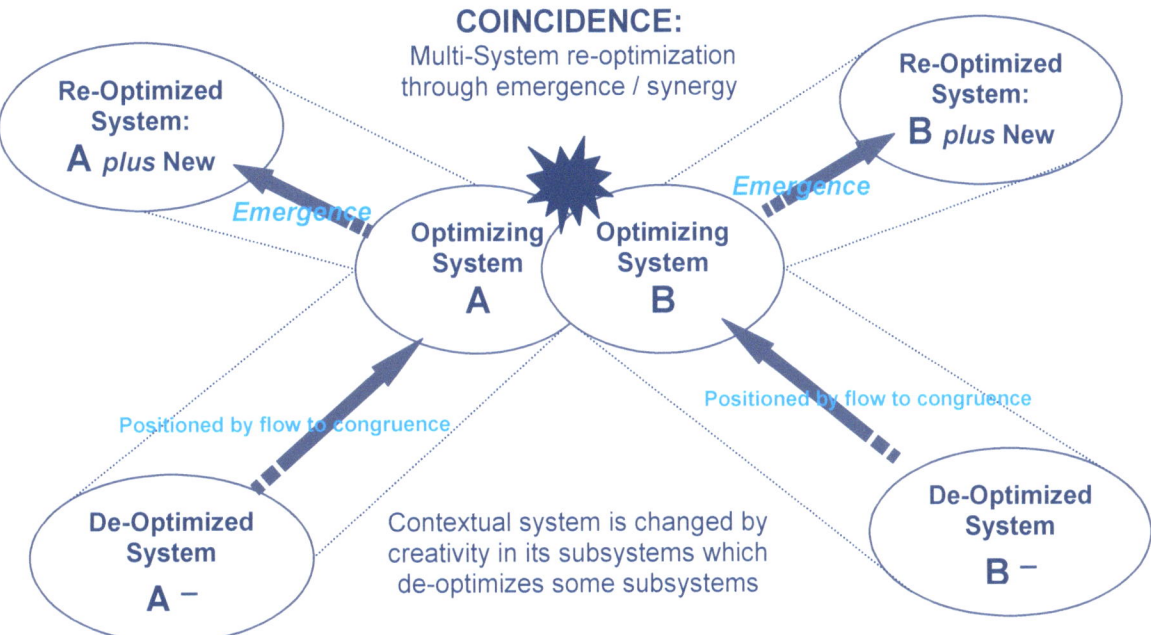

Coincidences: multi-system re-optimizations

To create coincidences: Subsystems have to all be moving with the flow to congruence of their shared contextual system to be orchestrated to collide with the best available subsystems for emergence to merge their information to advantage for multi-system re-optimization.

Corollary: Coincidences are ideal indicators of the flow to congruence – the force which is harnessed in the paradigm.

Emergence: Nature's tendency to organize unpredictable and complex things out of simple components whereby the whole is greater than the sum of its parts.

Dynamics of a Quantum Leap

PRE-LEAP
Integrated Stable State or internal congruence

POST-LEAP
Integrated Stable State or internal congruence.

OLD BELIEF TEMPLATE

OLD REALITY

PLUS **NEW INFO**

Emergence
Direction congruent with the generative flow of the contextual system: external congruence

NEW BELIEF TEMPLATE

NEW REALITY

INTERNAL CONGRUENCE
A naturality-based state. Discernible through patterns of naturality expansion, talent-based flow, expressions of one's art, and spontaneous knowledge, spontaneous creativity

EXTERNAL CONGRUENCE
Discernible through patterns of coincidences, flow events, and the following drives which are a subsystem's links to the flow to congruence of its contextual system: drives for creativity, growth, frontiering, resonance, flow state, emotional highs, knowledge.

A QUANTUM LEAP IS A TEMPLATE EXCHANGE CAUSING A REALITY EXCHANGE

It is a system reincarnation at a more advanced state

© 2006 Lauren Holmes

COMPONENTS OF THE INTEGRATED TARGET PARADIGM - 1

DYNAMICS Maximizing actions	DRIVES links to maximization	META-COMPETENCIES capabilities from dynamics/drives

System Organization:
a congruence dynamic
a self-organizing dynamic
a systems-based dynamic
a templating dynamic
an emergence dynamic
 	
Multi-System Organization:
an adaptation dynamic
a co-evolution dynamic
an expanding
   consciousness dynamic
a flow-within-flow dynamic
   (subsystems achieve
   congruence with their
   contextual system
 	
Improved Performance and Functionality:
a quantum leap dynamic
a frontier-pursuit dynamic
a creation/creativity dynamic
a flow dynamic
an evolution dynamic
a knowledge-pursuit dynamic
	Drives to
	   internal congruence
	   external congruence
	
	flow state
	   (our peak-performance
	   / peak-evolution state
	   of int/ext congruence)
	naturality
	   (internal congruence)
	expanded natural core
	   (growth congruence)
	resonance
	   (frequency congruence)
	meaning
	positive emotions
	adapt
	learn
	new knowledge
	emergence
	co-evolve
	frontiering
	creativity/creation
	achievement
	self-expression
		Systems-Based Approach
		systems thinking, systems-based operation, systems-based emotional intelligence, belief system management, quantum leaping, expanded consciousness, conceptual skills, templating
		
		Continuous Development
		accelerating growth, co-evolution, re-optimization, agility, fluidity, expanding self-expression, learning/adaptation agility, belief upgrading, expanding consciousness
		
		Cognitive Capabilities
		learning agility, knowing, conceptual skills, abstract thinking, expanding consciousness, internally referenced, expanding self-expression and self-awareness, emotional intelligence, deductive reasoning, pattern recognition
		
		Mastering the Unknown
		frontiering, creating, innovating, systems thinking, informationless decision-making, abstract thinking, conceptual skills, expanded consciousness
		
		Performance Improvement
		talent-based flow and other peak performance states, accelerated implementation, advancement by nonlinear quantum leaps, systems thinking, systems-based operation, expanding self-expression, learning/adaptation agility

© 2006 Lauren Holmes

COMPONENTS OF THE INTEGRATED TARGET PARADIGM - 2

KEY THEMES TRACKED FOR HARNESSING THE FLOW OF SYSTEMS TO CONGRUENCE
unpaid work theme, knowledge-pursuit theme, frontier-pursuit theme, creativity-pursuit theme, learning-pursuit theme, meaning-pursuit theme, talent-based flow state events theme, resonance events theme, positive emotion events theme, spontaneous knowledge events theme, creative invention events theme, spontaneous creativity events theme, theme of talent-based projects which had many coincidences and flow events.

HIGHLIGHTS OF THE TARGET PARADIGM

Advancing by wholes: Promotes: systems-based thinking and operation; a quantum leap process; template-based change management; coincidences; spontaneous knowledge; spontaneous creativity; spontaneous self-organization. Used to adapt and enhance human systems such as a leader, a follower, an organizational system, a market system, or leadership development.

Re-optimization, adaptation, co-evolution: All paradigm dynamics and drives serve these never-ending goals synergistically and opportunistically.

Flow-within-flow: Paradigm is powered by the flow of systems to congruence internally and externally.

Talent-based flow: The peak-performing/peak-evolving goal state of being which capitalizes on natural mechanisms built in to support a system's natural talents and passions.

Evolution direction: Human systems intensify around their natural core through an endless series of expansion quantum leaps rather than advance linearly.

Belief Engineering: Each human system and its reality are a single system defined by a single belief template. Change beliefs to change both the system and its reality. Beliefs can be known from reality patterns. Leading conditioned reflexes triggered by problem events internally and externally activate an automatic belief template upgrade process. Reality is used as a self-correcting feedback system.

THE LEADERING™ PARADIGM SHIFT

Quantum leaps to internalize subsets of an integrated paradigm belief system result in an integrated system of leader drives, reflexes and meta-competencies

RECORDING 7

Operating from your natural core enables internal and external systems to partner the way they have evolved to – a synergy which enables performance beyond the sum of the parts. Extraordinary achievement results.

5   THE PARADIGM SHIFT PROCESS   continued

7. **The Leadering™ Quantum Leap Process**   50 minutes   10 figures

   This recording:
   - describes the uses of Leadering's paradigm-based quantum leap process such as (a) the Leadering™ paradigm shift, (b) routine operation within the paradigm, (c) for quickly and safely advancing human systems, (c) the continuous re-optimization or maximization of human systems, (d) organizational change management, (e) creativity and creation, (f) penetrating new territory, (g) when it is impossible to re-optimize a system through a linear process, (h) when it is impossible to keep a system safe through all of the linear transition states between point A and B. It is safer, faster and more efficient to move from one stable state to another stable state in nonlinear ways if necessary with a quantum leap, and so on.
   - explains the steps of the quantum leap process in detail to develop proficiency with them.
   - begins to install the expertise, know-how, belief systems, identities, emotions, fluidity, and nonlinearity to improve quantum leap performance for the rest of the quantum leaps required for both the paradigm shift and later for operating successfully within the Leadering™ paradigm.
   - begins the installation of conditioned reflexes to quantum leap in response to trigger events internally or externally.
   - provides a workout at the Leadering™ frequency gym

THE LEADING™ PARADIGM SHIFT

Quantum leaps to internalize subsets of an integrated paradigm belief system result in an integrated system of leader drives, reflexes and meta-competencies

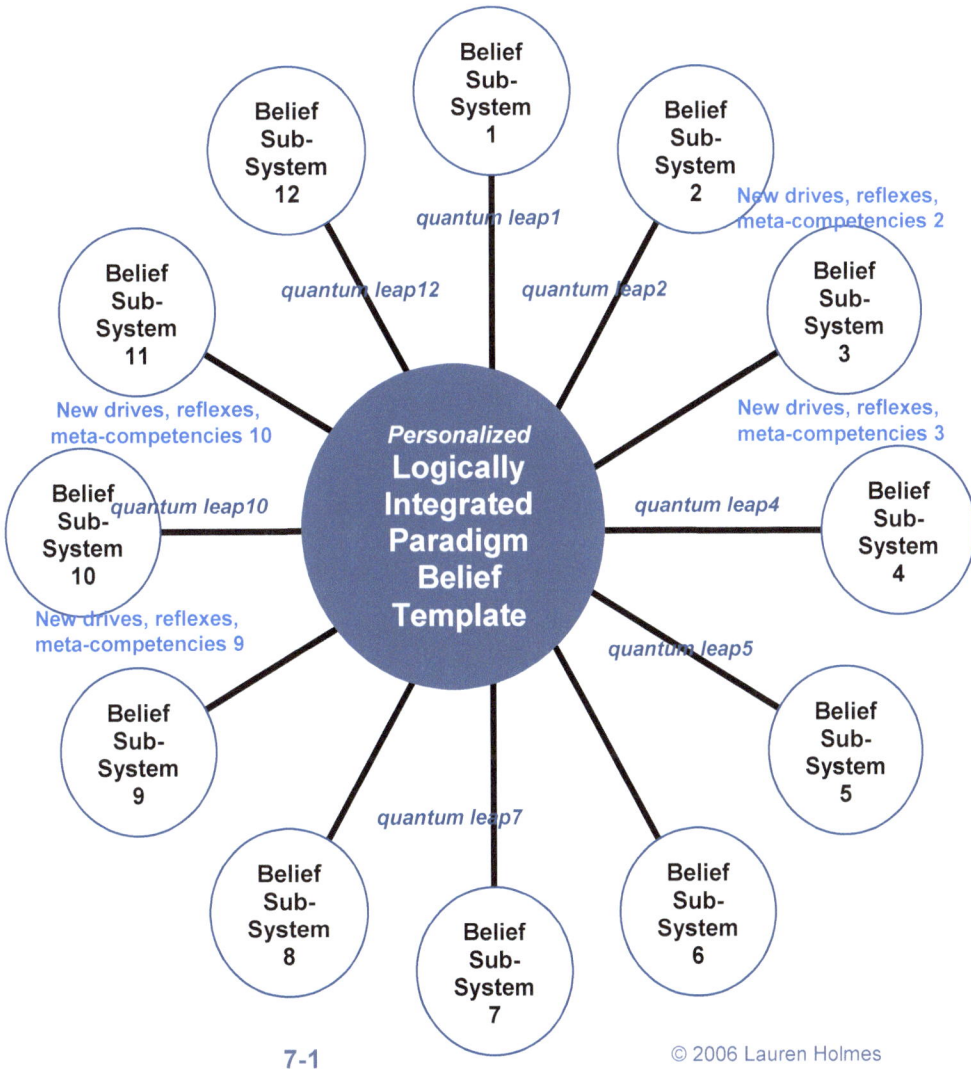

INTERNAL CONGRUENCE: Centered on the Natural Core
The only foundation for leader and personal strength

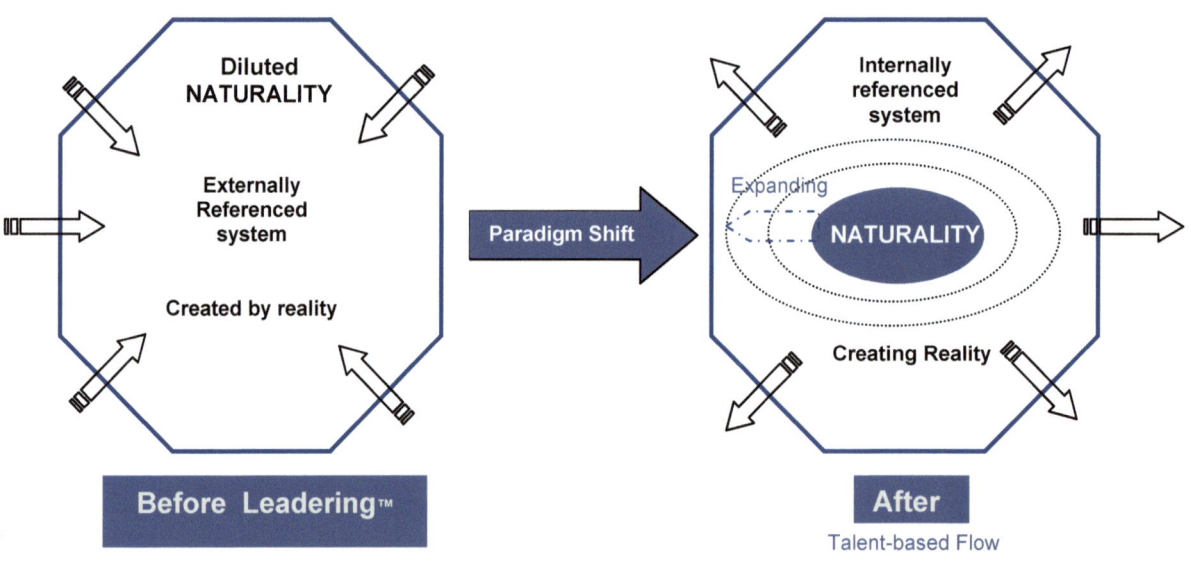

EXTERNAL CONGRUENCE: Flow-Within-Flow

Co-evolving subsystems in talent-based flow synergistically merge into the flow of their shared contextual system which is also seeking its own state of talent-based flow or congruence.

A Flow-within-Flow Example: THE IDEAL HUMAN CAPITAL STRATEGY.
Maximize an individual or organizational system in talent-based flow while they are contributing to the talent-based flow state of the company system.

Subsystems maximized in flow state merge with the flow to the <u>peak-performing / peak-advancing flow state</u> of the system of which they are a part.

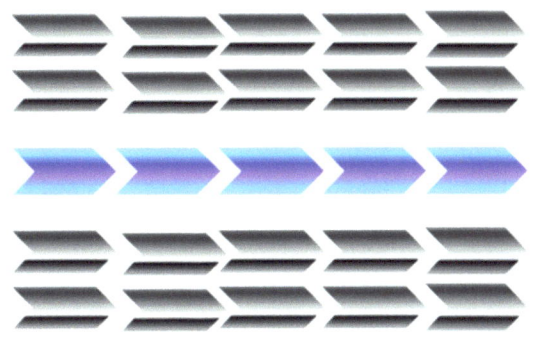

COMPONENTS OF THE INTEGRATED TARGET PARADIGM - 1

DYNAMICS Maximizing actions	DRIVES links to maximization	META-COMPETENCIES capabilities from dynamics/drives

System Organization:
a congruence dynamic
a self-organizing dynamic
a systems-based dynamic
a templating dynamic
an emergence dynamic
 	
Multi-System Organization:
an adaptation dynamic
a co-evolution dynamic
an expanding consciousness dynamic
a flow-within-flow dynamic
   (subsystems achieve congruence with their contextual system
 	
Improved Performance and Functionality:
a quantum leap dynamic
a frontier-pursuit dynamic
a creation/creativity dynamic
a flow dynamic
an evolution dynamic
a knowledge-pursuit dynamic
	Drives to
	  internal congruence
	  external congruence
	
	flow state
	  (our peak-performance / peak-evolution state of int/ext congruence)
	naturality
	  (internal congruence)
	expanded natural core
	  (growth congruence)
	resonance
	  (frequency congruence)
	meaning
	positive emotions
	adapt
	learn
	new knowledge
	emergence
	co-evolve
	frontiering
	creativity/creation
	achievement
	self-expression
		Systems-Based Approach
		systems thinking, systems-based operation, systems-based emotional intelligence, belief system management, quantum leaping, expanded consciousness, conceptual skills, templating
		
		Continuous Development
		accelerating growth, co-evolution, re-optimization, agility, fluidity, expanding self-expression, learning/adaptation agility, belief upgrading, expanding consciousness
		
		Cognitive Capabilities
		learning agility, knowing, conceptual skills, abstract thinking, expanding consciousness, internally referenced, expanding self-expression and self-awareness, emotional intelligence, deductive reasoning, pattern recognition
		
		Mastering the Unknown
		frontiering, creating, innovating, systems thinking, informationless decision-making, abstract thinking, conceptual skills, expanded consciousness
		
		Performance Improvement
		talent-based flow and other peak performance states, accelerated implementation, advancement by nonlinear quantum leaps, systems thinking, systems-based operation, expanding self-expression, learning/adaptation agility

COMPONENTS OF THE INTEGRATED TARGET PARADIGM - 2

KEY THEMES TRACKED FOR HARNESSING THE FLOW OF SYSTEMS TO CONGRUENCE
unpaid work theme, knowledge-pursuit theme, frontier-pursuit theme, creativity-pursuit theme, learning-pursuit theme, meaning-pursuit theme, talent-based flow state events theme, resonance events theme, positive emotion events theme, spontaneous knowledge events theme, creative invention events theme, spontaneous creativity events theme, theme of talent-based projects which had many coincidences and flow events.

HIGHLIGHTS OF THE TARGET PARADIGM

Advancing by wholes: Promotes: systems-based thinking and operation; a quantum leap process; template-based change management; coincidences; spontaneous knowledge; spontaneous creativity; spontaneous self-organization. Used to adapt and enhance human systems such as a leader, a follower, an organizational system, a market system, or leadership development.

Re-optimization, adaptation, co-evolution: All paradigm dynamics and drives serve these never-ending goals synergistically and opportunistically.

Flow-within-flow: Paradigm is powered by the flow of systems to congruence internally and externally.

Talent-based flow: The peak-performing/peak-evolving goal state of being which capitalizes on natural mechanisms built in to support a system's natural talents and passions.

Evolution direction: Human systems intensify around their natural core through an endless series of expansion quantum leaps rather than advance linearly.

Belief Engineering: Each human system and its reality are a single system defined by a single belief template. Change beliefs to change both the system and its reality. Beliefs can be known from reality patterns. Leadering conditioned reflexes triggered by problem events internally and externally activate an automatic belief template upgrade process. Reality is used as a self-correcting feedback system.

Dynamics of a Quantum Leap

PRE-LEAP
Integrated Stable State or internal congruence

POST-LEAP
Integrated Stable State or internal congruence.

OLD BELIEF TEMPLATE

OLD REALITY

PLUS NEW INFO

Emergence

Direction congruent with the generative flow of the contextual system: external congruence

NEW BELIEF TEMPLATE

NEW REALITY

INTERNAL CONGRUENCE
A naturality-based state. Discernible through patterns of naturality expansion, talent-based flow, expressions of one's art, and spontaneous knowledge.

EXTERNAL CONGRUENCE
Discernible through patterns of coincidences, flow events, and the following drives which are a subsystem's links to the flow to congruence of its contextual system: drives for creativity, growth, frontiering, resonance, flow state, emotional highs, knowledge.

A QUANTUM LEAP IS A TEMPLATE EXCHANGE CAUSING A REALITY EXCHANGE

It is a system reincarnation at a more advanced state

© 2006 Lauren Holmes

THE LEADERING™ QUANTUM LEAP PROCESS

Design it!   Feel it!   Be it!

PRE-LEAP
1. Choose the right quantum leap or post-leap state
2. Define the post-leap state with clarity
3. Define the post-leap state without previous limitations or toxicity
4. Emotionally template the post-leap state
5. Add the information to fuel emergence
6. Expect the unexpected post-leap

LEAP
1. Release the linear connection to the past
2. Feel yourself 100% fluid
3. Feel the post-leap state
4. Feel who the "post-leap you" will be
5. Commit to the quantum leap
6. Make an abrupt, no-return, reincarnation
7. Trigger spontaneous self-organization by intent

POST-LEAP
1. Operate as if the quantum leap was successful
2. Walk around as the person with the post-leap reality
3. Hold this new identity until reality restructures
4. Ignore evidence of events created by the old template
5. Trigger cascading quantum leaps by intent
6. Establish quantum leaping as a way of life
7. Consolidate your new quantum leap expert beliefs

EVENT PATTERNS TRACKED FOR THEMES
These patterns are indicative of the flow to internal and external congruence or the flow to flow

In the target paradigm, the life-long patterns of the following 'talent-based' or 'work' events are analyzed for themes indicating the flow to generative congruence or flow internally or externally:

- **an unpaid work theme** based on patterns of events in which you freely give away "work" that others would charge for or that you are so passionate about that you would pay for the opportunity to do.
- **a knowledge-pursuit theme** based on patterns of events of seeking knowledge passionately and willingly for the application of key talents (learning-pursuit theme)
- **a spontaneous knowledge theme** based on patterns of events in which spontaneous knowledge emerged to support the application of key talents
- **a frontier-pursuit theme** based on patterns of events of new territories of growth, learning and achievement the system was drawn to pursue for the application of key talents
- **a creativity-pursuit theme** based on patterns of events of preferred creative expression or creative expression which you or system was drawn to pursue for the application of key talents along with events in which creativity or creative invention or innovation spontaneously emerged for the application of key talents
- **a talent-based creative expression theme** based on patterns of events of creative expression in which your passion and enthusiasm were inflamed
- **a meaning-pursuit theme** based on patterns of events of work or achievements or contributions considered a meaningful application of key talents
- **the theme(s) of talent-based flow states** indicated by patterns of events whereby you went into flow state during the application of key talents
- **a naturality expansion theme** indicated by patterns of expansions or intensifications of your system around its core to greater impact on reality - the key direction of growth and advancement of any system in the Leadering™ paradigm.
- **a flow-to-flow theme, theme(s) of projects** requiring the application of key talents which were supported by lots of coincidences, flows, spontaneous knowledge / creativity
- **a resonance theme** based on patterns of subjects or activities for the application of key talents with which you resonated
- **a positive emotion theme** based on patterns of events in which passion, excitement, and enthusiasm emerged during the application of key talents

All of the above themes indicate when a system is integrated into the flow to congruence.

FIVE PERSONAL FORMULAS
for operating in the target Leadering™ paradigm

Based on the themes of the event patterns tracked in the paradigm, the following 5 formulas will emerge to help participants determine how to capitalize on the flow to flow of all human systems.

Your key talents are a system of your strongest capabilities which you are passionate about using and improving which advance reality in some way. This system is what is being acted upon by the flow to flow and your addictive drives.

ADVANCING YOUR SYSTEM

1. **Talent-based lifetime development formula** or personal evolution formula

2. **Greatest lifetime level of talent-based operation**: the culmination of living one's lifetime development formula.

ADVANCING OTHER SYSTEMS TO ADVANCE YOUR SYSTEM

3. **Talent-based leadership formula**: leadership as an expression of one's lifetime development formula

4. **Talent-based leadership development formula**: merging one's lifetime development formula with one's talent-based leadership formula.

5. **Greatest lifetime talent-based operating level as a leader**: based on the previous 4 formulas.

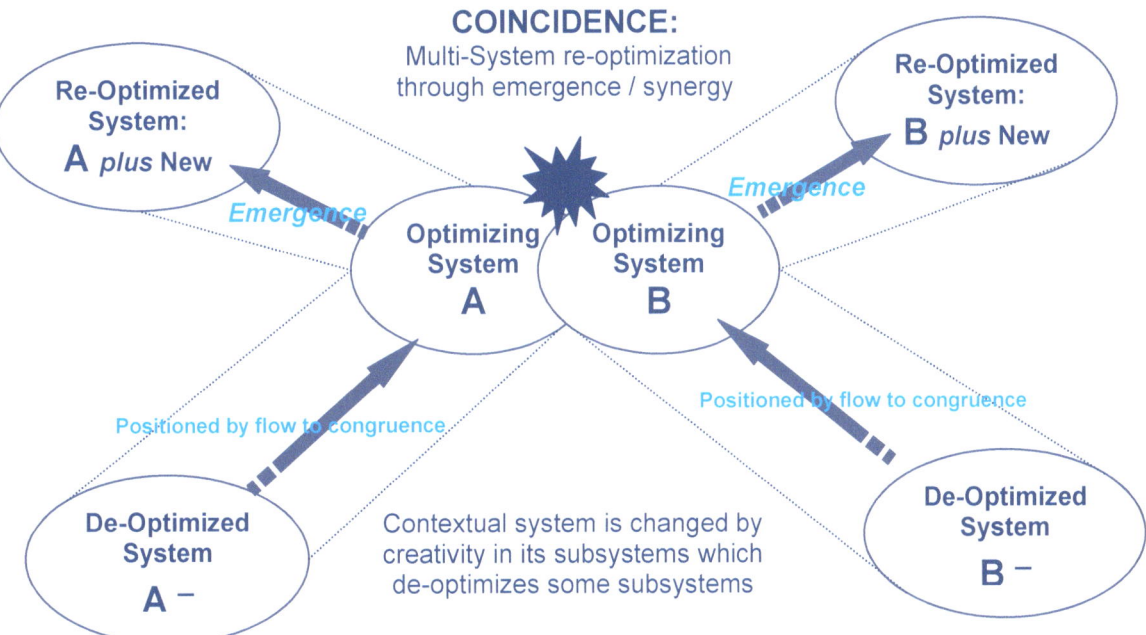

Coincidences: multi-system re-optimizations

To create coincidences: Subsystems have to all be moving with the flow to congruence of their shared contextual system to be orchestrated to collide with the best available subsystems for emergence to merge their information to advantage for multi-system re-optimization.

Corollary: Coincidences are ideal indicators of the flow to congruence – the force which is harnessed in the paradigm.

Emergence: The appearance of a property or feature not previously observed as a functional characteristic of the system: Nature's tendency to organize unpredictable and complex things out of simple components whereby the whole is greater than the sum of its parts. An automobile is an emergent property of its interconnected parts.

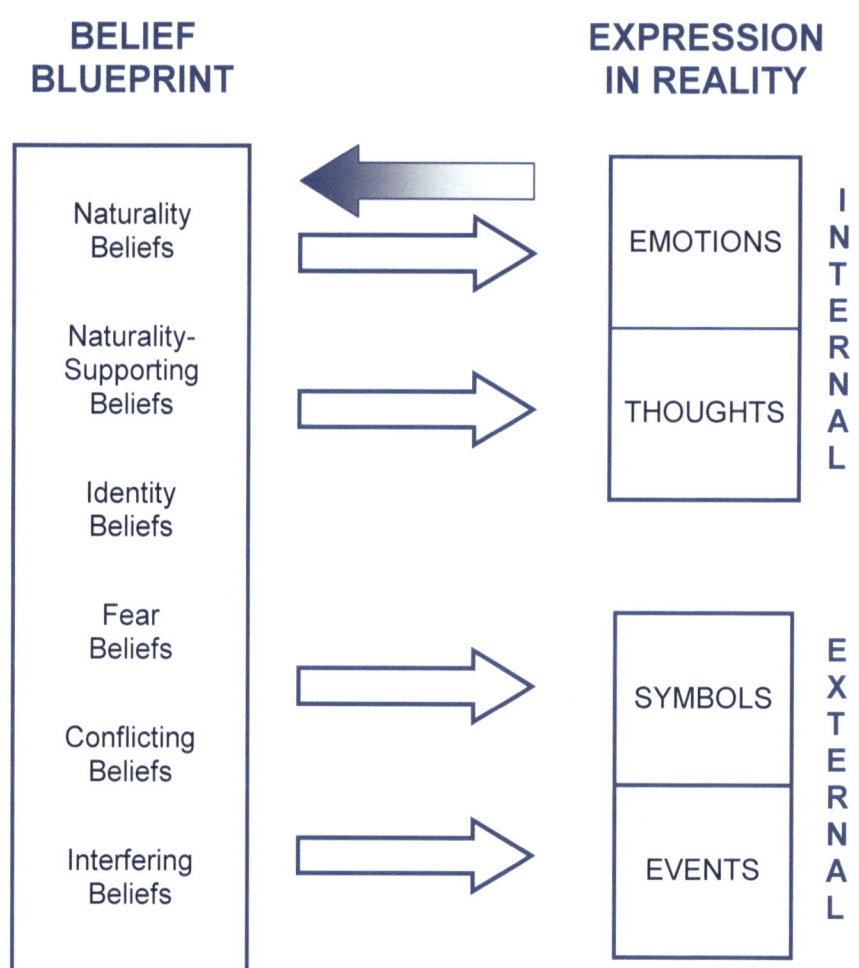

BELIEFS CREATE REALITY

The quantum leap to a 100% self-created and belief-created reality initiates the cascading quantum leaps presented as an example of how to increase the magnitude of impact of a quantum leap expert.

© 1993 Lauren Holmes
Excerpted from *Peak Evolution* (Lauren Holmes, 2001)

NATURAL QUANTUM LEAPS CLUSTER IN THE FLOW

The advantage of operating in talent-based flow within the talent-based flow of the contextual system

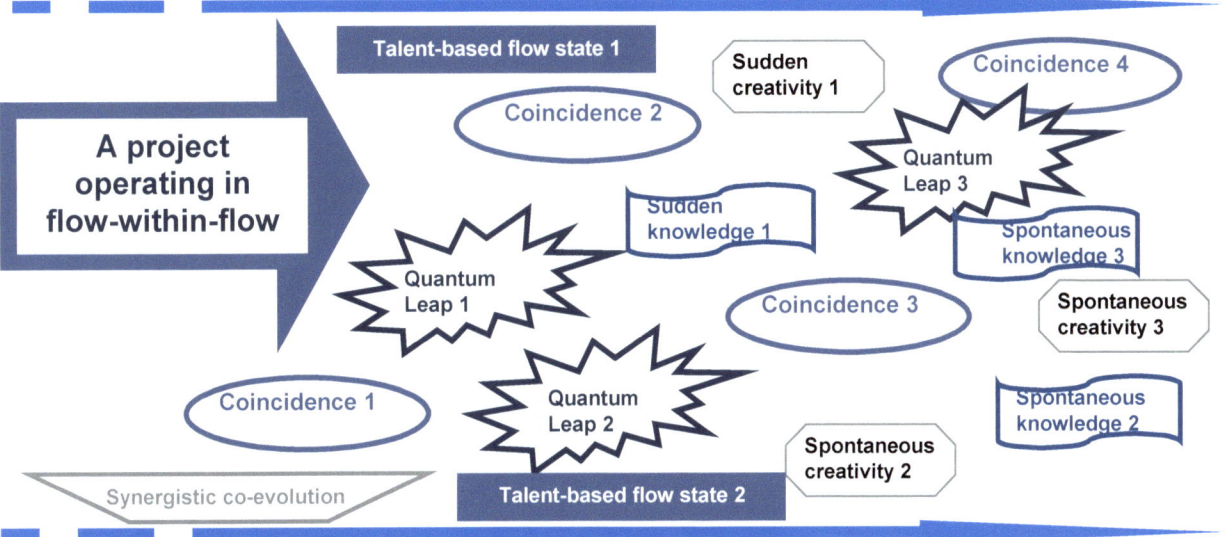

Flow to Congruence   or   Flow-to-Flow

**Flow to Congruence   or   Flow-to-Flow   or   Flow to Fusion
or   projection of your talent-based life themes into the future**

Increasing functionality with each flow experience:
- expanding consciousness and conceptual capacity
- peak performance
- peak evolution
- increasing creative capability
- expansion / intensification / enlargement of the system's natural creative expression

Proof of the Leadering™ paradigm – Proof of the accuracy of your 5 formulas
If you are operating in talent-based flow and the clustering of natural quantum leaps above emerge in your reality, then you have proof that the Leadering paradigm™ and nature's machinery inside and outside of you do indeed operate in the way Leadering™ describes.

5 THE PARADIGM SHIFT PROCESS continued

8. **The Quantum Leap to Quantum Leap Expert:**   74 minutes   6 figures
   This is the first identity quantum leap (as per audios 20-23)

   Leadering's quantum leap process detailed in the previous recording has been customized in this audio for a specific quantum as the means to test drive the tool as well as to develop expertise for its use in the paradigm shift process and later for driving the Leadering™ machinery.

   The specific quantum leap is to a quantum leap expert who routinely advances himself/herself or the systems in their reality by wholes from one stable state to the next using a belief template exchange process. The goal is for each participant to become a quantum leap expert with the belief template, conditioned reflexes, experiential learning, fluidity, and emotional memory of the process. This will enable each individual to not only effectively accomplish all of the quantum leaps in the Leadering™ paradigm shift but the ongoing personal quantum leaps of one's own system or systems led.

   This is the first quantum leap of many in the Leadering™ paradigm necessary for assimilating the multitude of beliefs, dynamics, and information required for the paradigm shift. This quantum leap is designed to quickly provide you with the expertise necessary for using Leadering's quantum leap tool. This first quantum lays the foundations for excelling at all of the other quantum leaps in the Leadering™ program.

   This entire recording is the quantum leap. It includes the new information, beliefs, emotions for the emergence process that energizes the quantum leap. As you learn to 'quantum leap' your system, you will be able to apply the same techniques to other human systems. Even if it is not your goal, you will have the means to become adept with breakthrough methodologies for leadership, organizational change, people development, and goal achievement. You will learn how to maximize human systems for profound achievement - for your goals or theirs.

   Significant time is spent defining the post-leap state. This includes:
   - defining the identity of a quantum leap expert
   - identifying the ways in which quantum leap expertise can develop with practice to increase functionality, expertise and performance. The progression of expertise as one gains experience with quantum leaps is laid out. The growth continuums built into becoming a quantum leap expert are projected.
   - installing the conditioned reflexes to automatically quantum leap given specific circumstances internally and externally.
   - defining the identities of belief engineer, emergence expert, pathfinding expert, expert with cascading quantum leaps or multi-system quantum leaps or quantum leaps of increasing magnitude and complexity,
   - increasing fluidity and nonlinearity

Dynamics of a Quantum Leap

PRE-LEAP
Integrated Stable State or internal congruence

POST-LEAP
Integrated Stable State or internal congruence.

OLD BELIEF TEMPLATE
OLD REALITY

PLUS **NEW INFO**

Emergence → Direction congruent with the generative flow of the contextual system: external congruence

NEW BELIEF TEMPLATE
NEW REALITY

INTERNAL CONGRUENCE
A naturality-based state. Discernible through patterns of naturality expansion, talent-based flow, expressions of one's art, and spontaneous knowledge.

EXTERNAL CONGRUENCE
Discernible through patterns of coincidences, flow events, and the following drives which are a subsystem's links to the flow to congruence of its contextual system: drives for creativity, growth, frontiering, resonance, flow state, emotional highs, knowledge.

A QUANTUM LEAP IS A TEMPLATE EXCHANGE CAUSING A REALITY EXCHANGE

It is a system reincarnation at a more advanced state

© 2006 Lauren Holmes

THE LEADERING™ QUANTUM LEAP PROCESS

Design it!   Feel it!   Be it!

PRE-LEAP
1. Choose the right quantum leap or post-leap state
3. Define the post-leap state with clarity
3. Define the post-leap state without previous limitations or toxicity
4. Emotionally template the post-leap state
5. Add the information to fuel emergence
6. Expect the unexpected post-leap

LEAP
1. Release the linear connection to the past
2. Feel yourself 100% fluid
3. Feel the post-leap state
4. Feel who the "post-leap you" will be
5. Commit to the quantum leap
6. Make an abrupt, no-return, reincarnation
7. Trigger spontaneous self-organization by intent

POST-LEAP
1. Operate as if the quantum leap was successful
2. Walk around as the person with the post-leap reality
3. Hold this new identity until reality restructures
4. Ignore evidence of events created by the old template
5. Trigger cascading quantum leaps by intent
6. Establish quantum leaping as a way of life
7. Consolidate your new quantum leap expert beliefs

© 1998 Lauren Holmes

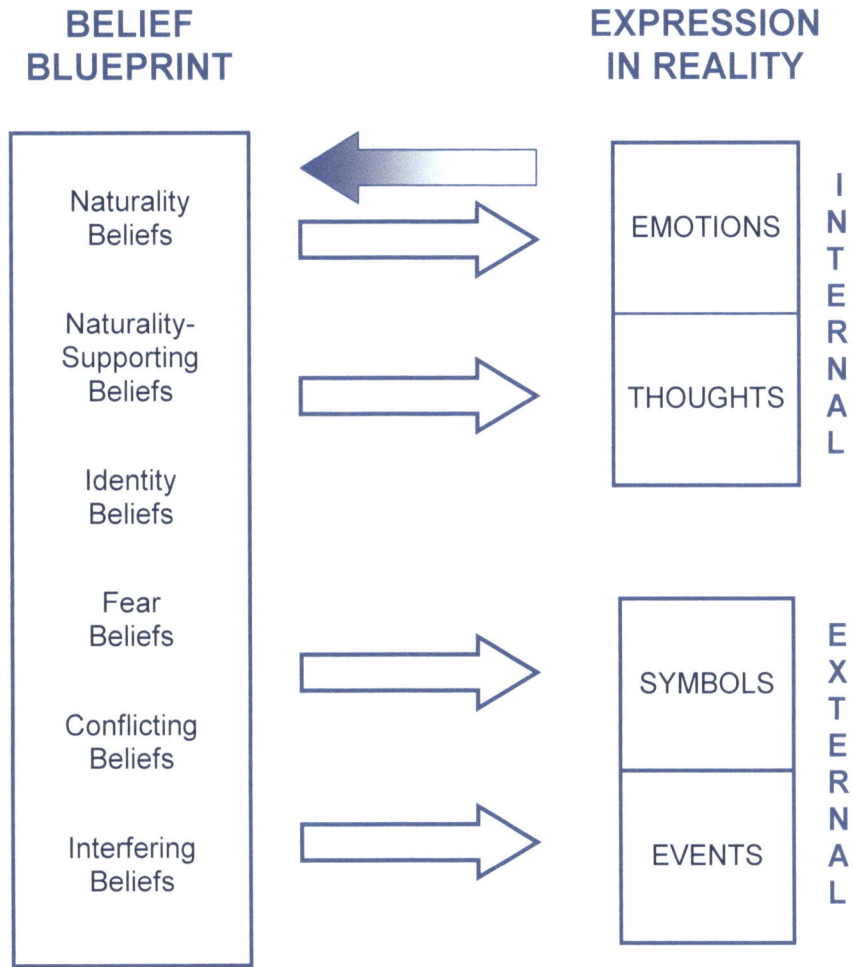

The quantum leap to a 100% self-created and belief-created reality initiates the cascading quantum leaps presented as an example of how to increase the magnitude of impact of a quantum leap expert.

8-3 © 1995 Lauren Holmes
Excerpted from *Peak Evolution* (Lauren Holmes, 2001)

CREATING WORLD LEADERS

YOUR REALITY → ORGANIZATION → INDUSTRY → BUSINESS ECOSYSTEM → CIVILIZATION

POWER MUST INCREASE TO:

Imprint **Beliefs** → Unify **Identities** → Increase **Creations**

© 1995 Lauren Holmes

NATURAL QUANTUM LEAPS CLUSTER IN THE FLOW

The advantage of operating in talent-based flow within the talent-based flow of the contextual system

Flow to Congruence   or   Flow-to-Flow

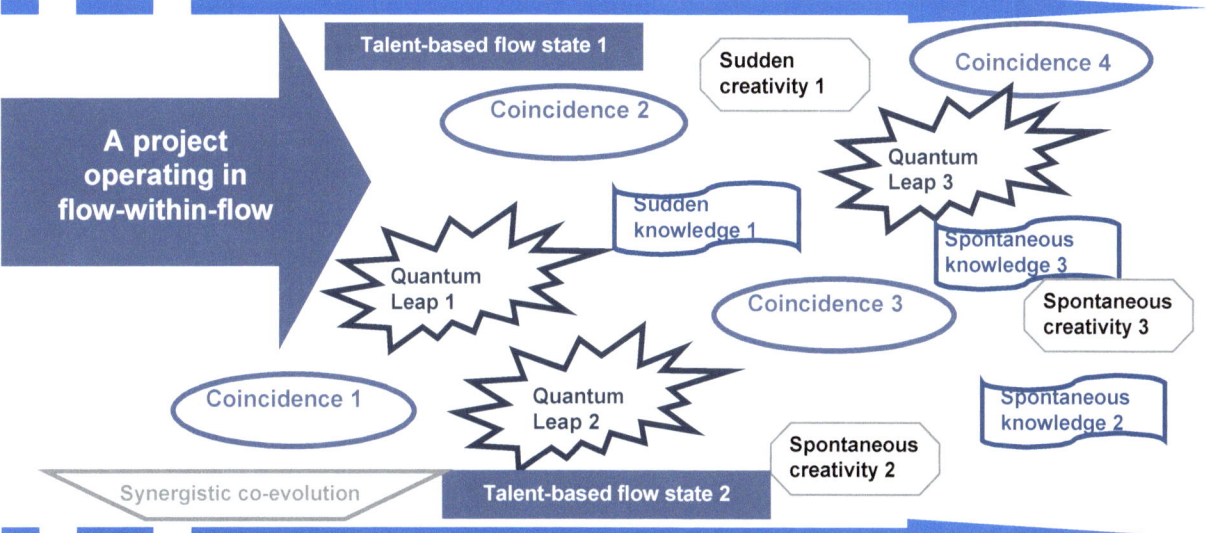

Flow to Congruence   or   Flow-to-Flow   or   Flow to Fusion
or   projection of your talent-based life themes into the future

Increasing functionality with each flow experience:
- expanding consciousness and conceptual capacity
- peak performance
- peak evolution
- increasing creative capability
- expansion / intensification / enlargement of the system's natural creative expression

Proof of the Leadering™ paradigm – Proof of the accuracy of your 5 formulas
If you are operating in talent-based flow and the clustering of natural quantum leaps above emerge in your reality, then you have proof that the Leadering paradigm™ and nature's machinery inside and outside of you do indeed operate in the way Leadering™ describes.

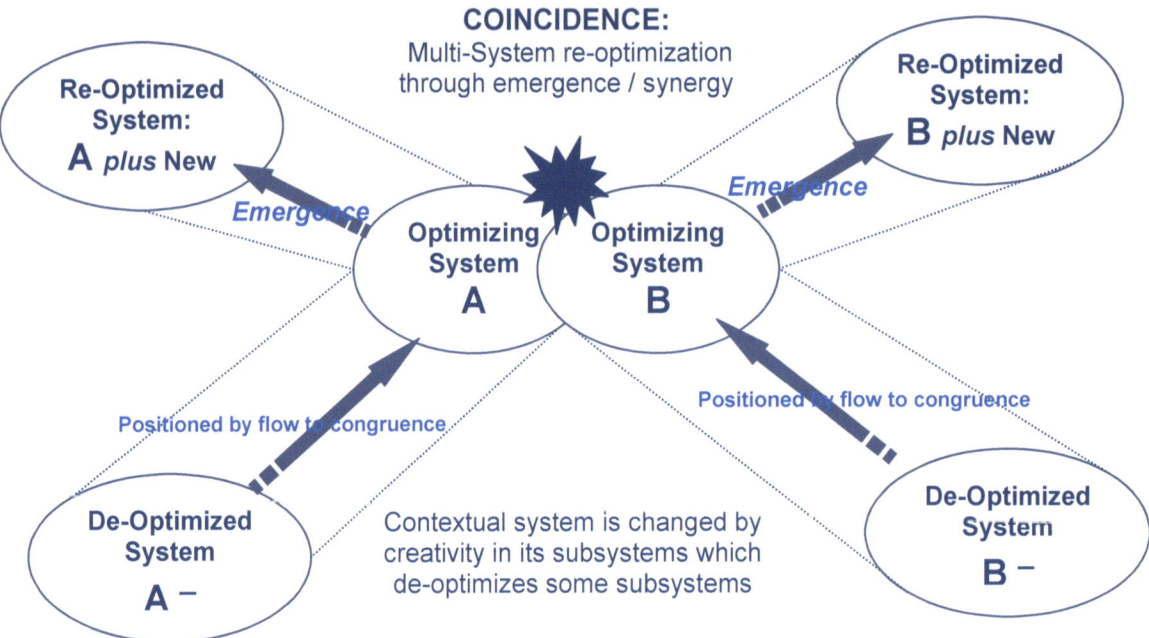

Coincidences: multi-system re-optimizations

To create coincidences: Subsystems have to all be moving with the flow to congruence of their shared contextual system to be orchestrated to collide with the best available subsystems for emergence to merge their information to advantage for multi-system re-optimization.

Corollary: Coincidences are ideal indicators of the flow to congruence – the force which is harnessed in the paradigm.

Emergence: The appearance of a property or feature not previously observed as a functional characteristic of the system: Nature's tendency to organize unpredictable and complex things out of simple components whereby the whole is greater than the sum of its parts. An automobile is an emergent property of its interconnected parts.

LEADERING VISUALS ONE
Paradigm Shift to Peak Legacy

NOTE: Leadering's quantum leap process only works within the Leadering™ paradigm where you drive a multi-system, multi-dynamic Leadering™ machinery personalized to how natural forces are acting on your system and the human systems you choose to advance or capitalize on to achieve your goals.

NOTE: Leadering's paradigm personalization exercise recordings may be begun any time after this *Quantum Leap to Quantum Leap Expert*. Within the progression of the recordings gradually building pressures to catalyze the paradigm shift, the exercises have actually been recorded to follow Section 6 (next) about the system of 15 integrated leader drives and dynamics embedded within the paradigm. However, using the Leadering™ frequency workout gym™ built into each recording will put you into a better frequency and expansion of perspective for doing the exercises than trying to do them in your normal consciousness. The exercises will be much easier if you work on them after being expanded and centered by a recording.

6 THE FIFTEEN PARADIGM LEADER DRIVES
to maximize human systems for goal achievement

LEADERS EXTEND NATURE: the 15 dynamics of the Leadering™ systems maximization toolkit
1 presentation that has been broken into 8 parts.
The same 21 figures are shared by each of these 8 recordings:

9. **15 Leader Drives:**
   - 9.1 Introduction — 23 minutes — 21 figures
   - 9.2 Systems mindset: congruence, systems-based, expanded consciousness — 22 minutes — 21 figures
   - 9.3 Advancement mechanics: quantum leap, templating, self-organizing, emergence — 22 minutes — 21 figures
   - 9.4 Advancement directions: knowledge-pursuit — 16 minutes — 21 figures
   - 9.5 Advancement directions: adaptation, evolution — 17 minutes — 21 figures
   - 9.6 Leader drives quantum leap preparation and initiation, plus the part that the frontier-pursuit drive, creation / creativity-pursuit drives play in all the dynamics — 22 minutes — 21 figures
   - 9.7 Co-evolution, talent-based flow, flow-to-flow plus additional information for the frontier-pursuit drive and the creation / creativity-pursuit drives — 55 minutes — 21 figures
   - 9.8 Quantum leap to operating with the 15 leader drives as a way of life. — 57 minutes — 21 figures

15 PARADIGM LEADER DRIVES: to maximize human systems for goal achievement

LEADERS EXTEND NATURE'S SYSTEMS MAXIMIZATION PROCESS:
   the 15 dynamics of the Leadering™ systems maximization toolkit
The leader dynamics lectures are really one process ending in a quantum leap that is building throughout the 8 component recordings. The same 21 figures are therefore shared by each of the 8 Leader Drives recordings.

RECORDING 9.1

Leadering™ is an unprecedented performance technology which enables a lifetime legacy more profound, more meaningful, and more impactful than you thought you were capable of.

6 THE FIFTEEN PARADIGM LEADER DRIVES
to maximize human systems for goal achievement

9.1

The 15 Leader Drives: 23 minutes 21 figures
INTRODUCTION:
This presentation takes a big-picture perspective to demonstrate how leadership mirrors and is an extension of nature's systems management process described in *the Leadering™ Paradigm* presentations.

Leadership is re-written as (i) an extension of nature's systems maximization process described in *the Leadering™ Paradigm* presentations and as (ii) a copy of nature used as a metaphor.
- how companies (human systems) would be run by this redefined leadership is presented.
- the ideal career strategy (paid peak evolution) is extrapolated from this leader redefinition as well
- the leadership redefinition is explored in terms of the 15 dynamics. For example: (a) quantum leap leadership (b) creational leadership (c) frontiering leadership™ (d) emergence leadership (e) flow leadership and the flow evolutionary continuum (f) evolution leadership (g) follower leadership (h) power leadership (i) unity leadership, and (j) world leadership.
- the second Leadering™ quantum leap is launched which will build throughout all 8 of the *Leader Drives* recordings.

6   THE FIFTEEN PARADIGM LEADER DRIVES continued
to maximize human systems for goal achievement

THE TRANSLATION OF THE NATURE'S 15 DYNAMICS INTO LEADER DYNAMICS
to capitalize on existing natural forces acting on human systems:

9.2

    The 15 Leader Drives: 22 minutes   21 figures
    SYSTEMS MINDSET: drives for congruence, systems-based, expanded consciousness
- Everything in the paradigm is a system, including individuals, organizations, and processes.
- Operating in the flow to congruence and stretching to view interacting systems causes consciousness to expand.

9.3

    The 15 Leader Drives: 22 minutes   21 figures
    ADVANCEMENT MECHANICS: drives for quantum leaping, templating, self-organizing, emergence
- These are nonlinear system upgrade mechanisms.
- Leaders (human system maximizers) orchestrate abrupt nonlinear system advancements, adaptations, co-evolutions, and re-optimizations using mechanisms available in the flow to congruence.
- They operate as belief engineers, cultural engineers, reality architects, quantum leap leaders, and emergence leaders

9.4

    The 15 Leader Drives: 16 minutes   21 figures
    ADVANCEMENT DIRECTIONS: knowledge-pursuit drive
- This drive serves as a key determinant of the underlying talent-based growth path of any human system.
- Leaders (human system maximizers) harness a system's innate drives for advancing its talent-based expression of the key talents at its core in order to achieve multi-system goals and maximization

Recordings 9.1-9.8: 15 Leader Drives 48

RECORDING 9.5 to 9.6

Because Leadering™ copies and capitalizes on nature's systems maximization process, powerful natural forces, capabilities, and mechanisms are available to extend the functionality of any human system so that it can perform beyond its potential.

6   THE FIFTEEN PARADIGM LEADER DRIVES continued
to maximize human systems for goal achievement

9.5

The 15 Leader Drives: 17 minutes   21 figures
ADVANCEMENT DIRECTIONS: drives for adaptation, evolution
   adaptation drive:
an externally driven adjustment to advances in the shared contextual system caused by the adaptation / evolution of other subsystems. These are a chain reaction as the creativity of one system to adjust to changes in its environment triggers creative solutions from other systems adjusting to the contextual change caused by the first. Nature and leaders merely orchestrate a creative dance of co-adapting and co-evolving systems.
   evolution drive:
'Growth' and 'learning' provide information to help human systems achieve their existing potential with their existing machinery. 'Evolution' advances that potential. 'Evolution' upgrades the existing machinery and potential. Human systems advance by (1) quantum-leap intensifications of their natural core and (2) belief template upgrades: upgraded potential / functionality
In the Leadering™ paradigm, adaptation is externally driven and evolution is internally driven.

9.6

The 15 Leader Drives: 22 minutes   21 figures
QUANTUM LEAP PREPARATION
DRIVES FOR THE UNKNOWN: the frontier-pursuit and creation-pursuit drives
- This presentation is entirely dedicated to preparation for the quantum leap begun in the introduction. A description is provided for all of the complex elements which could be considered for the desired post-leap state.
- An integrated review of the 15 drives is provided to help define one's ideal post-leap state for operating as nature does in maximizing and advancing human systems: their interrelationship and their application to leadership, and the advancement and maximization of systems alone or together.
- The recording is designed to let tensions build to fuel the next quantum leap as the translation of the 15 paradigm dynamics to leader drives continues.
- Drives for the unknown - frontier pursuit and creativity/pursuit drives are introduced as part of the integrated view of the operation of the machinery composed of the 15 drives.

6 THE FIFTEEN PARADIGM LEADER DRIVES continued
to maximize human systems for goal achievement

9.7

The 15 Leader Drives: 55 minutes 21 figures
ADVANCEMENT DIRECTIONS: co-evolution, talent-based flow, flow-to-flow plus
DRIVES FOR THE UNKNOWN: the frontier-pursuit and creation-pursuit drives

- The co-evolution drive is an internally driven system upgrade achieved by capitalizing on external upgrading systems using opportunistic synergy, lockstep advancement, or mixing and matching pieces from multiple systems to feed the emergence process which fuels quantum leaps of human systems.

- Flow to congruence is officially changed to flow-to-flow- because of the all encompassing status of the talent-based flow drive. This drive is metaphorically similar to white light with all of the other drives/colours being subservient to its achievement.

- The flow drive will therefore upgrade all of the discussions of the 15 dynamics/drives to this point and will, in fact, rewrite figure 9g-5. Your understanding of the Leadering™ paradigm will be shifted upward to a new cohesive whole and a new integrated sophistication. This upgrade will allow more effective application of the Leadering™ paradigm as a cohesive multi-dimensional force.

- The drives for the unknown are presented in more detail. These are the essence of leadership, entrepreneurship, innovation, and career creation
  - a frontier-pursuit drive: penetrating the unknown.
  - a creation / creativity-pursuit drive: bringing the unknown into existence.

These 2 dynamics are requisite to the successful operation of all 15 drives/ dynamics. All 15 drives require the drives to penetrate the unknown or bring the new into existence. The drives for the unknown are the drives behind the other 15 dynamics. All 15 dynamics are about the unknown.

Similarly, all of the natural forces in nature's systems maximization process are about bringing something new into existence or penetrating new territory (bringing a new territory into existence). So is leadership. Nature is endless creativity. So is leadership. Leadership or the maximization of human systems can therefore harness natural forces for goal achievement or bringing new realities into existence. multi-system context for goal achievement.

It is evident from this recording that Leadering™ rewrites today's disciplines for leadership, leadership development, performance improvement, organization change, entrepreneurial / intrapreneurial development, and management science.

Because the Leadering™ paradigm is logically interconnected, parts of the paradigm can be deduced by knowing other parts. Eventually you will have a critical mass of knowledge about the paradigm which catalyzes the paradigm shift.

9.8

The 15 Leader Drives: 57 minutes 21 figures
QUANTUM LEAP to operating with the 15 leader drives as a way of life.
This quantum leap has been building over the 8 recordings in the *Leader Drives* segment. It includes the application of the 15 drives in the Leadering™ systems maximization toolkit to corporate leadership. This example of multi-system orchestration and advancement within the Leadering™ paradigm is used to help define the post-leap state of the quantum leap. Participants are encouraged to extrapolate the corporate metaphor to their own multi-system context for goal achievement. The term '*leader*' and '*system maximizer*' are used interchangeably in the Leadering paradigm.

It is evident from this recording that Leadering™ rewrites today's disciplines for leadership, leadership development, performance improvement, organization change, entrepreneurial / intrapreneurial development, and management science.

COMPONENTS OF THE INTEGRATED TARGET PARADIGM - 1

DYNAMICS Maximizing actions	DRIVES links to maximization	META-COMPETENCIES capabilities from dynamics/drives

System Organization:
a congruence dynamic
a self-organizing dynamic
a systems-based dynamic
a templating dynamic
an emergence dynamic
 	
Multi-System Organization:
an adaptation dynamic
a co-evolution dynamic
an expanding consciousness dynamic
a flow-within-flow dynamic
(subsystems achieve congruence with their contextual system
 	
Improved Performance and Functionality:
a quantum leap dynamic
a frontier-pursuit dynamic
a creation/creativity dynamic
a flow dynamic
an evolution dynamic
a knowledge-pursuit dynamic
	Drives to
	internal congruence
	external congruence
	
	flow state
	   (our peak-performance / peak-evolution state of int/ext congruence)
	naturality
	   (internal congruence)
	expanded natural core
	   (growth congruence)
	resonance
	   (frequency congruence)
	meaning
	positive emotions
	adapt
	learn
	new knowledge
	emergence
	co-evolve
	frontiering
	creativity/creation
	achievement
	self-expression
		Systems-Based Approach
		systems thinking, systems-based operation, systems-based emotional intelligence, belief system management, quantum leaping, expanded consciousness, conceptual skills, templating
		
		Continuous Development
		accelerating growth, co-evolution, re-optimization, agility, fluidity, expanding self-expression, learning/adaptation agility, belief upgrading, expanding consciousness
		
		Cognitive Capabilities
		learning agility, knowing, conceptual skills, abstract thinking, expanding consciousness, internally referenced, expanding self-expression and self-awareness, emotional intelligence, deductive reasoning, pattern recognition
		
		Mastering the Unknown
		frontiering, creating, innovating, systems thinking, informationless decision-making, abstract thinking, conceptual skills, expanded consciousness
		
		Performance Improvement
		talent-based flow and other peak performance states, accelerated implementation, advancement by nonlinear quantum leaps, systems thinking, systems-based operation, expanding self-expression, learning/adaptation agility

© 2006 Lauren Holmes

COMPONENTS OF THE INTEGRATED TARGET PARADIGM - 2

KEY THEMES TRACKED FOR HARNESSING THE FLOW OF SYSTEMS TO CONGRUENCE
unpaid work theme, knowledge-pursuit theme, frontier-pursuit theme, creativity-pursuit theme, learning-pursuit theme, meaning-pursuit theme, talent-based flow state events theme, resonance events theme, positive emotion events theme, spontaneous knowledge events theme, creative invention events theme, spontaneous creativity events theme, theme of talent-based projects which had many coincidences and flow events.

HIGHLIGHTS OF THE TARGET PARADIGM

Advancing by wholes: Promotes: systems-based thinking and operation; a quantum leap process; template-based change management; coincidences; spontaneous knowledge; spontaneous creativity; spontaneous self-organization. Used to adapt and enhance human systems such as a leader, a follower, an organizational system, a market system, or leadership development.

Re-optimization, adaptation, co-evolution: All paradigm dynamics and drives serve these never-ending goals synergistically and opportunistically.

Flow-within-flow: Paradigm is powered by the flow of systems to congruence internally and externally.

Talent-based flow: The peak-performing/peak-evolving goal state of being which capitalizes on natural mechanisms built in to support a system's natural talents and passions.

Evolution direction: Human systems intensify around their natural core through an endless series of expansion quantum leaps rather than advance linearly.

Belief Engineering: Each human system and its reality are a single system defined by a single belief template. Change beliefs to change both the system and its reality. Beliefs can be known from reality patterns. Leadering conditioned reflexes triggered by problem events internally and externally activate an automatic belief template upgrade process. Reality is used as a self-correcting feedback system.

INTERNAL CONGRUENCE: Centered on the Natural Core
The only foundation for power as an individual and a leader

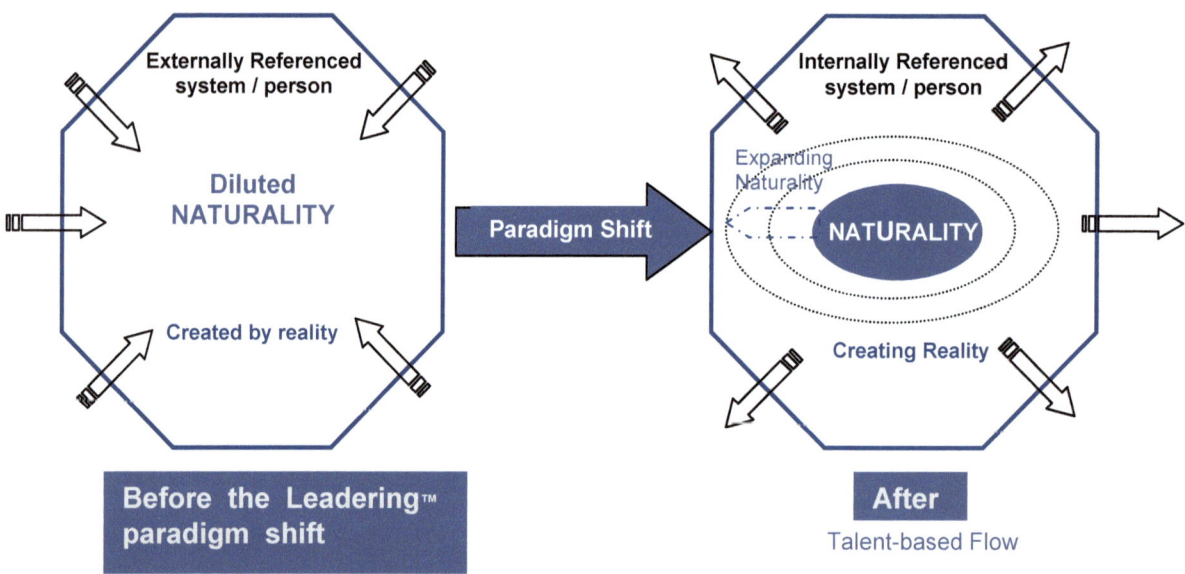

Generative congruence is the goal of systems in the target paradigm to operate with **systems integrity internally** and with **systems integration externally**. Congruence means that systems are consistent and in agreement and correspondence. The integration of systems inside a healthy body is an example of the congruence goal.

The fact that human systems are always trying to achieve internal and external congruence within a continuously advancing context creates a flow to congruence or a congruence dynamic which can be harnessed for maximizing, advancing, co-evolving and co-adapting individual and organizational systems.

Every paradigm dynamic or leader dynamic contributes to the achievement of generative congruence. The Leadering paradigm shift clicks systems into congruence internally and externally and sets them up to sustain that congruence.

EXTERNAL CONGRUENCE: Flow-Within-Flow

Co-evolving subsystems in talent-based flow synergistically merge into the flow of their shared contextual system which is also seeking its own state of talent-based flow or congruence.

A Flow-within-Flow Example: **THE IDEAL HUMAN CAPITAL STRATEGY**.
Maximize an individual or organizational system in talent-based flow while they are contributing to the talent-based flow state of the company

Subsystems maximized in flow state merge with the flow to the peak-performing / peak-advancing flow state of the system of which they are a part.

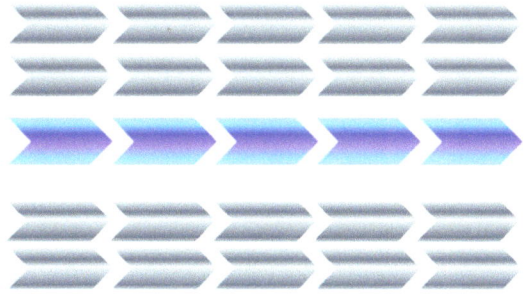

Competencies taught in traditional Leadership Programs
which Leadering™ Meta-Competencies Improve

Notice how most are designed to improve the flow of systems to congruence
based on the leader dynamics or paradigm dynamics of Leadering™

PLANNING
strategic planning
tactical planning
goal setting and communication
develop a shared vision
create a customer-focus
align people/organizations to strategy
translating strategy
execute strategic priorities
create clarity and focus
holistic/systems thinking
conceptualization
synthesis
manage attention
provide frameworks of reference

FUNCTIONS
financial management
marketing/sales management
HR management
IT management
operations management
customer relationship mgt (CRM)
project management
performance management
knowledge management
information management
systems management
managing up and down
command and control
stewardship
business acumen

MANAGING TALENT
hiring talent
build capability
develop competency / skills
develop talent
develop leaders
develop distributed leadership
mentor / coach
cultural imprinting
promote life-long learning
succession planning
assess performance
develop emotional intelligence
leading by example
teach/mentor the strategic art

ADVANCING
change management
implement ideas/goals
cultivate organizational learning, adaptivity and agility
performance improvement
process improvement
drive continuous improvement
generate/commercialize ideas
cultivating creativity/innovation
innovation adoption
product development/delivery
problem management
decision-making
develop / deliver value
leverage diversity
leverage resources
leverage technology
risk management
communicate the vision
deal with uncertainty/ambiguity
entrepreneurship/intrapreneurship
transformation
business process reengineering

ACHIEVING
motivate, inspire
empower
develop/align reward systems
create a sense of urgency
drive committed action
influence
communicate
establish credibility
gain commitment
establish accountability
establish consistency
maintain balance
get results
manage meaning
drive performance through shared vision, values, and accountability

COLLABORATING
clustering
build strategic alliances
team building
relationship building/maintaining
community building
generate alignment
consensus building
globalization
build social networks
manage across networks
lead across boundaries
integrate
promote collaboration / synergy
participative management
resolve conflict
influencing and negotiating
political acumen

© 2006 Lauren Holmes

Systems Management used by Nature and Natural Leaders

Nature pressures all human systems into generative congruence internally and externally. Successful leaders do the same thing.

The 14 paradigm dynamics or leader dynamics below promote the 15th dynamic: the flow of systems to generative congruence internally and externally. Congruence is the driving force of the target paradigm of Leadering™.

FLOW to GENERATIVE CONGRUENCE dynamic *(left margin)*

SYSTEMS MINDSET

A systems-based dynamic
Everything in the paradigm is a system, including individuals, organizations, and processes.

An expanding consciousness dynamic
Operating in the flow to congruence and stretching to view interacting systems causes consciousness to expand.

ADVANCEMENT MECHANICS

A quantum leap dynamic
A templating dynamic
A self-organizing dynamic
An emergence dynamic
Leaders orchestrate abrupt nonlinear system advancements, adaptations, co-evolutions, and re-optimizations using mechanisms available in the flow to congruence. They operate as belief engineers, cultural engineers, reality architects, quantum leap leaders, and emergence leaders:
NONLINEAR UPGRADE MECHANISMS

An evolution dynamic
'Growth' and 'Learning' help human systems achieve their existing potential. 'Evolution' advances that potential. Human systems advance by (1) quantum-leap intensifications of their natural core and (2) belief template upgrades: UPGRADED POTENTIAL / FUNCTIONALITY

ADVANCEMENT DIRECTIONS

A knowledge-pursuit dynamic
Leaders harness a system's innate drives for advancing its talent-based expression in order to achieve multi-system goals and maximization:
EVOLUTIONARY PATH DETERMINANT

An adaptation dynamic
Externally driven adjustment to advances in the shared contextual system caused by the adaptation / evolution of other subsystems:
CHAIN REACTION: THE DANCE

A co-evolution dynamic
Internally driven system upgrade achieved by capitalizing on external upgrading systems: OPPORTUNISTIC SYNERGY + LOCKSTEP ADVANCEMENT

A talent-based flow dynamic (internal)
A flow-within-flow dynamic (hierarchical)
The flow to internal/external congruence:
PEAK-PERFORMING / PEAK-EVOLVING STATE

DYNAMICS FOR MASTERING THE UNKNOWN:
the essence of leadership, entrepreneurship, innovation, and career creation
1. **A creation / creativity-pursuit dynamic:** Bring unknown into existence.
2. **A frontier-pursuit dynamic:** Penetrate unknown systems.
NATURE IS ENDLESS MULTI-SYSTEM CREATIVITY - LEADERSHIP IS AN EXTENSION

These dynamics form the toolkit for maximizing any human system in the paradigm whether the system is an individual, organization, market, civilization, or process such as leadership development, career management, or organizational change.

Figure 5 © 2006 Lauren Holmes

LEADER DYNAMICS for advancing systems within the Flow to Congruence

CONGRUENCE DYNAMIC COMPONENTS:

1. **SYSTEMS MINDSET:**
   - Systems-based dynamic
   - Expanding consciousness to systems mindset

2. **ADVANCEMENT MECHANICS**
   - quantum leap dynamic
   - templating dynamic
   - self-organization dynamic
   - emergence dynamic

3. **ADVANCEMENT DIRECTIONS**
   - knowledge pursuit dynamic (talent-based)
   - adaptation dynamic
   - evolution dynamic
   - co-evolution dynamic
   - talent-based flow dynamic
   - flow-within-flow dynamic
   - expanding consciousness dynamic

4. **DYNAMICS FOR THE UNKNOWN**
   the essence or definition of leadership, entrepreneurship, innovation, and career creation
   - frontiering™ dynamic: penetrate unknown systems
   - creation/creativity dynamic: bring unknown systems into existence

© 2006 Lauren Holmes

Leader dynamics indicating
ADVANCEMENT DIRECTIONS

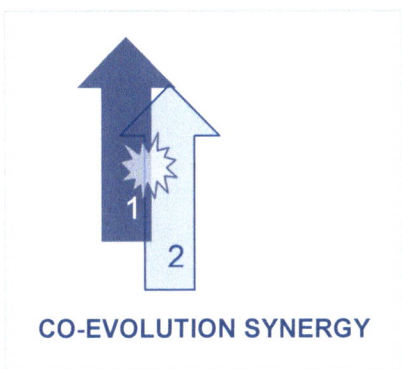

CO-EVOLUTION SYNERGY

ADAPTATION CREATIVITY

Quantum leaps in the direction of the knowledge-pursuit theme

Pre-leap → Post-leap

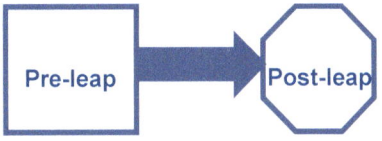

NATURAL TALENTS

EVOLUTION DIRECTIONS

Quantum leaps that expand / intensify / increase
- creativity
- creative expression of talents
- frontiering
- expanded consciousness
- congruence
- impact

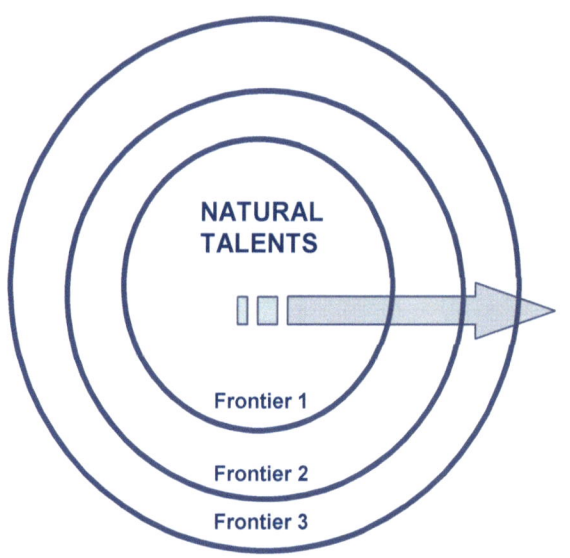

Leader dynamics indicating ADVANCEMENT DIRECTIONS

KNOWLEDGE-PURSUIT DYNAMIC

Pursuit of new knowledge which allows one to break through new frontiers of using one's natural talents to the fullest thus achieving the maximum creative expression of the system

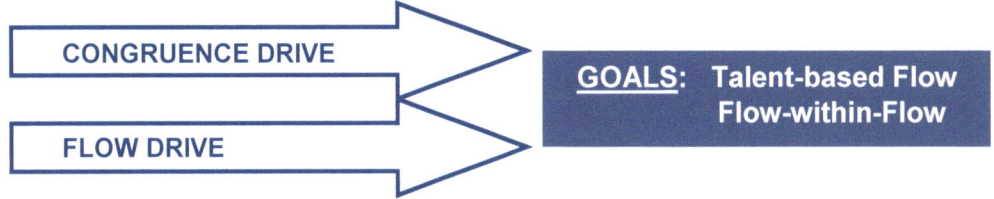

THE FLOW DRIVE = THE CONGRUENCE DRIVE

The **flow to congruence** or **the congruence-pursuit drive**
is identical to **the talent-based, flow-pursuit drive**.

Therefore all of the dynamics contributing to the flow to congruence
identified in Figure 5 are also contributing to the achievement of talent-based
flow - the peak-performance / peak-evolution state of any human system.

**100% talent-based flow state is Leadering's goal state
for you and for any systems you choose to lead.**

9-5E   © 2006 Lauren Holmes

Talent-Based Flow State = Internal Generative Congruence

The flow state which occurs while doing activities using
the talents one is most passionate about using and improving

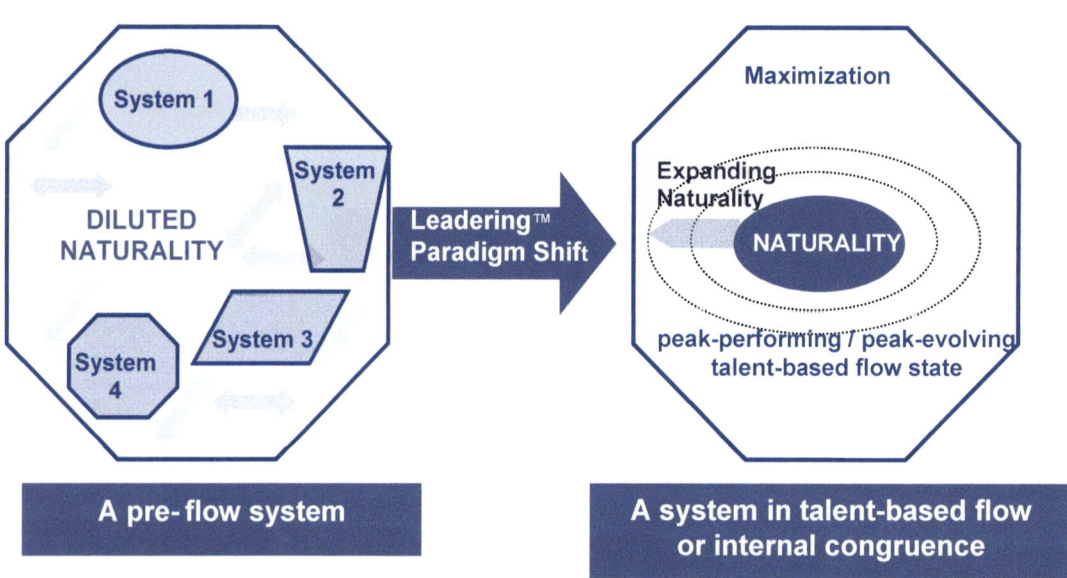

Fragmented and competing systems. No integration, internal cohesiveness or congruence.

Fully integrated around one's naturality, natural talents, and creative expression (one's 'art').

A pre-flow system

A system in talent-based flow or internal congruence

Clicking into flow state is a quantum leap to congruence, peak performance and peak evolution which upgrades one's system with each experience.

Talent-based flow is based on using one's greatest talents to do 'work' one is predisposed to pursue and to improve, and which is personally addicting to one's system. Only system resources required for the task at hand are activated. Peak performance results from the singular focus of all of the body's resources.

Flow is addicting. The more you experience it, the more you want to experience it. The admission price for entering flow state is to be stretched beyond your existing capabilities. Therefore flow perpetually advances a system. It puts it into a state of peak evolution.

Talent-based flow state results in increased functionality, upgraded potential, and expanded consciousness and cognitive abilities.

© 2006 Lauren Holmes

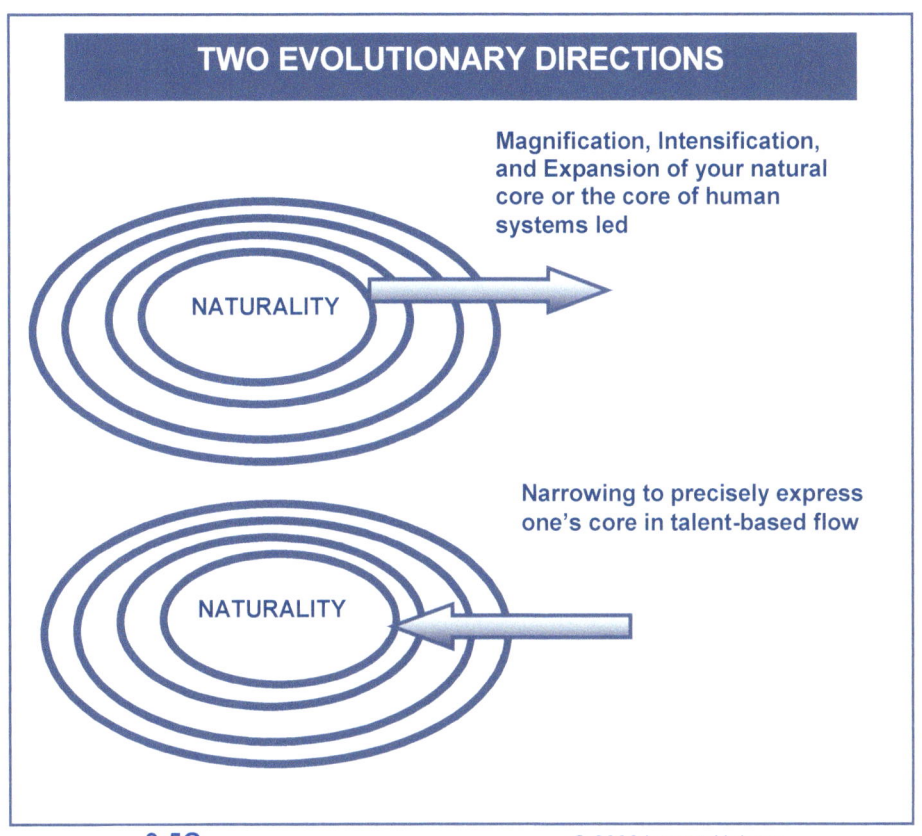

OUR FLOW ENGINE

KEY EVOLUTIONARY DIRECTION DETERMINANTS

OUR CORE FLOW DRIVE COMPLEX

Talent-based flow is addicting because its component drives are addicting:

Our key talent-based drives: *our flow engine*
- flow-pursuit drive
- creativity-pursuit drive
- creative-expression or self-expression drive
- frontier-pursuit drive
- knowledge-pursuit drive
- meaning-pursuit drive

Our secondary talent-based drives:
- quantum leap drive
- evolution drive
- co-evolution drive
- self-organization drive

These addictive drives integrate and unify to form a personalized synergistic thrust within each of us:
our flow engine

EVENT PATTERNS TRACKED FOR THEMES
These patterns are indicative of the flow to internal and external congruence or the flow-to-flow

In the target paradigm, the life-long patterns of the following 'talent-based' or 'work' events are analyzed for themes indicating the flow to generative congruence or flow internally or externally:

- **an unpaid work theme** based on patterns of events in which you freely give away "work" that others would charge for or that you are so passionate about that you would pay for the opportunity to do.
- **a knowledge-pursuit theme** based on patterns of events of seeking knowledge passionately and willingly for the application of key talents (learning-pursuit theme)
- **a spontaneous knowledge theme** based on patterns of events in which spontaneous knowledge emerged to support the application of key talents
- **a frontier-pursuit theme** based on patterns of events of new territories of growth, learning and achievement the system was drawn to pursue for the application of key talents
- **a creativity-pursuit theme** based on patterns of events of preferred creative expression or creative expression which you or system was drawn to pursue for the application of key talents along with events in which creativity or creative invention or innovation spontaneously emerged for the application of key talents
- **a talent-based creative expression theme** based on patterns of events of creative expression in which your passion and enthusiasm were inflamed
- **a meaning-pursuit theme** based on patterns of events of work or achievements or contributions considered a meaningful application of key talents
- **the theme(s) of talent-based flow states** indicated by patterns of events whereby you went into flow state during the application of key talents
- **a naturality expansion theme** indicated by patterns of expansions or intensifications of your system around its core to greater impact on reality - the key direction of growth and advancement of any system in the Leading™ paradigm.
- **a flow-to-flow theme, theme(s) of projects** requiring the application of key talents which were supported by lots of coincidences, flows, spontaneous knowledge / creativity
- **a resonance theme** based on patterns of subjects or activities for the application of key talents with which you resonated
- **a positive emotion theme** based on patterns of events in which passion, excitement, and enthusiasm emerged during the application of key talents

All of the above themes indicate when a system is integrated into the flow to congruence.

FIVE PERSONAL FORMULAS
for operating in the target Leadering™ paradigm

Based on the themes of the event patterns tracked in the paradigm, the following 5 formulas will emerge to help participants determine how to capitalize on the flow to flow of all human systems.

Your key talents are a system of your strongest capabilities which you are passionate about using and improving which advance reality in some way. This system is what is being acted upon by the flow to flow and your addictive drives.

ADVANCING YOUR SYSTEM

1. **Talent-based lifetime development formula** or personal evolution formula
2. **Greatest lifetime level of talent-based operation**: the culmination of living one's lifetime development formula.

ADVANCING OTHER SYSTEMS TO ADVANCE YOUR SYSTEM

3. **Talent-based leadership formula (or systems maximizer formula)** leadership as an expression of one's lifetime development formula
4. **Talent-based leadership development formula**: merging one's lifetime development formula with one's talent-based leadership formula.
5. **Greatest lifetime talent-based operating level as a leader**: based on the previous 4 formulas.

THE NATURE – HUMAN DRIVE CONTINUUM

All successful human systems must have links into the flow to congruence and their maximization in flow state. These links are our human drives.

The drives in humans are the same as nature's drives.
These are the same dynamics found in nature and our Leadering paradigm.

The drives in humans and the dynamics in nature compose a single systems maximization continuum

LEADERING DYNAMICS from nature's systems management	LEADERING DRIVES for Leadering™ systems management

a generative congruence dynamic
 	
SYSTEMS MINDSET
a systems-based dynamic
an expanding consciousness dynamic
 	
ADVANCEMENT MECHANICS
a quantum leap dynamic
a templating dynamic
a self-organizing dynamic
an emergence dynamic
 	
ADVANCEMENT DIRECTIONS
a knowledge-pursuit dynamic
a systems adaptation dynamic
an evolution dynamic
a co-evolution dynamic
a flow dynamic
a flow-within-flow dynamic
 	
DYNAMICS FOR MASTERING
THE UNKNOWN
a creation/creativity dynamic
a frontiering dynamic™
	OUR FLOW ENGINE
	
	TALENT-BASED ADDICTIVE DRIVES
	which are attempting to keep us and the human systems we compose operating in peak performance and peak evolution within the flow to congruence of the larger system of which we are a part.
	
	congruence-pursuit drive
	  • internal congruence
	  • external congruence
	  • resonance (frequency congruence)
	  • drive to self-organization and order
	  • drive to naturality (internal congruence)
	flow-pursuit drive:
	  (our peak-performance / peak-evolution
	  state of internal congruence)
	a flow-within-flow drive:
	  (for subsystems to merge with the
	  congruence/flow of a larger system)
	creativity-pursuit drive
	  • drive to self-expression
	  • drive to achievement
	frontier-pursuit drive
	knowledge-pursuit drive
	  • learning-pursuit drive
	meaning-pursuit drive
	positive-emotion pursuit drive
	evolution-pursuit drive
	
	LESS TALENT-BASED and ADDICTIVE DRIVES
	adaptation-pursuit drive
	a quantum leap drive
	a templating drive
	an emergence drive
	a co-evolution drive
	expanding consciousness drive
	systems-based drive

© 2006 Lauren Holmes

FLOW-WITHIN-FLOW = External Congruence

A subsystem in talent-based flow is integrated into the flow of its contextual system to its own state of talent-based flow or congruence.

A Flow-within-Flow Example: THE IDEAL HUMAN CAPITAL STRATEGY. Maximize an individual or organizational system in talent-based flow while they are contributing to the talent-based flow state of the company system.

Subsystems maximized in flow state merge with the flow to the peak-performing / peak evolving flow state of the system of which they are a part.

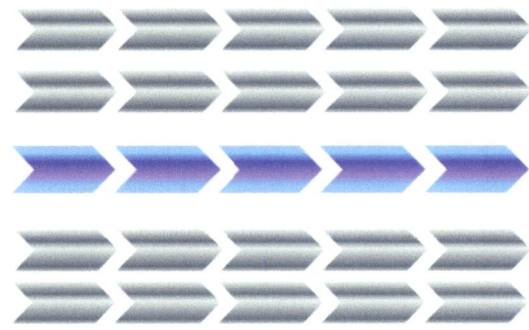

© 2006 Lauren Holmes

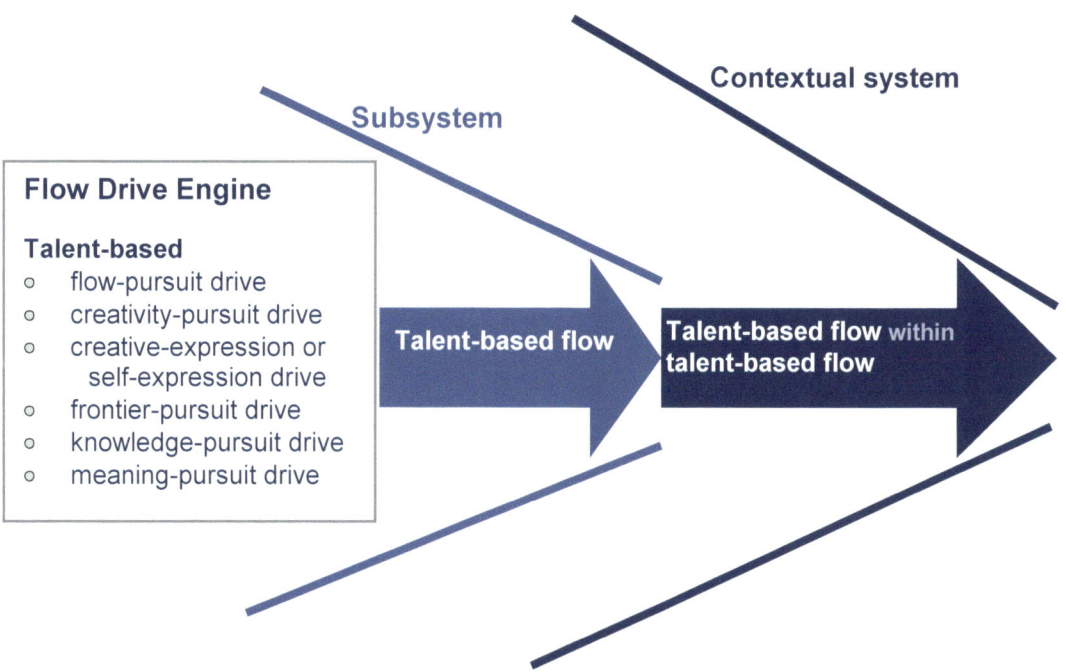

There is a single synergistic, adaptive, and co-evolutionary flow of human systems to maximization and survival. We are linked to this flow through drives addicting us to using our key talents. This core drive complex forms a flow engine trying to maximize us now and in the future by pulling us to use our key talents in our peak-performing and peak-evolving flow state: the flow-to-flow.

9-5M © 2006 Lauren Holmes

The advantage of operating in talent-based flow within the talent-based flow of the contextual system

Flow to Congruence or **Flow-to-Flow**

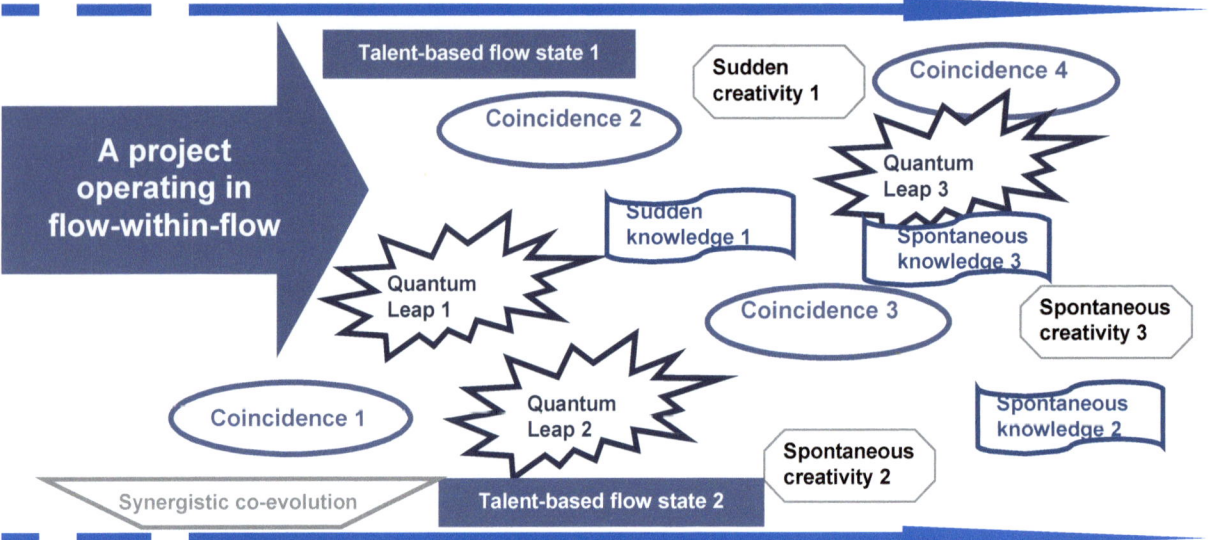

Flow to Congruence or **Flow-to-Flow** or **Flow to Fusion**
or   projection of your talent-based life themes into the future

---

Increasing functionality with each flow experience:
- expanding consciousness and conceptual capacity
- peak performance
- peak evolution
- increasing creative capability
- expansion / intensification / enlargement of the system's natural creative expression

Proof of the Leadering™ paradigm – Proof of the accuracy of your 5 formulas
If you are operating in talent-based flow and the clustering of natural quantum leaps above emerge in your reality, then you have proof that the Leadering paradigm™ and nature's machinery inside and outside of you do indeed operate in the way Leadering™ describes.

Leadering™ Reactivates Leader Drives
We are all born with the drives that energize natural leaders

Drives for creativity, innovation, frontiering™, advancement, learning, achievement, adaptation, self-expression, and talent-based flow

Our drives hook us to nature's endless evolutionary flow
with all the other successful living systems.

All are drives for penetrating the unknown or bringing the unknown into existence — the essence of leadership —

A NASA test for hiring innovative engineers and scientists
was given to 1,600 children as they aged:
  Leader drives at age   5:   98%
  Leader drives at age 10:   30%
  Leader drives at age 15:   12%
  Leader drives of 280,000 adults: 2%

Leader drives are culturally deterred.

The Leadering™ paradigm shift *reactivates* the drives underlying natural leadership

9-5P   © 2003 Lauren Holmes

Systems Management used by Nature and Natural Leaders

FLOW to GENERATIVE CONGRUENCE DRIVE

FLOW to FLOW DRIVE – THE FLOW ENGINE

Nature pressures all human systems into generative congruence internally and externally. Successful leaders do the same thing.

The 14 paradigm dynamics or leader drives below promote the 15th drive: the flow of systems to generative congruence internally and externally. Congruence is the driving force of the target paradigm of Leadering™.

SYSTEMS MINDSET

A systems-based drive
Everything in the paradigm is a system, including individuals, organizations, and processes.

An expanding consciousness drive to oneness. Consciousness expands due to operating in the flow to congruence and stretching to view interacting systems.

ADVANCEMENT MECHANICS

A quantum leap drive
A templating drive
A self-organizing drive
An emergence drive
Leaders orchestrate abrupt nonlinear system advancements, adaptations, co-evolutions, and re-optimizations using mechanisms available in the flow to congruence. They operate as belief engineers, cultural engineers, reality architects, quantum leap leaders, and emergence leaders:
NONLINEAR UPGRADE MECHANISMS

ADVANCEMENT DIRECTIONS

A knowledge-pursuit drive*
Leaders harness a system's innate drives for advancing its talent-based expression in order to achieve multi-system goals and maximization:
EVOLUTIONARY PATH DETERMINANT

An adaptation drive*
Externally driven adjustment to advances in the shared contextual system caused by the adaptation / evolution of other subsystems:
CHAIN REACTION: THE DANCE

An evolution drive*
'*Growth*' and '*Learning*' help human systems achieve their existing potential. '*Evolution*' advances that potential. Human systems advance by (1) quantum-leap intensifications of their natural core and (2) belief template upgrades: UPGRADED POTENTIAL / FUNCTIONALITY

A co-evolution drive*
Internally driven system upgrade achieved by capitalizing on external upgrading systems: OPPORTUNISTIC SYNERGY + LOCKSTEP ADVANCEMENT

A talent-based flow drive* (internal)
A flow-within-flow drive* (hierarchical)
The flow to internal/external congruence:
PEAK-PERFORMING / PEAK-EVOLVING STATE

DRIVES FOR THE UNKNOWN:
the essence of leadership, entrepreneurship, innovation, and career creation
1. **A frontier-pursuit drive*:** Penetrate unknown systems.
2. **A creation / creativity-pursuit drive*:** Bring unknown into existence.
   NATURE IS ENDLESS MULTI-SYSTEM CREATIVITY - LEADERSHIP IS AN EXTENSION

These dynamics form the toolkit for maximizing any human system in the paradigm whether the system is an individual, organization, market, civilization, or process such as leadership development, career management, or organizational change.

9- 5 upgraded © 2006 Lauren Holmes * addicting talent-based drives

Leadering™ Leadership Development Directions

LEADERING™ AMPLIFIES LEADER DRIVES

© copyright 1995 Lauren Holmes

Manager	Transitional Change Leader	Transformational Change Leader	Creational Leader / Frontiering Leader™
Run an existing business as is	Linearly advance an existing business • Incremental upgrades • Harvest	Nonlinearly advance an existing business • Turnarounds • Explosive Growth • Merge 2 existing businesses	Create the unknown **or** Penetrate the unknown • Business startups • Pioneering / Frontiering™ • Re-engineering • New ventures • Innovation

As leader drives strengthen, leader impact increases:
INCREASED DRIVES to change – creativity/creation – frontiering™
INCREASED BELIEF CHANGES MADE ➔

| Systems maintenance | Increasing systems advancement | | Systems Creation: including new systems from re-grouping existing systems |

Managers run existing systems ➔ Leaders create and advance human systems

As individuals advance along the leadership development continuum,
their ability to advance reality increases.
If there is no change in beliefs, there is no change in reality.
If there is no change on reality, leadership has not occurred.
The magnitude of change is the measure of leadership in the Leadering™ paradigm.

10 to 18 TRANSFERRED to *Leading Visuals Two*

7 PERSONALIZING THE LEADERING™ PARADIGM

I FLOW MAXIMIZATION EXERCISES

These exercises may be started any time after the Paradigm Shift Launch but cannot be completed before completing the Paradigm-Based Leadership segment

10. Big-Picture positioning for developing your 5 maximizing formulas
    22 minutes   15 figures
    ADVANCING YOUR SYSTEM
        Formula 1: Talent-based lifetime development formula
        Formula 2: Greatest lifetime level of talent-based operation as an individual
    ADVANCING YOUR SYSTEM BY ADVANCING OTHER HUMAN SYSTEMS
        Formula 3: Talent-based leadership formula
        Formula 4: Talent-based leadership development formula
        Formula 5: Greatest life-time level of talent-based operation as a leader or systems maximizer
11. Introduction to the 5 Leadering™ maximizing formulas
    18 minutes   12 figures
12. Advice for the core determination exercises for identifying one's 5 operating formulas for the Leadering™ paradigm   11 minutes   4 figures
13. Life Themes Exercises   48 minutes   5 figures
14. System Categories Exercises   36 minutes   28 figures
15. Growth built into the Leadering™ paradigm   23 minutes   19 figures
16. Key Talents Exercises   21 minutes   17 figures
17. Your 5 personalized Formulas for operating
    in the Leadering™ paradigm: intro   51 minutes   19 figures
18. 5 Formulas Specifics - Exercises for determining each of your 5 formulas for maximizing within the Leadering™ paradigm   34 minutes   18 figures

    Formula 1: 14 figures   Formula 3: 17 figures   Formula 5: 13 figures
    Formula 2:   8 figures   Formula 4: 18 figures

10 to 18 TRANSFERRED to *Leading Visuals Two*

Leadering prescribes new operating modes to capitalize on your upgraded functionality and normalized state resulting from the paradigm shift.

8 PERSONALIZING THE LEADERING™ PARADIGM

II BELIEF MAXIMIZATION EXERCISES: to promote flow maximization
These exercises may be started any time after the Paradigm Shift Launch but cannot be completed before completing the 15 paradigm-based Leader Drives segment

19. Belief Maximization Introduction   (ID quantum leaps)   108 minutes   41 figures
    10 Identity Quantum Leap Tool Categories are introduced as a means to more quickly and precisely define post-leap states that you wish to achieve:
       natural identity, goal-driven identity (+flow-driven+ corporate), belief clearing, multi-system, Leadering™ toolkit, (+ Leadering™ meta-competencies), quantum leaps to states of being: assimilated expert and projected expert

    Part 1: An introduction to belief engineering and the belief maximization process in the Leadering™ paradigm (35 minutes). It is ideal to have the right beliefs to support the maximization, growth and application of your key talents and your system core and the flow-to-flow. Various mechanisms for achieving this goal are introduced.

    Part 2: An introduction to the specific Leadering™ tools and exercises that will be used to personalize the paradigm further for you by ensuring that your changeable beliefs are supportive of your innate beliefs and the rest of the core of your system. The more integrated and cohesive your system is, the more power you have to achieve your goals.

    This is a very ambitious overview of some very new material. If you find it overwhelming, do not be concerned. Each category of identity quantum leap will be discussed in greater detail in separate recordings. This is just an opportunity to see what is coming and to see how it all fits together. Remember, the Leadering™ format is (a) big-picture overview then (b) examination of relevant parts, then (c) big-picture integration of the new parts into the whole again.

    10 identity quantum leap tools are introduced to Leadering's system maximization toolkit as a means to increase functionality and to quickly and precisely achieve desired goal realities.

THE LEADERING™ PARADIGM SHIFT

Quantum leaps to internalize subsets of an integrated paradigm belief system result in an integrated system of leader drives, reflexes and meta-competencies

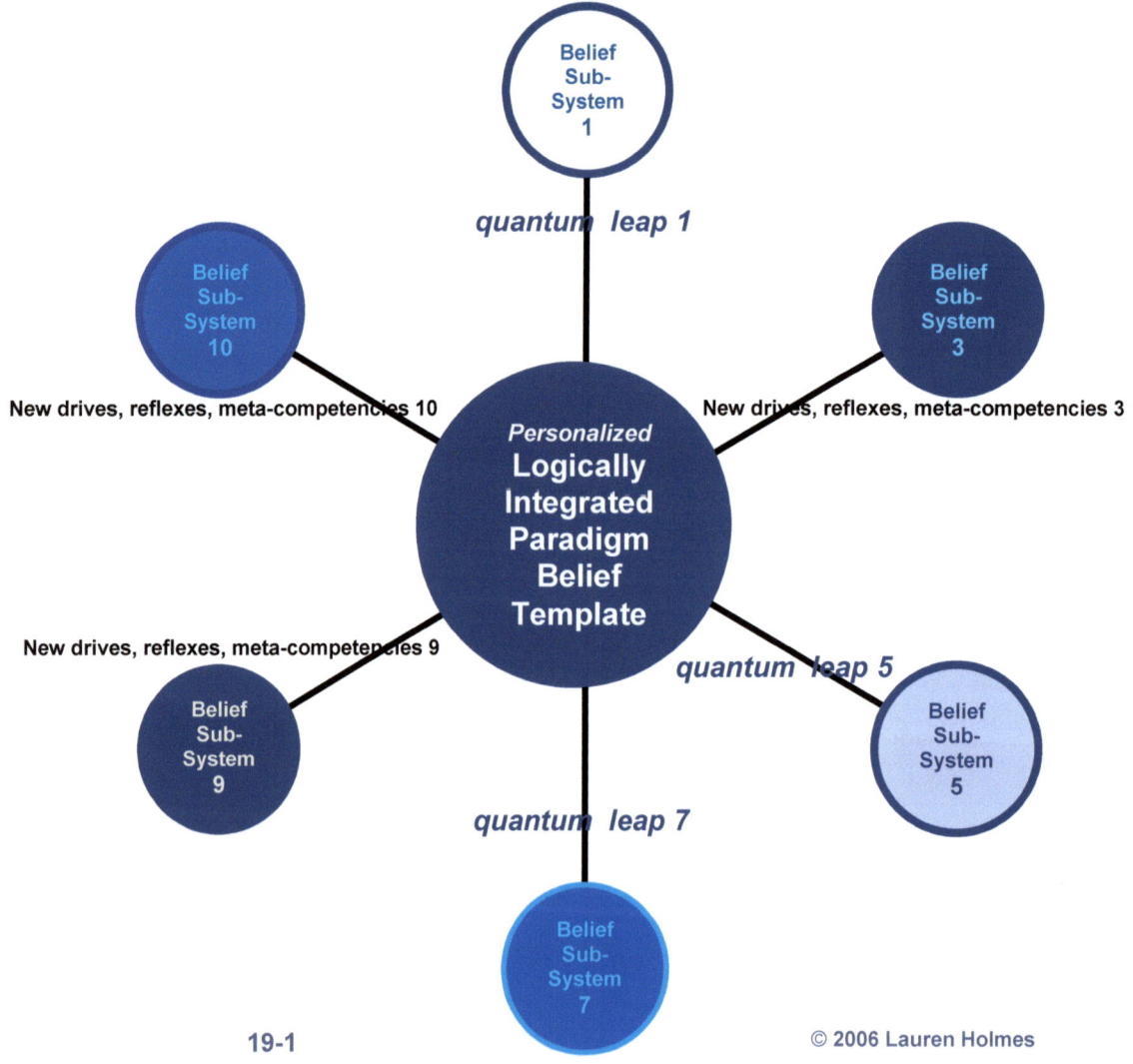

© 2006 Lauren Holmes

Recording 19: Belief Maximization Exercises 76

THE LEADERING™ CORE CONGRUENCE EXERCISES

These exercises are designed to identify the core of your system which is being acted upon by natural forces inside and outside of you so you can comply with and capitalize on them and avoid operating contrary to them.

FLOW MAXIMIZATION EXERCISES
for maximum performance and advancement

Life Theme exercises
- key talent determination
- flow to flow determination

Key talent Determination exercises
- system-based key talent exercise
- various other exercises

5 Talent-Based Operating Formulas exercises
1: your lifetime development formula
2: your greatest lifetime achievement formula
3: your natural leader formula
4: your leadership development formula
5: your greatest leader performance formula

YOUR FLOW ENGINE:

Natural forces inside and outside of you act on your core

YOUR CORE CONSISTS OF:

1. **KEY TALENTS**

2. **ADDICTIVE DRIVES**
pulling you to use your key talents

*Note: Your key talents and associated drives are the immutable beliefs below. They continuously
- create your reality and
- are being acted upon by the flow-to-flow and Leadering's built-in growth continuums which amplify core impact.

BELIEF MAXIMIZATION EXERCISES
for Core Congruence

Belief Template Analysis and Upgrade:
- beneficial belief determination:
  ideal talent-based and flow-based beliefs
  identity beliefs, reality creation beliefs
- problem belief determination:
  fear beliefs, toxic beliefs, conflicting beliefs
- event-driven template upgrade process
- quantum leap template exchange process:
  goal-packaging identities, reincarnation

Action Learning Experimentation
- proving beliefs create reality
- improving belief engineering in your own and other systems
- improving template determination / design
- quantum leap experimentation

YOUR BELIEF TEMPLATE

Your belief template governs both you and your reality as a single system

Beliefs are information storage units like genes

3. **IMMUTABLE BELIEFS**
(innate gene-based beliefs)
These define the essence of your system and why it came together in the first place. These beliefs are genetically based and inherent to the built-in creative expression of your system. See *Note above.

4. **CHANGEABLE BELIEFS**
ideally designed to support the key talents, addictive drives, and immutable beliefs to maximize your performance, development, and survival in biological terms. The goal is core congruence.

19-2A

© 2006 Lauren Holmes

*im·mu·ta·ble: unchanging or unchangeable: not changing or not able to be changed

CORE CONGRUENCE: The Changeable Beliefs

AUTOMATIC REALITY CREATION

IMMUTABLE or GENE-BASED BELIEFS

The beliefs behind the key talents and drives innate to your system core and flow engine.

Consistent with the flow-to-flow.

Adaptive realities are created automatically and continuously to amplify core through Leadering's built-in growth continuums.

Life Themes, Key Talent, and 5 Formula

CHANGEABLE

1. SUPPORTIVE

Promote flow to flow and Leadering's built-in growth continuums which amplify core expression and advancement for your system core.

Belief Upgrade Exercises

2. INTERFERING

Block flow to flow and built-in growth continuums required to maximize and advance core talents and drives

Belief Clearing Exercises

Leadering's single systems management toolkit can also be applied to belief systems.

Belief changes are achieved by quantum leap. It is easier to exchange a belief template than to try to change beliefs already logically integrated and interlinked into systems.

19-2B

© 2006 Lauren Holmes

The advantage of operating in talent-based flow within the talent-based flow of the contextual system

Flow to Congruence   or   Flow-to-Flow

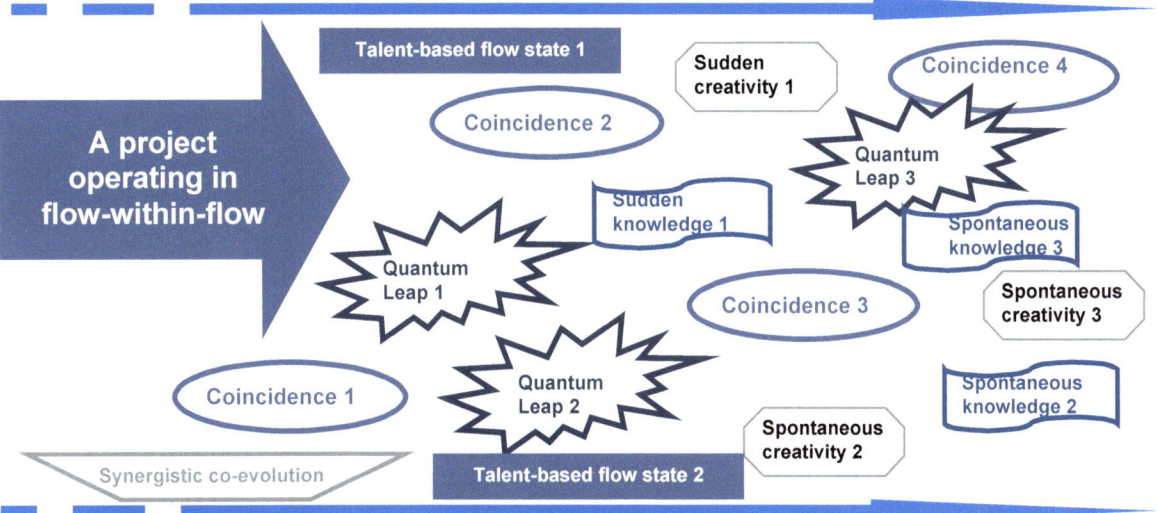

**Flow to Congruence   or   Flow-to-Flow   or   Flow to Fusion
or   projection of your talent-based life themes into the future**

Increasing functionality with each flow experience:
- expanding consciousness and conceptual capacity
- peak performance
- peak evolution
- increasing creative capability
- expansion / intensification / enlargement of the system's natural creative expression

Proof of the Leadering™ paradigm – Proof of the accuracy of your 5 formulas
If you are operating in talent-based flow and the clustering of natural quantum leaps above emerge in your reality, then you have proof that the Leadering paradigm™ and nature's machinery inside and outside of you do indeed operate in the way Leadering™ describes.

The REALITY-DRIVEN to CORE-DRIVEN Quantum Leap

- the quantum leap from externally to internally referenced
- a quantum leap to the core-driven advancement of systems in the Leading™ paradigm

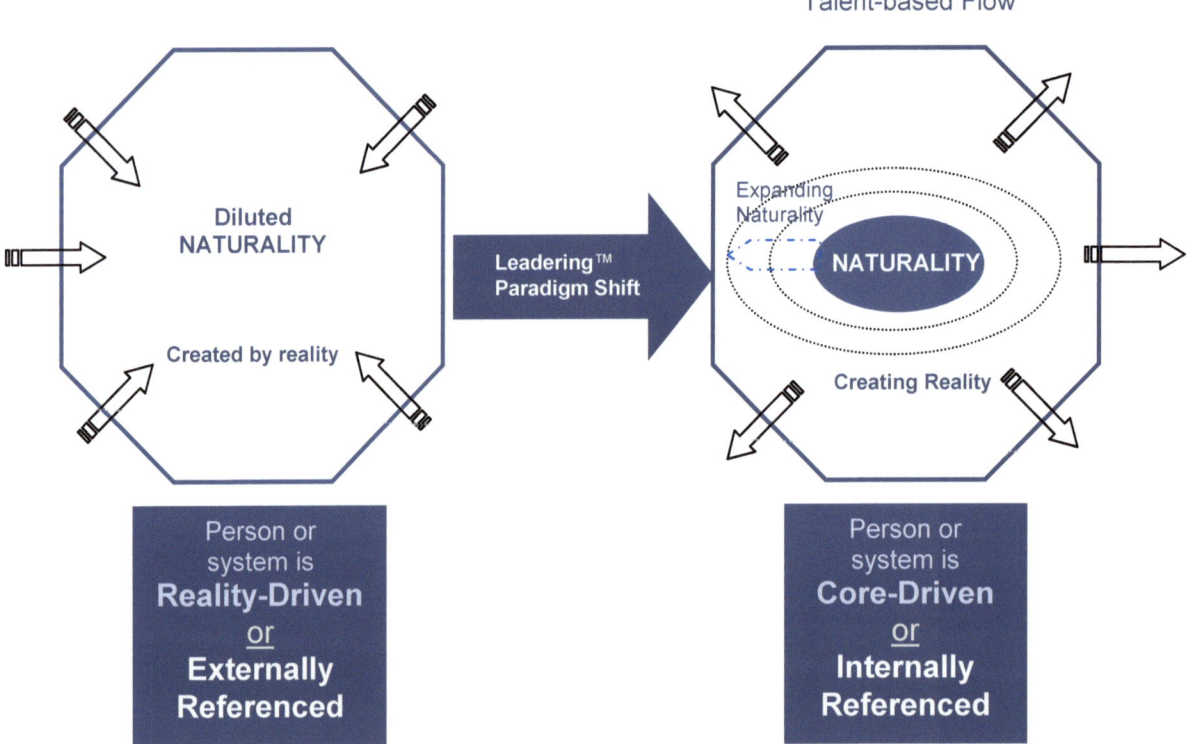

Re-boot your system onto its natural core to drive the Leading™ machinery

In the Leading™ paradigm, beliefs create reality. You and your reality are a single system created and run by a single belief template. Therefore, the quantum leap from externally referenced and created by the people and events in your reality to internally referenced and creating your reality is critical to leadership, entrepreneurship, innovation, peak performance and precise reality creation. This is a quantum leap from reality-driven to core-driven. It is the pivotal quantum leap to operating in the driver's seat of the Leading™ machinery in a paradigm which must be personalized to your system.

The natural forces, mechanisms and dynamics which compose the Leading™ machinery are acting on your natural core. To use them, you need your system to be centred on that core.

Recording 19: Belief Maximization Exercises 80

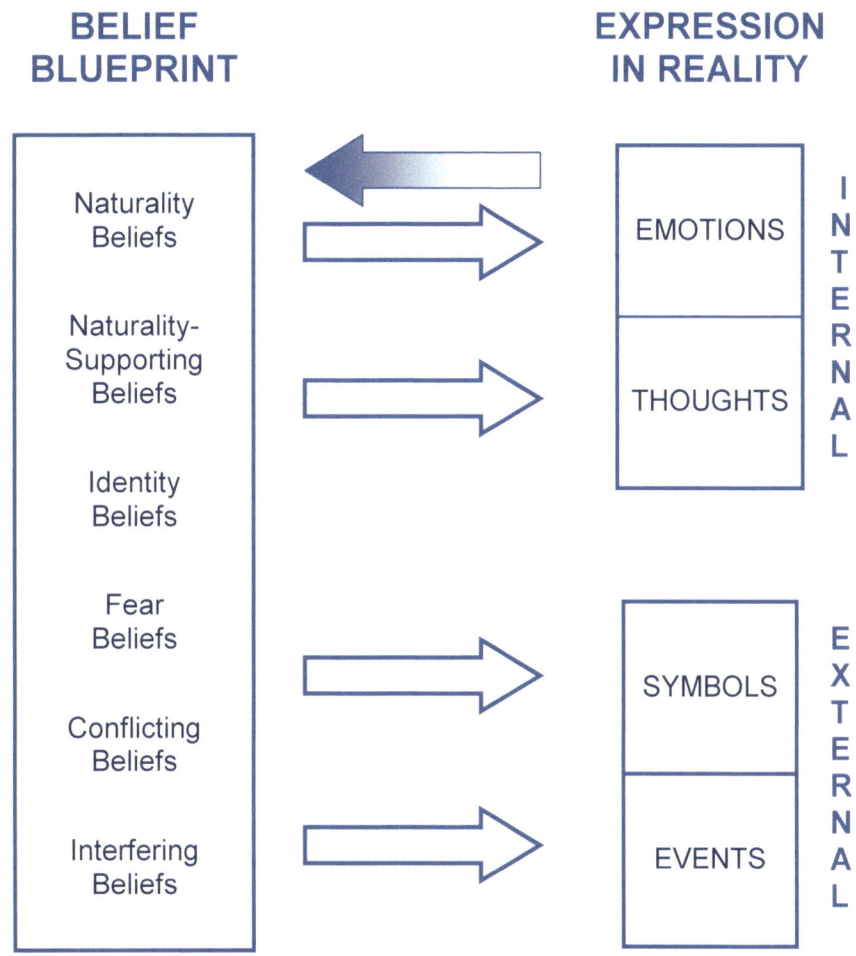

19-2E   © 1993 Lauren Holmes
Excerpted from *Peak Evolution* (Lauren Holmes, 2001)

CORE-DRIVEN: A Recurring Theme In Nature

Human systems in the Leadering™ paradigm are <u>core-driven</u> or <u>template-driven</u>. Change the core to change both the system and its reality:
- the part contains the information for the whole
- the microcosm mirrors the macrocosm
- the core defines the system and its reality
- David Bohm: the implicate order defines the explicate order: the unseen defines the seen

A LIST OF RELEVANT FIGURES TO FOLLOW:
Visual metaphors for a core-driven reality and core-driven leadership

Figure 3B	Nucleus to an atom
Figure 3C	Nucleus to a cell
Figure 3C	DNA to a nucleus to a cell
Figure 3D:	Cell to a human body
Figure 3E:	DNA replication
Figure 3F:	Our belief template to our reality
Figure 3G:	Beliefs in the core-driven Leadering paradigm
Figure 3H:	Leader versus systems led: as in hierarchical or traditional leadership
Figure 3I:	Leadering's core-driven leadership: Change the template to change the system and its reality
Figure 3J:	Traditional Leadership versus Leadering's core-driven leadership
Figure 3K:	Leadering's core-driven leadership: Another view

© 2006 Lauren Holmes

NUCLEUS: the Core of the Atom

- The smallest unit of matter having all the characteristics of that element.
- Consisting of a dense, central, positively charged nucleus surrounded by a system of electrons.

19-3B © 2006 Lauren Holmes

NUCLEUS: the core of every Human Cell
DNA: the core of every Cell Nucleus

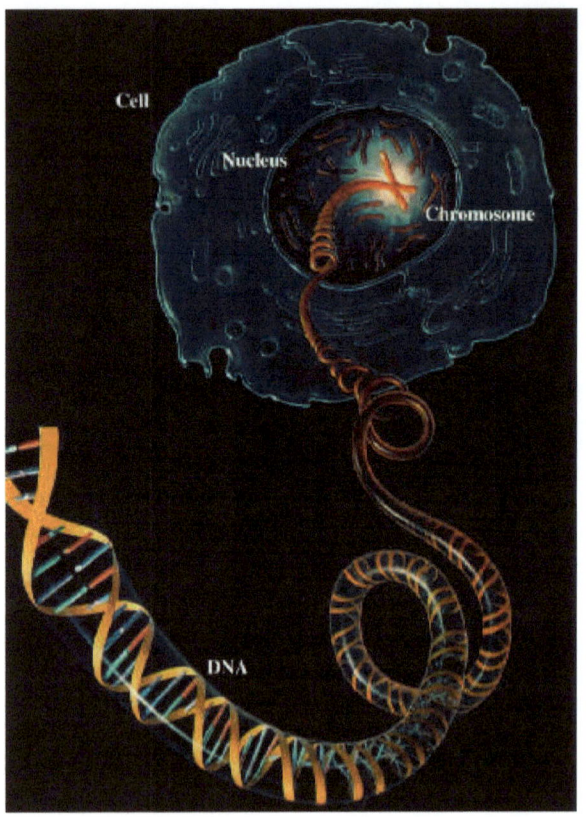

This is a diagram of a typical cell from the human body. In this picture you can get a sense of where the DNA resides in the cell as well as how it is organized in the nucleus. Double-stranded DNA is organized into chromosomes. Chromosomes are situated in the nucleus and the membrane bound nucleus is found in the cell.

If every cell in your body has a nucleus or natural core, it makes sense that you too have a natural core or template for you and your reality.

"The part contains the information for the whole" is a recurring theme throughout the universe. As the part, you would therefore contain the template for your whole system which includes you and your reality. This repetitious recurrence is at the foundation of Leadering's single systems management toolkit for all human systems.

Copyright © The National Human Genome Research Institute

Recording19:   Belief Maximization Exercises   84

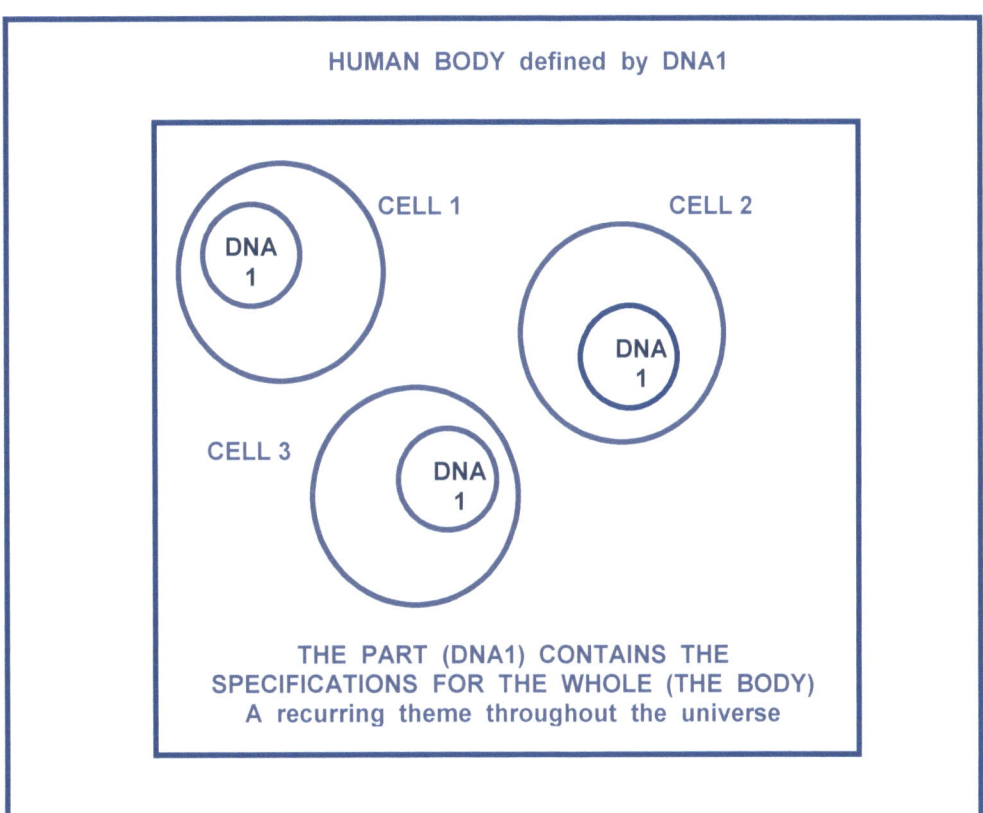

The DNA in every cell of the human body is identical. It contains all of the specifications for defining the whole human body: the part contains the information for the whole.

In our nature metaphor for the Leading paradigm, the belief template operates in the same way as DNA: **the core belief template contains the specifications for the reality experienced which includes your physical body.**

The effective leader of an organizational system or company strives to have each person have the same DNA or belief template as this metaphor to create a cohesive force to achieve organizational goals.

19-3D   © 2006 Lauren Holmes

DNA Transcription

Another nature metaphor

a metaphor for how the beliefs in your belief template create reality in the Leadering™ paradigm

DNA transcription is used for

- transcribing one DNA from another or
- transcribing a DNA to a messenger RNA

It relies on the **principle of complementarity** with respect to matching up nucleic acids:

> A attracts U.
> G attracts C.
> T attracts A
> C attracts G

A core-driven leader acts as the DNA or belief template for
- his/her system and its their reality
- the systems s/he chooses to lead to create/achieve goal realities

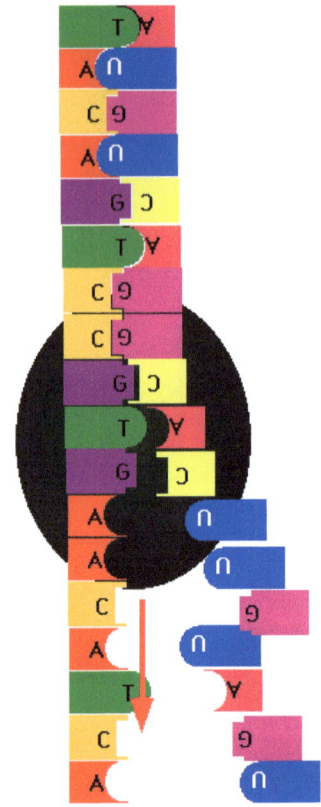

Copyright © Paul Decelles 1995, 2002
http://staff.jccc.net/pdecell/proteinsynthesis/transcript.html

© 2006 Lauren Holmes

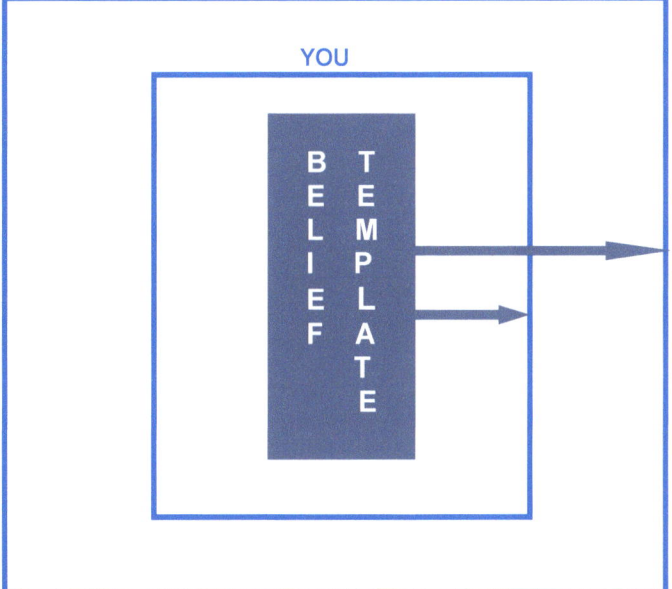

Elements in reality are replicated from beliefs using the same transcription process metaphorically as DNA uses to replicate itself, instruct RNA and protein synthesis. The result is a belief-created reality instructed by the immutable beliefs which are linked to your genes and changeable beliefs which you can design to support natural processes working on your system internally and externally.

HIERARCHICAL LEADERSHIP

TRADITIONAL LEADER-AT-THE-TOP MODEL
one leader acting on one or more individuals

19-3G

© 2006 Lauren Holmes

LEADING, CREATING and ACHIEVING in the PARADIGM

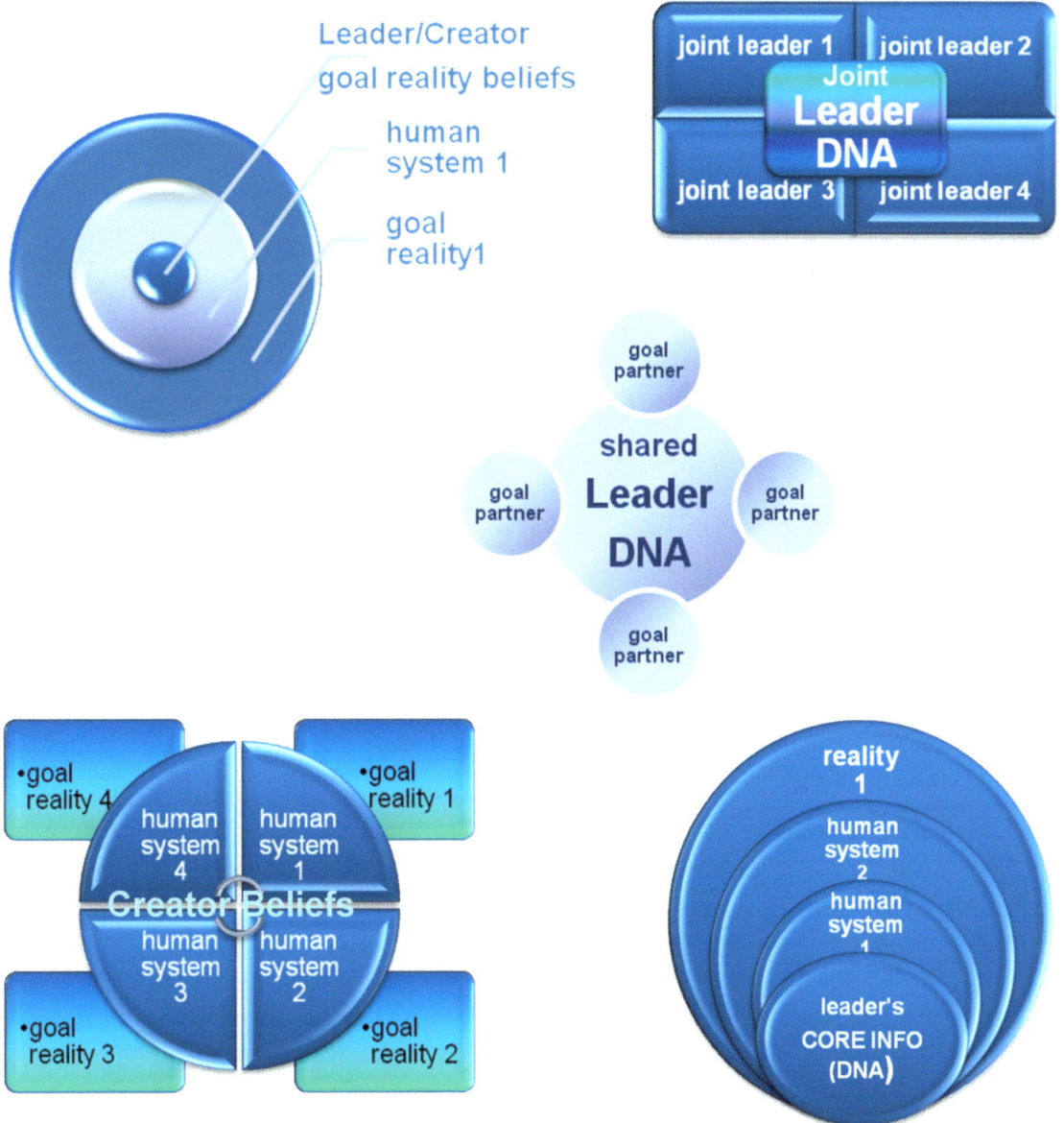

SYSTEMS-BASED or CORE-BASED LEADING, CREATING and ACHIEVING in the LEADERING™ PARADIGM

Reality creation is accomplished by one or more leaders or system maximizers creating the core 'DNA' for defining the new goal reality system based on a belief template shared by multiple systems. **You and your reality are a system.**
Merge yourself and relevant systems to a single system for *peak legacy*.

Leadering™ Simplifies Leadership to its Dynamics

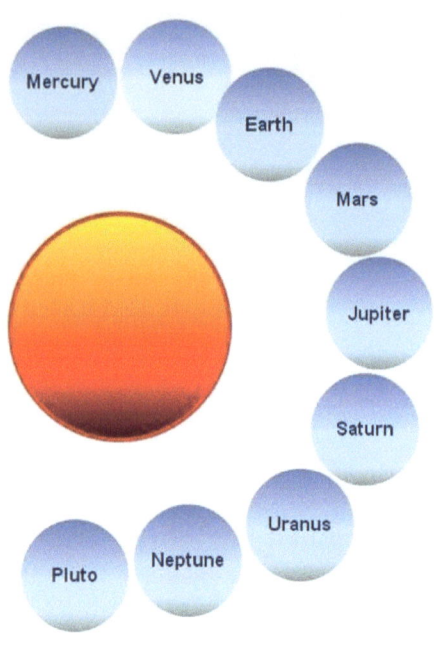

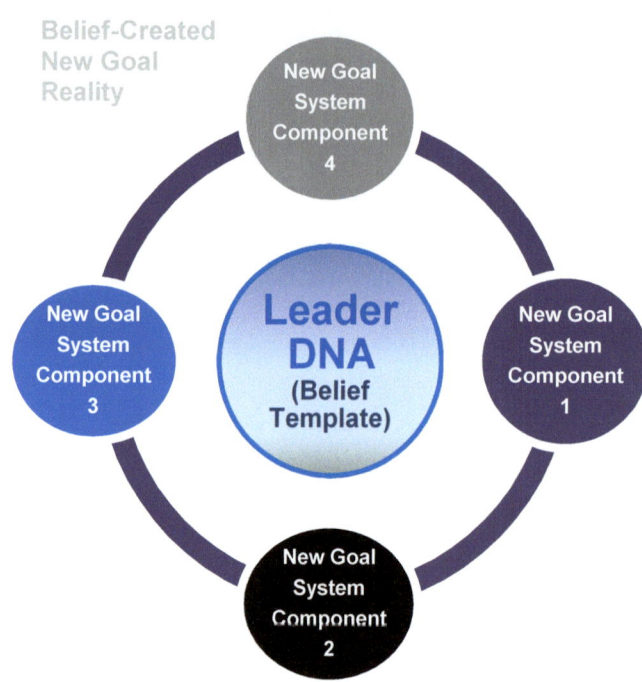

Traditional Leadership
Metaphor: Sun-Planet Relationship

The sun locks the planets in by force. It directs planet movement. However, the cores of the planets are unchanged by the sun and the core of the sun is unchanged by the planets. Neither the sun nor the planets benefit from each other. There is no synergy whereby the whole is greater than the sum of the parts.

Leadering's Core-Based Leadership
Metaphor: DNA or genes defining a human cell

In the Leadering Paradigm, a leader's beliefs and decision-making systems are replicated in individual or organizational systems so that their natural operation will result in achieving a goal in the same way the leader would accomplish it personally.

Rather than a leader acting on others, leaders with their follower individuals and systems operate as a single integrated system with a shared belief template for creating the goal reality. It is about multi-system reality creation.

The leader's belief template must be strong enough and clear enough to define this new multi-component system and its goal reality. A non-leader can use the same approach to capitalize on relevant human systems. By extending one's capabilities with those of other systems one can achieve beyond one's potential.

Beliefs create reality in the Leadering paradigm. Just as in nature, there must always be a blueprint or information structure defining the expression. Human cells and the human body are examples. Beliefs (not thoughts) are how we lock in the new blueprint or, metaphorically, the new DNA. If the information structure does not change inside, nothing will express differently outside . . . . no matter how much action is taken. This is why passionate entrepreneurs can succeed where brilliant experts fail.

CORE-DRIVEN LEADING and ACHIEVING

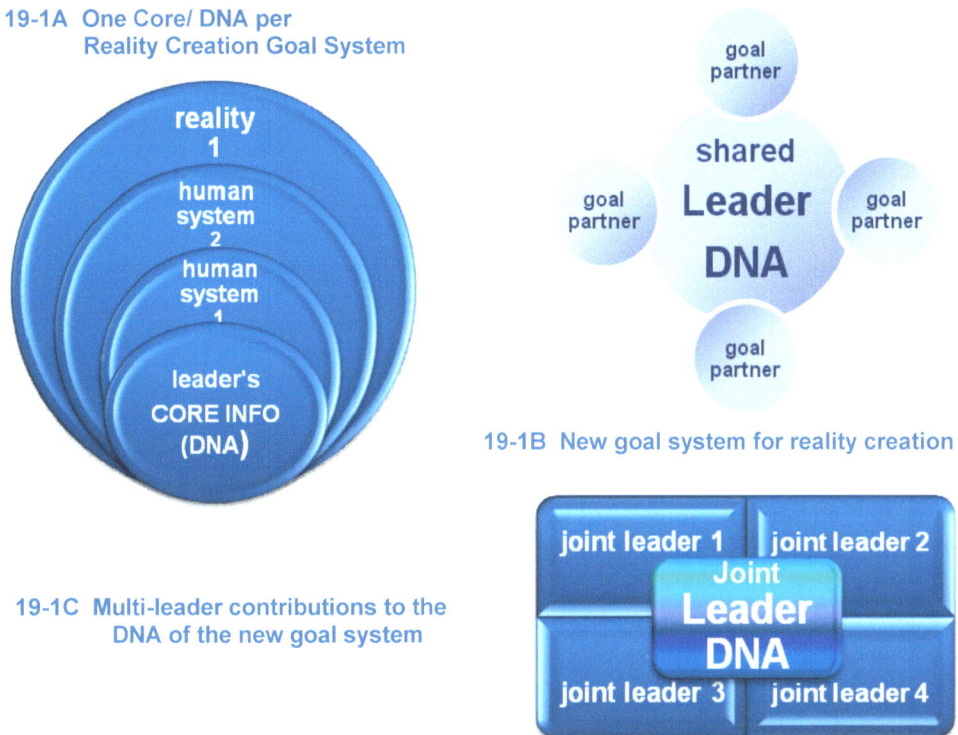

19-1A One Core/ DNA per Reality Creation Goal System

19-1B New goal system for reality creation

19-1C Multi-leader contributions to the DNA of the new goal system

Core change for reality change
One's core belief template creates both you and your reality in the Leadering paradigm. Your core will also create the reality of the human systems you wish to lead or harness for goal achievement. This is a new understanding of *leading from within*.

Leaders (or those maximizing human systems for goal achievement) must define the reality of human systems they choose to lead by becoming their core or, metaphorically, their DNA, the information structure that defines those systems. The leader and the harnessed human systems must become a single system defined by the core belief template of the leader. For outward change, leaders must first focus inward with rigid clarity to empower the imprinting of beliefs inside of others.

Core-Driven Leadership is *belief-template-driven* leadership.
Leadering™ prescribes changing the core information structure that defines each human system in order to create that system's goal reality by reflection.

The DNA in the genes of all our cells defines the reality of the expression of a physical body. The comparable defining information structure in the Leadering paradigm is the belief template of each human system in the collective required for the goal reality creation. Change the internal belief structure to change human systems in order to change the reality experienced. No change inside, no change outside. In physicist David Bohm's terminology: the *implicate* defines the *explicate*.

The goal achievement process must refocus accordingly. Instead of a focus on getting people from point A to B, or through activities 1 to 10, a core-driven creator concentrates on changing the belief template defining each of the systems required to help to achieve his/her goal reality. Coincidences, flow events, synergistic systems, and quantum leaps will cluster accordingly in reality. Progress accelerates as a reflection of the change in core information.

INCREASING MAGNITUDE OF IMPACT ON BELIEF SYSTEMS

© copyright 1995 Lauren Holmes

LEADERING™ promotes LEADER DRIVES and BELIEFS

Manager	Transitional Change Leader	Transformational Change Leader	Creational Leader / Frontiering Leader™
Run an existing business as is	**Advance an existing business linearly** • Incremental upgrades • Harvest	**Change an existing business nonlinearly** • Turnarounds • Explosive Growth • Merge 2 existing businesses	**Create the unknown or Penetrate the unknown** • Business startups • Pioneering / Frontiering™ • Re-engineering • New ventures / Innovation

As leader drives strengthen, leader impact increases:
INCREASED DRIVES to change – creativity/creation – frontiering™
INCREASED BELIEF CHANGES MADE

Systems maintenance	Increasing systems advancement		Systems Creation: new and new from grouping existing systems

Managers run existing systems ➡ Leaders advance and create systems

As managers advance along the leadership development continuum,
their ability to advance reality increases.
Their ability to make belief changes increases.
If there is no change in beliefs, there is no change in reality.
If there is no change in reality, leadership has not occurred.
The magnitude of change achieved in reality is the measure of leadership strength.

© 1995 Lauren Holmes

INCREASING MAGNITUDE OF IMPACT ON BELIEF SYSTEMS

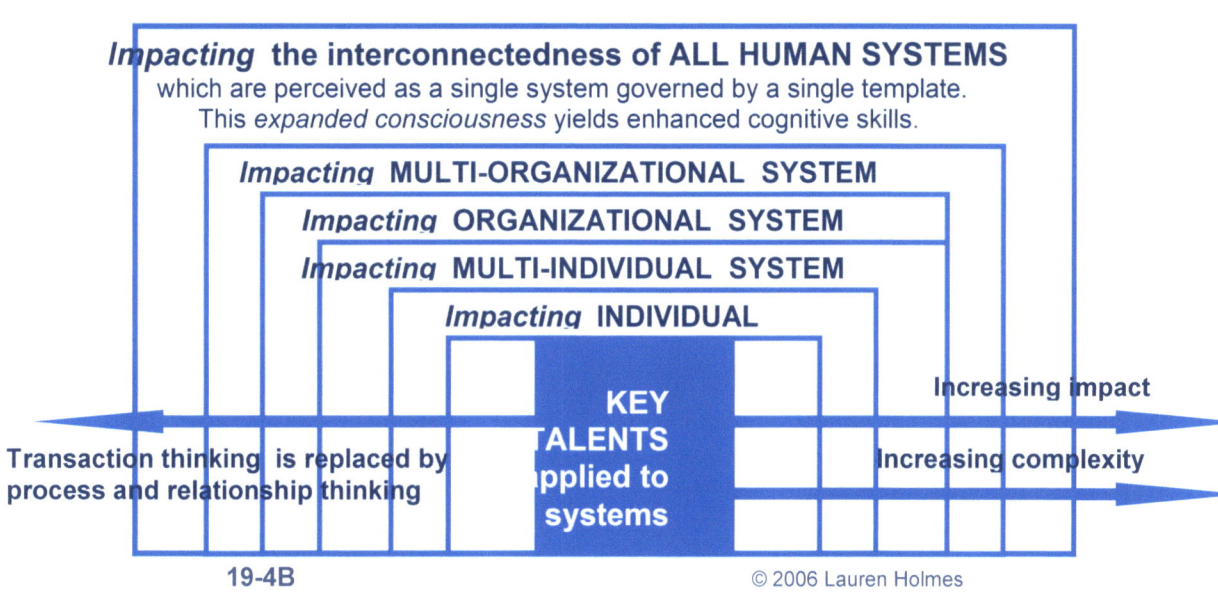

19-4B © 2006 Lauren Holmes

CREATING WORLD LEADERS

| YOUR REALITY | ORGANIZATION | NDUSTRY | BUSINESS ECOSYSTEM | CIVILIZATION |

POWER MUST INCREASE TO:

Imprint Beliefs → Unify Identities → Increase Creations

19-4C © 1995 Lauren Holmes

LEADERING™ BELIEF ENGINEERING TOOLS
for the 'Changeable Core Beliefs' requisite to core maximization

THREE CATEGORIES OF BELIEF UPGRADE TOOLS to

- upgrade your "*Changeable Core Beliefs*" to support the maximum performance and advancement of your core. (figure 19-2B)
- clear the interfering beliefs which are creating unpreferred realities: problem beliefs, conflicting beliefs, fear beliefs, and beliefs interfering with the built-in growth continuums. (figure19- 2B)
- add layers of advantageous beliefs such as goal-driven identities and core-expansion identities (figures 19-7 and 19-8)

1. QUANTUM LEAPS

Quantum leaps are belief system exchanges. Changed beliefs result in a changed reality. Quantum leaps are power tools in Leadering's single systems management toolkit. There are no quantum leaps without a change in beliefs. (figures 19-9 and 19-10)

2. REALITY PARTNERING:

Belief determination, reinforcement and upgrade (figure 19-11):
- Event-driven belief upgrades: events in reality serve as triggers for a conditioned reflex to quantum leap to upgrade your beliefs (figure 19-12)
- Reality is a self-correcting feedback system
- Action learning experimentation

3. LEADERING™ SYSTEMS MAXIMIZATION TOOLKIT AND MACHINERY

Talent-based flow state merged with the flow to flow and the Leadering™ machinery:
- Installs and strengthens beliefs supportive of the maximum advancement and performance of your system
- Activates the belief systems supporting your key talents and core to create adaptive realities promoting the built-in growth continuums
- De-activates interfering beliefs allowing them to atrophy from disuse over time

Identity Quantum Leap Categories
Install belief systems using identities as the post leap

8 IDENTITY QUANTUM LEAP CATEGORIES

A. Natural identity quantum leaps (immutable beliefs)
  A. Subset: Growth or expansion identity quantum leaps

B. Goal-driven identity quantum leaps
  B. Subset: Flow-driven identity quantum leaps

C. Leadering™ toolkit identity quantum leaps
  C. Subset: Leadering™ meta-competency identity quantum leaps

D. Identity quantum leaps to replace problem beliefs

E. Corporate Identity Quantum Leaps

IDENTITY QUANTUM LEAP BASICS:

1. Identities are integrated systems of beliefs.

2. Beliefs, like genes in the nucleus of a cell, are information storage units which define the core of any human system.

3. All advancement of human systems in the Leadering™ paradigm requires a change of beliefs. Leaders are therefore belief engineers.

4. Internalize the 'feel' or emotional template of your desired post-leap identity to lock in the belief upgrades which will change reality to coincide with those new beliefs. (figure 19-2E)

5. Assume you or systems you lead have operated with the proposed post-leap identity successfully for 10 years.

6. Your selected post leap must be consistent with the direction of the flow to flow for natural forces to energize the leap.

Natural Identity Quantum Leaps
Install belief systems using identities as the post leap

A. YOUR NATURAL IDENTITY QUANTUM LEAP:

Leadering™ re-centres your system onto its natural core and then expands that core.

- Quantum leap to the talent-based core defined by the 5 Leadering™ operating formulas
  Quantum leap to talent-based living and talent-based flow state.

- Quantum leap from externally referenced and created by your reality to internally referenced and creating your reality.
  Quantum leap from reality-driven to core-driven.

- Quantum leap to the core-driven approach required to drive the Leadering™ machinery.
  Re-boot your system into the driver's seat of your personalized Leadering™ machinery

- Re-boot your system onto its core consistent with pressures by natural forces and built-in growth continuums

- Apply natural identity quantum leaps to other systems to facilitate the achievement of their goals and yours.

AA: GROWTH OR EXPANSION IDENTITY QUANTUM LEAPS

Once your system has been re-centred onto its natural core, establish one post-leap identity after the next for the next expansion of your core. Use your 5 Leadering™ operating formulas and especially formulas 2 and 5 to keep your growth identities consistent with the flow to flow.

Assume you have successfully been each of these identities for 10 years. Each identity penetrates the next frontier of applying your key talents in compliance with the built-in growth continuums operating in the Leadering™ paradigm. You can think of these post-leap growth identities as talent-based identities. They relate to the advancement of your key talents (figure 19-6A, 19-6B, and 19-6C)

Goal-Driven Identity Quantum Leaps
Install belief systems using identities as the post leap

B. GOAL-DRIVEN IDENTITY QUANTUM LEAPS (figures 2B, 2E, 19-7, and 19-8)

Partner adaptive "goal-driven identities" with your "natural identity"
You can use quantum leaps as a form of reincarnation to package your natural identity in such a way that it will help you to achieve immediate goals by quickly changing reality.

For the best results you still need to honour the direction of the flow to flow and your natural core with its key talents and drives and immutable beliefs. Goals and quantum leaps will only be supported by natural forces when you are being true to the system and its contextual system.

Both your natural identity and any goal-driven identities with which you choose to package yourself are massive systems of beliefs which will therefore impact reality more dramatically than changing one belief at a time. As a result, goals are achieved more quickly.

BB. FLOW-DRIVEN IDENTITY QUANTUM LEAPS

Flow-driven identities arise opportunistically from the flow to flow when you set a new goal. **These flow-driven post-leap identities are absorbed from models, information systems, and people and events flowing in to you as part of the flow to flow when you set goals consistent with that flow.**

Once you set a goal which complies with the flow to flow and the advancement of your key talents through new frontiers, you have launched the support of natural forces, natural quantum leaps like coincidences, spontaneous knowledge, spontaneous creativity, and facilitative events, and the flow of supportive information systems. All of these could cumulatively suggest all or part of your post-leap identity or the ultimate solution to your immediate goal.

The flow-to-flow always orchestrates synergy and co-evolution and co-adaptation. It is only logical then that co-evolving systems will move into your vicinity which will support the goal for your system that you have selected consistent with the flow-to-flow.

Leadering™ Toolkit Identity Quantum Leaps
Install belief systems using identities as the post leap

C. LEADERING™ TOOLKIT IDENTITY QUANTUM LEAPS

Examples of belief systems or identities used for the reality-driven to core-driven quantum leap and operating in the Leadering™ paradigm.
Examples:

1. *Quantum Leap Expert* **revisited** from your current level of capability and experience to push the envelope on your expertise. Template exchange is belief engineering

2. Quantum leap to the identity of a **person who owns and operates his/her reality** so that you and your reality are a single system.

3. Quantum leap to *Reality Creation Expert* and to be able to change your belief template or system at will in order to change yourself and your reality advantageously in the shortest possible time.

4. Quantum leap to *Belief Engineering Expert* able to quickly change belief systems whether changing your own beliefs, your children's, or an organization's culture.

5. Quantum leap to **Emotional Engineering Expert:** a visioneer who constructs visions which engage people through their emotions which changes their beliefs and thus their realities and the reality of the organization.

6. Quantum leap to your formulas 2 and 5. These are the identities of you at your maximum as an individual and as a leader respectively.

7. Quantum leap to one or more of *the following identities* as relevant:
   - a leader
   - a high performer
   - a career master
   - a system maximizer
   - a systems co-evolution expert or system advancement master
   - an entrepreneur or intrapreneur
   - an innovator or a creative

Leadering™ Meta-Competency Identity Quantum Leaps
Install belief systems using identities as the post leap

CC: LEADERING™ META-COMPETENCY IDENTITY QUANTUM LEAPS

Use the identity quantum leap tool on an ongoing basis for internalizing all of the leader meta-competencies being cultivated by the Leadering™ program (figure 19-5Fb). Examples:

1. Quantum leap to a **frontiering™ expert**: an individual who has been successfully penetrating new territory for the last 10 years and has now become a frontiering addict. While the Leadering™ program itself is a workout gym for this since no one can absorb it all.

   It is necessary for you to be stretched in order to advance your system. If you never go into the deep end of the pool, how will you learn the skills to survive when you cannot touch bottom. A large integrated system of beliefs must be internalized to become a master of the unknown.

2. Quantum leap to being **someone who has well developed conceptual skills or someone who has operated in unity consciousness** for the last 10 years who is able to see the interconnectedness, dynamic flow, and co-evolution of all human systems and tap into that flow. It is akin to merging with what David Bohm calls the holomovement.

3. Quantum leap to a **growth expert or continuous advancement expert**, with the ability to orchestrate systems through the built-in growth continuums in the Leadering™ paradigm to their ultimate maximization.

19-5Fa © 2006 Lauren Holmes

META-COMPETENCIES cultivated by Leadering™

Systems-Based Approach
systems thinking, systems-based operation, systems-based emotional intelligence, belief system management, quantum leaping, expanded consciousness, conceptual skills, templating

Continuous Development
accelerating growth, co-evolution, re-optimization, agility, fluidity, expanding self-expression, learning/adaptation agility, belief upgrading, expanding consciousness

Cognitive Capabilities
learning agility, knowing, conceptual skills, abstract thinking, expanding consciousness, internally referenced, expanding self-expression and self-awareness, emotional intelligence, deductive reasoning, pattern recognition

Mastering the Unknown
frontiering™, creating, innovating, systems thinking, informationless decision-making, abstract thinking, conceptual skills, expanded consciousness

Performance
talent-based flow and other peak performance states, accelerated implementation, advancement by nonlinear quantum leaps, systems thinking, systems-based operation, expanding self-expression, learning/adaptation agility

19-5Fb   © 2006 Lauren Holmes

Interfering Belief Replacement Identity Quantum Leaps
Install belief systems using identities as the post leap

D. IDENTITY QUANTUM LEAPS FOR PROBLEM BELIEF REPLACEMENT

Only activated problem beliefs which are creating unpreferred realities right now in the present need to be cleared. Old inactive problem beliefs will eventually atrophy from disuse and no longer create unpreferred realities - especially as you spend time in talent-based flow state. Only supportive beliefs and positive emotions are activated in talent-based flow.

1. **Post-leap identities without the pre-leap problems:** Quantum leap to a post-leap identity without the problem beliefs creating the problem reality. (figure 19-2B)

2. **Event-driven belief upgrade tool:** Use unpreferred events in reality to instantly trigger a conditioned reflex to have you quantum leap to an identity without the problem beliefs creating these events. (figure 19-12)

3. **Clear problem beliefs by *systems*:** Beliefs travel in packs or schools. Use identity belief systems to quantum leap to eliminate whole systems of interconnected problem beliefs. You need to clear them as a system or they keep resurrecting themselves from the remnants of the interconnections. Quantum leap to **jettison a key culturally induced conflicting belief complex,** the only belief clearing that has to be done right now before the ongoing cleanup.

4. **New goal syndrome:** Belief clearing as a conditioned reflex after setting a new goal-driven identity. New goals activate all relevant beliefs in your belief template. As a result, new goals may activate beliefs you have not yet cleared which create unpreferred realities. Use the problem realities to trigger a conditioned reflex to routinely reinforce your post leap to facilitate belief clearings of the problem beliefs that are activated by goal setting.
On the positive front, new goals also trigger the flow-driven identity quantum leaps and natural quantum leaps and facilitative events.

5. **Identifying interfering beliefs from problem event clusters:** The belief most interfering with your immediate advancement along Leadering's built-in growth continuums creates a cluster of problem events which will increase in number and severity over time. Use the clustering to trigger a conditioned reflex to reinforce your quantum leaps to natural and goal-driven identities which do not include the offending belief.

Corporate Goal-Driven Identity Quantum Leaps
Install belief systems using identities as the post leap

E. CORPORATE GOAL-DRIVEN IDENTITY QUANTUM LEAPS

Capitalize on existing identities and identity uses:

Historically, corporations have used identities
- **to unify:** individuals, teams, departments, companies, customer relationships, marketplaces around a product or company or cause or project or marketing campaign
- **as goals to be pursued by linear process**

Capitalize on existing levers.
The below can thus be adapted for use in the Leadering™ paradigm:

GENERIC IDENTITY EXAMPLES
Belief systems usable for advancing corporate goals or realities include:
- vision
- branding
- cultural imprinting
- corporate image management
- organizational identity
- logo
- marketing campaign slogans

SPECIFIC IDENTITY EXAMPLES:
Corporate identity of :
- best company in the industry: best in class
- a top performance company
- best employer
- innovative company
- our employees are a community

Individual identity of:
- the top performing team
- change leader
- entrepreneur
- intrapreneur
- leader
- job titles

© 2006 Lauren Holmes

Recording 19: Belief Maximization Exercises 102

Nonlinear continuum direction

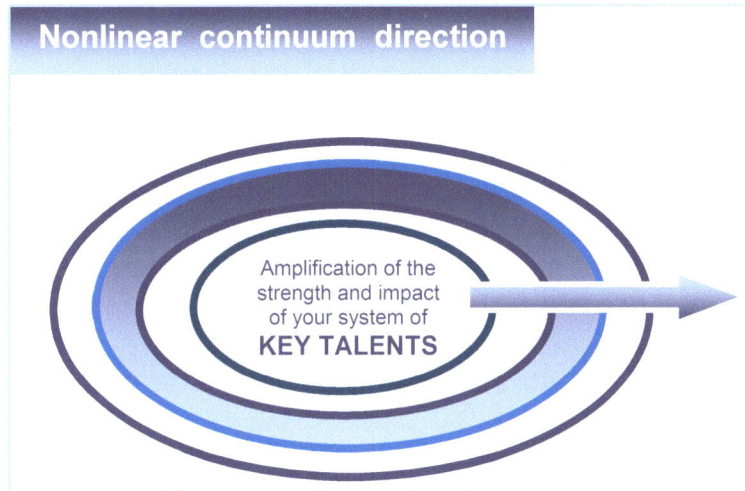

Amplification, Intensification, Expansion of your system's innate core. Core expansions in the Leading™ paradigm are achieved by quantum leap - a method for core replacement.

As your key talents expand as a result of operating in talent-based flow state and the flow to flow, your impact on reality increases. The magnitude of change you cause in reality increases. Your creative impact increases.

19-6A

© 2006 Lauren Holmes

Nonlinear reality advancement

YOUR SYSTEM CORE CREATES YOU and YOUR REALITY

You and your reality are a single system in the Leading™ paradigm. Realities are self-created by your system core.

Change your core to change your reality: the situations and events you will experience.

Formulas 1 and 2 not only advance your core but your reality or experience by reflection.

19-6B

© 2006 Lauren Holmes

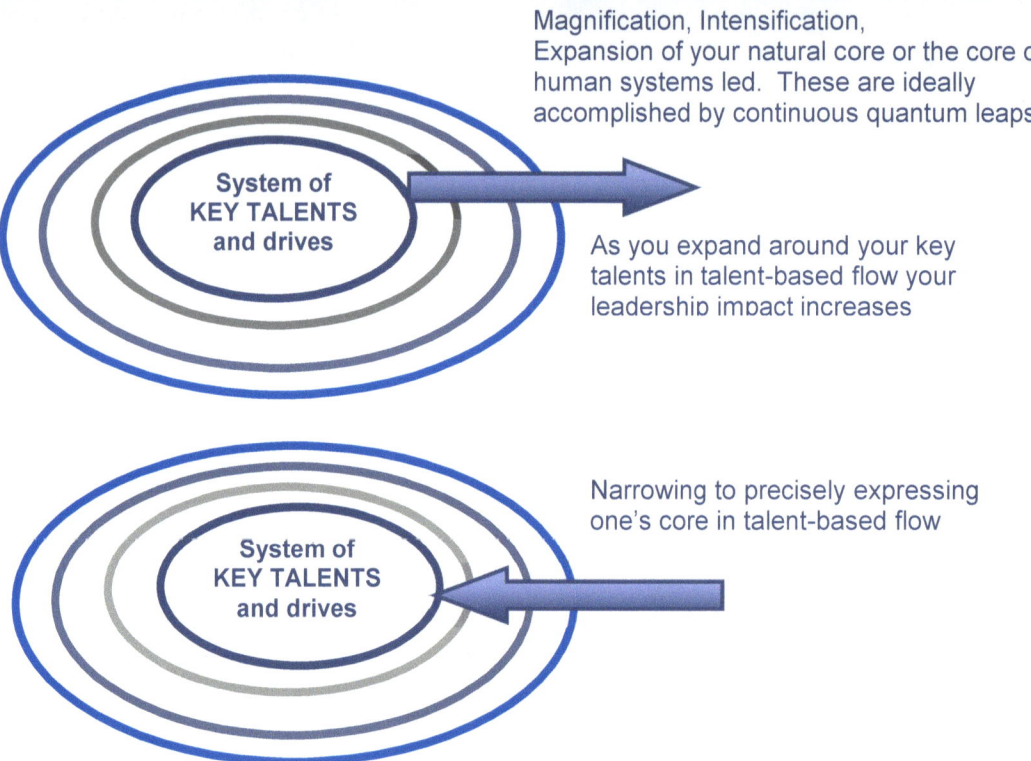

GOAL-DRIVEN IDENTITY QUANTUM LEAPS

Internalize the identity belief system of a person who has achieved a goal to make it a reality

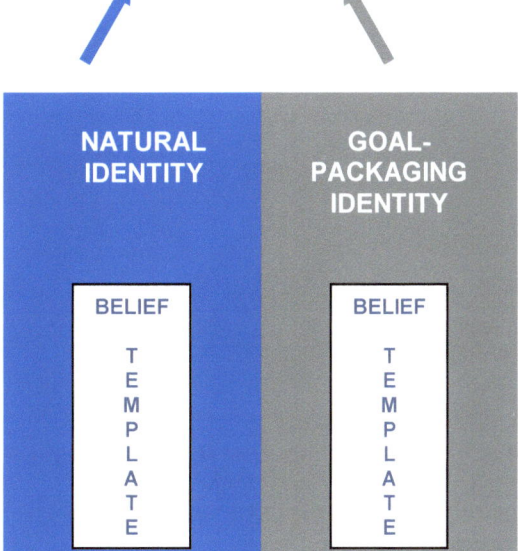

BELIEF-CREATED REALITY

NATURAL IDENTITY — BELIEF TEMPLATE

GOAL-PACKAGING IDENTITY — BELIEF TEMPLATE

Both systems of beliefs are creating your reality. Core congruence is therefore essential for precise reality creation.

Immutable Beliefs

A system of **Changeable Beliefs** which support the Immutable Beliefs to achieve a specific goal reality consistent with the flow to flow.

Identities are systems of beliefs. Beliefs create reality in the Leading™ paradigm. Therefore belief congruence ensures the greatest power and precision of reality creation. Since your natural identity, key talents and drives are predetermined, you will want changeable beliefs associated with the achievement of specific goals to be synergistic with your existing core.

Natural + Goal Identity Belief Systems

Goal-Driven Identity Quantum Leaps

GOAL REALITY A

GOAL-PACKAGING IDENTITY

a system of synergistic beliefs
designed to create a goal reality

NATURAL IDENTITY

the system of beliefs, key talents, and drives
upon which your system is founded

GOAL REALITY A

A system of beliefs is added to your natural identity beliefs to assist with the achievement of goals. These new beliefs are consistent with the creative expression and advancement of this natural identity with its system of beliefs, talents, and drives. Synergy or core congruence is requisite to effective creation of the goal reality.

Dynamics of a Quantum Leap

PRE-LEAP
Integrated Stable State or internal congruence

POST-LEAP
Integrated Stable State or internal congruence.

OLD BELIEF TEMPLATE

OLD REALITY

PLUS **NEW INFO**

Emergence

Direction congruent with the generative flow of the contextual system: external congruence

NEW BELIEF TEMPLATE

NEW REALITY

INTERNAL CONGRUENCE
A naturality-based state. Discernible through patterns of naturality expansion, talent-based flow, expressions of one's art, and spontaneous knowledge.

EXTERNAL CONGRUENCE
Discernible through patterns of coincidences, flow events, and the following drives which are a subsystem's links to the flow to congruence of its contextual system: drives for creativity, growth, frontiering, resonance, flow state, emotional highs, knowledge.

A QUANTUM LEAP IS A TEMPLATE EXCHANGE CAUSING A REALITY EXCHANGE

It is a system reincarnation at a more advanced state

© 2006 Lauren Holmes

THE LEADERING™ QUANTUM LEAP PROCESS

Design it!   Feel it!   Be it!

PRE-LEAP
1. Choose the right quantum leap or post-leap state
4. Define the post-leap state with clarity
3. Define the post-leap state without previous limitations or toxicity
4. Emotionally template the post-leap state
5. Add the information to fuel emergence
6. Expect the unexpected post-leap

LEAP
1. Release the linear connection to the past
2. Feel yourself 100% fluid
3. Feel the post-leap state
4. Feel who the "post-leap you" will be
5. Commit to the quantum leap
6. Make an abrupt, no-return, reincarnation
7. Trigger spontaneous self-organization by intent

POST-LEAP
1. Operate as if the quantum leap was successful
2. Walk around as the person with the post-leap reality
3. Hold this new identity until reality restructures
4. Ignore evidence of events created by the old template
5. Trigger cascading quantum leaps by intent
6. Establish quantum leaping as a way of life
7. Consolidate your new quantum leap expert beliefs

© 1998 Lauren Holmes

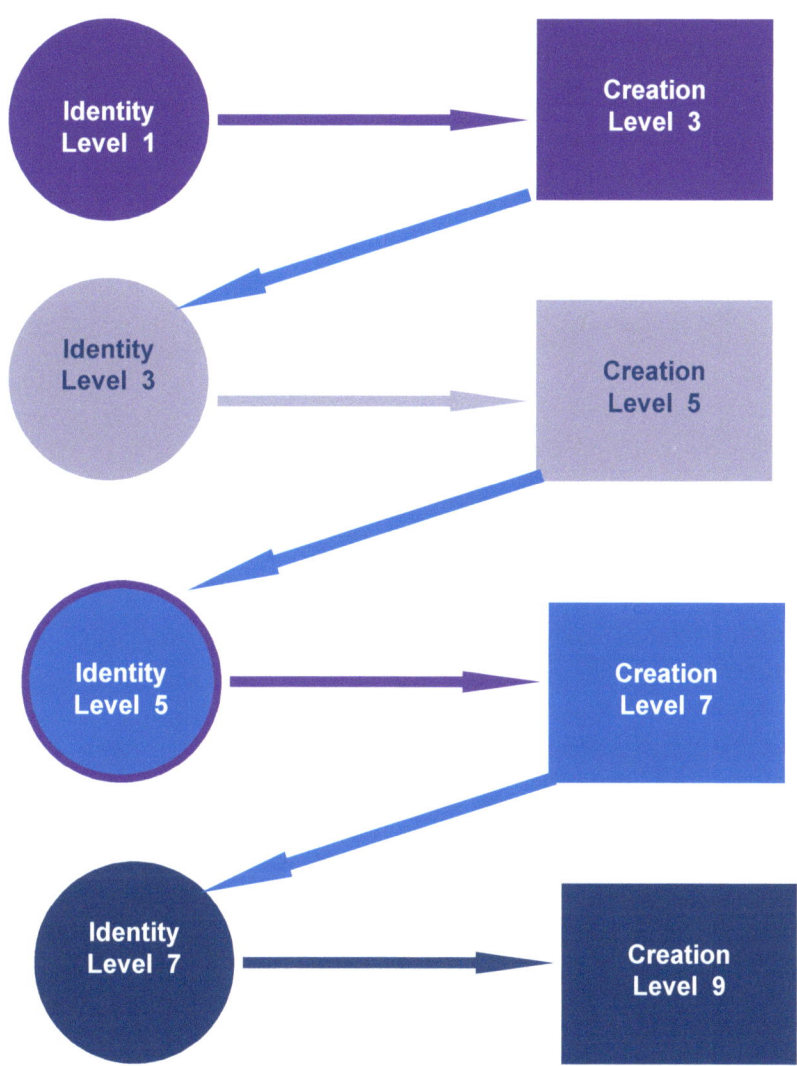

IDENTITY-AFFIRMING CREATION
Partnering with reality to speed advancement

Identity grows with its expression and shrinks with non-expression.
The 'larger' the identity, the larger, more specific the reality creation

**IDENTITY IS A SYSTEM OF BELIEFS.
BELIEFS CREATE REALITY IN THE LEADERING™ PARADIGM**

An Event-Driven Belief Template Upgrade Process

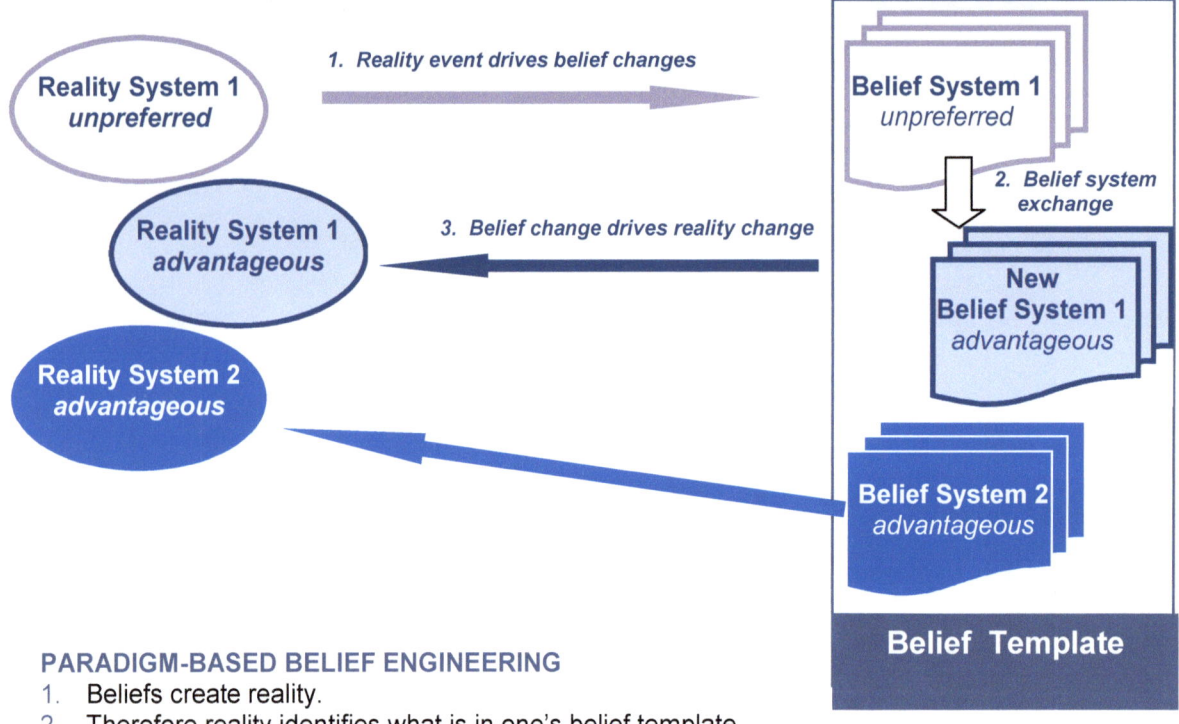

PARADIGM-BASED BELIEF ENGINEERING
1. Beliefs create reality.
2. Therefore reality identifies what is in one's belief template
3. Therefore unpreferred events in reality can be used to direct ongoing belief upgrades you make.

Benefits of the Belief Template Upgrade Process
1. for leadership strength, clarity and consistency
2. to enable the belief and emotion engineering requisite to leadership consistency, system advancement, and proficient change execution
3. to operate at full-power without dilution from interfering beliefs
4. for precise personal reality creation
5. for precise imprinting of culture and thus precise reality creation for large and/or complex organizational systems
6. for template-based change management of individual and organizational systems
7. to enable rapid-fire template rewrites in order to use the quantum leap or template exchange processes of the paradigm shift and Leadering™ paradigm modus operandi
8. to enable the quantum leap or template exchange from externally referenced to internally referenced that is critical to the creation and amplification of leaders.

LEADERING™ SYSTEMS MAXIMIZATION TOOLKIT

FLOW MAXIMIZATION TOOLS:

YOUR FLOW ENGINE: Capitalizing on the flow to flow or natural forces inside and outside of you act on your core for maximum performance and advancement
- **Quantum leaps** harnessing the power of the flow to flow
- **Partnering with internal and reality dynamics:** 15 dynamics (figure 19-13B)
- **Key talents and their addictive drives** (immutable beliefs)

BELIEF MAXIMIZATION TOOLS:

YOUR BELIEF TEMPLATE: Your belief template governs both you and your reality as a single system. Beliefs are information storage units like genes
- **Quantum leaps** or paradigm shifts or belief template exchanges
- **Partnering with reality events:** reality is a self-correcting feedback system
- **Changeable beliefs** in partnership with your immutable beliefs (innate gene-based beliefs associated with your key talents and addictive drives)

> **Byproduct:** THE META-COMPETENCIES OF LEADERS, ENTREPRENEURS, INNOVATORS AND HIGH ACHIEVERS

19-13A   © 2006 Lauren Holmes

15 LEADERING™ DYNAMICS
for advancing systems within the Flow-to-Flow

1. **SYSTEMS MINDSET:**
   - Systems-based dynamic
   - Expanding consciousness to systems mindset

2. **ADVANCEMENT MECHANICS**
   - **quantum leap dynamic**
   - templating dynamic
   - self-organization dynamic
   - emergence dynamic

3. **ADVANCEMENT DIRECTIONS**
   - knowledge pursuit dynamic (talent-based)
   - adaptation dynamic
   - evolution dynamic
   - co-evolution dynamic
   - talent-based flow dynamic
   - flow-within-flow dynamic
   - expanding consciousness dynamic

4. **DYNAMICS FOR THE UNKNOWN**
   the essence or definition of leadership, entrepreneurship, innovation, and career creation
   - frontiering dynamic™: penetrate unknown systems
   - creation/creativity dynamic: bring unknown systems into existence

© 2006 Lauren Holmes

> Leadering™ provides the functionality, toolkit, and strategies to enable you to be paid to grow along the natural growth paths you would pursue anyway given unlimited resources. This is the ultimate career strategy.

9 COMPLETING THE PARADIGM SHIFT

20. **Natural Identity quantum leaps (*immutable beliefs*)**   50 minutes   39 figures
    Subset: Growth or expansion identity quantum leaps
    Completing the Paradigm Shift: Natural identity quantum leaps (immutable beliefs)

    Operationalizing the Paradigm: Growth or expansion identity quantum leaps
    The transition from completing the paradigm shift to operating in the paradigm is made within this recording.

    Leadering's natural identity quantum leap tool is introduced as the means to reposition your system or any system you choose to advance to the natural core of the system. This is the only foundation for the peak performance of the system. It is used to help to maximize your changeable beliefs to support the innate or more hardwired parts of your core to maximize your system performance and advancement. Simultaneously, this discussion is used as a catalyst for completing the Leadering™ paradigm shift. All recordings after this one relate to paradigm operation and consolidating the paradigm into your life.

    As part of the final shift, and to build up the power of emergence to complete the paradigm shift, all key elements of the paradigm, paradigm operation, and driving the Leadering™ machinery are reviewed. They are presented in their most integrated form to ensure it is obvious how all of the elements function together and how you will operate in the Leadering™ paradigm.   A series of all-inclusive and very comprehensive diagrams and charts are provided to give you a visual of the integration of many parts.

    The goal is to try to build up the stresses in your system to change in order to power this final aspect of the paradigm shift or quantum leap that we have been working towards since the first recording. We want all of the elements of the paradigm foremost in your thinking to feed the quantum leap - to cause them to synthesize together into a machinery that you know how to drive. Remember, you don't have to be a mechanic to drive the car. The goal has always been to driving the machinery not to knowing how the engine operates. We used the complexity of how the engine operates to press natural levers in you for the paradigm shift.

Identity Quantum Leap Categories
Install belief systems using identities as the post leap

8 Identity Quantum Leap Tool Categories

PARADIGM SHIFT
1. Natural identity quantum leaps (*immutable beliefs*)

PARADIGM OPERATION
2. *Subset:* Growth or expansion identity quantum leaps
3. Goal-driven identity quantum leaps
4. *Subset:* Flow-driven identity quantum leaps
5. Corporate identity quantum Leaps
6. Identity quantum leaps to replace problem beliefs
7. Leadering™ toolkit identity quantum leaps
8. *Subset:* Leadering™ meta-competency identity quantum leaps
    Quantum leaps to goal 'states of being' rather than goal 'states':
       Subset: Assimilated Expert Identity quantum leaps
       Subset: Projected Expert Identity quantum leaps

IDENTITY QUANTUM LEAP BASICS:

1. Identities are integrated systems of beliefs.

2. Beliefs, like genes in the nucleus of a cell, are information storage units which define the core of any human system.

3. All advancement of human systems in the Leadering™ paradigm requires a change of beliefs. Leaders are therefore belief engineers.

4. Internalize the 'feel' or emotional template of your desired post-leap identity to lock in the belief upgrades which will change reality to coincide with those new beliefs.

5. Assume you or systems you lead have operated with the proposed post-leap identity successfully for 10 years.

6. Your selected post leap must be consistent with the direction of the flow to flow for natural forces to energize the leap.

© 2006 Lauren Holmes

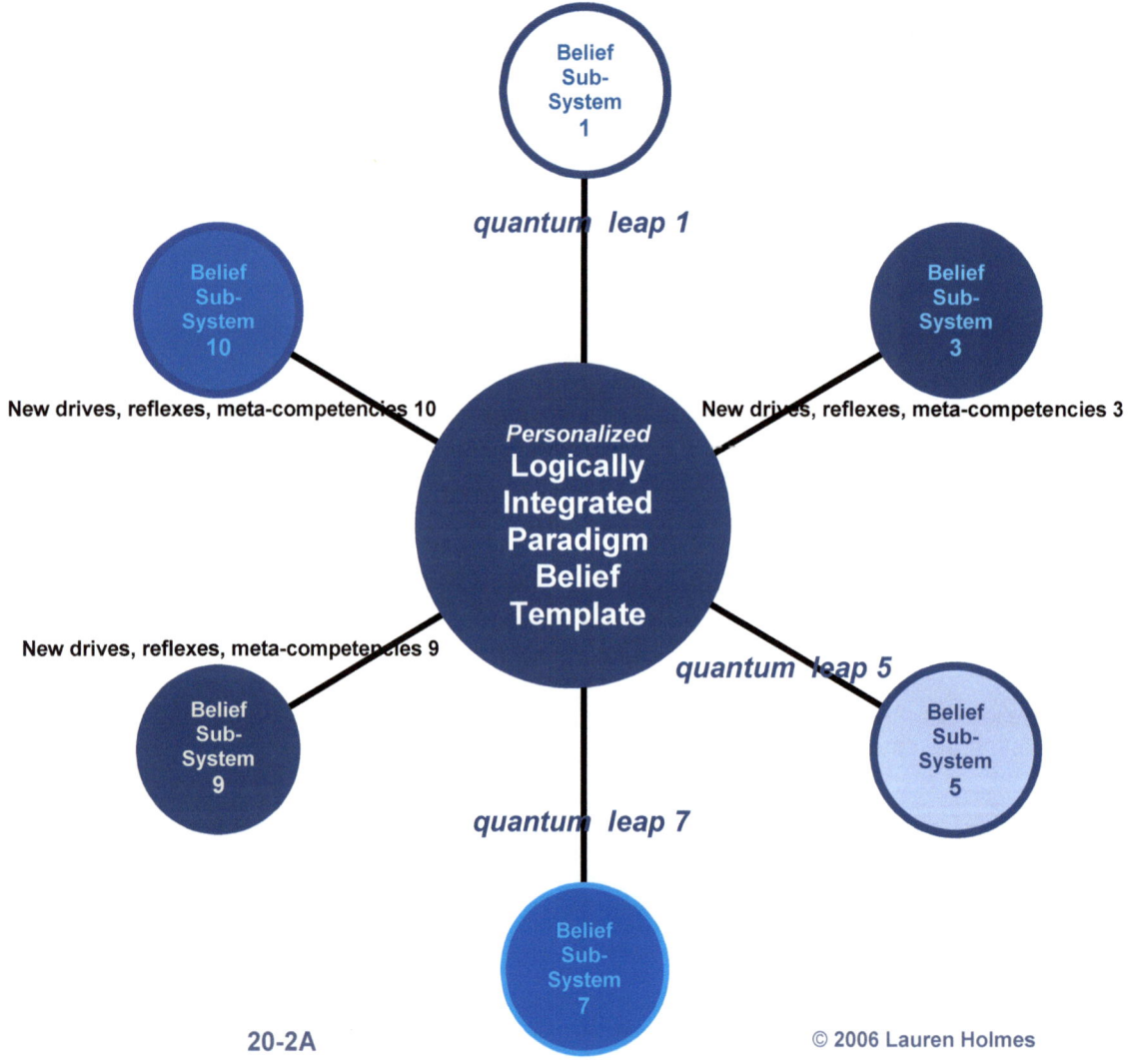

COMPONENTS OF THE INTEGRATED TARGET PARADIGM - 1

DYNAMICS Maximizing actions	DRIVES links to maximization	META-COMPETENCIES capabilities from dynamics/drives

System Organization:
a congruence dynamic
a self-organizing dynamic
a systems-based dynamic
a templating dynamic
an emergence dynamic
 	
Multi-System Organization:
an adaptation dynamic
a co-evolution dynamic
an expanding consciousness dynamic
a flow-within-flow dynamic
   (subsystems achieve congruence with their contextual system
 	
Improved Performance and Functionality:
a quantum leap dynamic
a frontier-pursuit dynamic
a creation/creativity dynamic
a flow dynamic
an evolution dynamic
a knowledge-pursuit dynamic
	Drives to
	  internal congruence
	  external congruence
	
	flow state
	  (our peak-performance / peak-evolution state of int/ext congruence)
	naturality
	  (internal congruence)
	expanded natural core
	  (growth congruence)
	resonance
	  (frequency congruence)
	meaning
	positive emotions
	adapt
	learn
	new knowledge
	emergence
	co-evolve
	frontiering
	creativity/creation
	achievement
	self-expression
		Systems-Based Approach
		systems thinking, systems-based operation, systems-based emotional intelligence, belief system management, quantum leaping, expanded consciousness, conceptual skills, templating
		
		Continuous Development
		accelerating growth, co-evolution, re-optimization, agility, fluidity, expanding self-expression, learning/adaptation agility, belief upgrading, expanding consciousness
		
		Cognitive Capabilities
		learning agility, knowing, conceptual skills, abstract thinking, expanding consciousness, internally referenced, expanding self-expression and self-awareness, emotional intelligence, deductive reasoning, pattern recognition
		
		Mastering the Unknown
		frontiering, creating, innovating, systems thinking, informationless decision-making, abstract thinking, conceptual skills, expanded consciousness
		
		Performance Improvement
		talent-based flow and other peak performance states, accelerated implementation, advancement by nonlinear quantum leaps, systems thinking, systems-based operation, expanding self-expression, learning/adaptation agility

© 2006 Lauren Holmes

COMPONENTS OF THE INTEGRATED TARGET PARADIGM - 2

KEY THEMES TRACKED FOR HARNESSING THE FLOW OF SYSTEMS TO CONGRUENCE

unpaid work theme, knowledge-pursuit theme, frontier-pursuit theme, creativity-pursuit theme, learning-pursuit theme, meaning-pursuit theme, talent-based flow state events theme, resonance events theme, positive emotion events theme, spontaneous knowledge events theme, creative invention events theme, spontaneous creativity events theme, theme of talent-based projects which had many coincidences and flow events.

HIGHLIGHTS OF THE TARGET PARADIGM

Advancing by wholes: Promotes: systems-based thinking and operation; a quantum leap process; template-based change management; coincidences; spontaneous knowledge; spontaneous creativity; spontaneous self-organization. Used to adapt and enhance human systems such as a leader, a follower, an organizational system, a market system, or leadership development.

Re-optimization, adaptation, co-evolution: All paradigm dynamics and drives serve these never-ending goals synergistically and opportunistically.

Flow-within-flow: Paradigm is powered by the flow of systems to congruence internally and externally.

Talent-based flow: The peak-performing/peak-evolving goal state of being which capitalizes on natural mechanisms built in to support a system's natural talents and passions.

Evolution direction: Human systems intensify around their natural core through an endless series of expansion quantum leaps rather than advance linearly.

Belief Engineering: Each human system and its reality are a single system defined by a single belief template. Change beliefs to change both the system and its reality. Beliefs can be known from reality patterns. Leadering conditioned reflexes triggered by problem events internally and externally activate an automatic belief template upgrade process. Reality is used as a self-correcting feedback system.

THE LEADING™ PARADIGM PLAYERS:
a talent-driven systems maximization toolkit

FORCES, DRIVES, DYNAMICS
a. **External Talent-based Natural Forces acting on your core:**
   - the 15 talent-based dynamics (Fig 20-4A-B)
   - the flow pursuit of the contextual system: the flow-to-flow or your flow engine (Fig20- 6A, 20-6C)

b. **Internal Talent-based Natural Forces acting on your core:**
   Addictive drives pressuring use of your key talents

c. **Built-in Talent-based Growth Continuums** to advanced functionality and performance (Fig 20-9, 20-9A-E)

d. **Talent-based Life Themes** (Fig 20- 5)

YOUR TALENT-BASED CORE
(Fig 20- 2D, 20-2E)
a. **Flow Maximization:** (Fig20- 6A, 20-6C)
   1. flow pursuit of your system
   2. key talents
   3. talent-based addictive drives
b. **Belief Maximization:**
   1. immutable beliefs
   2. changeable beliefs

A BELIEF-CREATED REALITY
Reality is a self-correcting feedback system

SYSTEM UPGRADES
a. Meta-Competencies of leaders, entrepreneurs, innovators, and high achievers (Fig 20-7)
b. Conditioned Reflexes (Fig 20-8A-B-C)
c. Enhanced Functionality
d. Beliefs

STRATEGIES
Five Talent-based Operating Formulas:
Advance your system: 1. lifetime development
2. greatest lifetime level of operation
Advance other systems to advance your system:
3. leadership   4. leadership development
5. greatest lifetime operating level as a leader
   (Fig 20-6A-C)

TECHNOLOGIES
a. System-Based Operation
b. Core-Driven Operation
c. Belief Engineering
d. Emotional Engineering
e. Reality Creation
f. Quantum Leap Technology (Fig 20-3A-B)
   Nature-Initiated Quantum Leaps (Fig 20-6C) imbedded in the flow to flow orchestrating you for
   - opportunistic synergy, co-evolution, co-adaptation, creative problem-solving, and flow-within-flow
   - natural quantum leaps such as coincidences (multi-system synergy, co-evolution, co-adaptation), sudden knowledge, sudden creativity, facilitating events, flow states

   Self-Initiated Quantum Leaps
   - Identity Quantum Leaps (20-1, 20-10A, 20-11A)

BELIEF UPGRADE TOOLS
a. Quantum Leaps
b. Paradigm Shift
c. Reality Partnering
d. Action Learning Experimentation
e. Leadering™ Systems Maximization Toolkit and Machinery

PARADIGM PERSONALIZATION EXERCISES

© 2006 Lauren Holmes

THE LEADERING™ CORE DETERMINATION EXERCISES

These exercises are designed to identify the core of your system which is being acted upon by natural forces inside and outside of you so you can comply with and capitalize on them and avoid operating contrary to them.

FLOW MAXIMIZATION EXERCISES
for maximum performance and advancement

Life Theme exercises
- key talent determination
- flow-to-flow determination

Key talent Determination exercises
- system-based key talent exercise
- various other exercises

5 Talent-Based Operating Formulas exercises
1: your lifetime development formula
2: your greatest lifetime achievement formula
3: your natural leader formula
4: your leadership development formula
5: your greatest leader performance formula

YOUR FLOW ENGINE:

Natural forces inside and outside of you act on your core

YOUR CORE CONSISTS OF:

1. **KEY TALENTS**

2. **ADDICTIVE DRIVES**
   pulling you to use your key talents

   *Note: Your key talents and associated drives are the immutable beliefs below. They continuously
   - create your reality and
   - are being acted upon by the flow to flow and Leadering's built-in growth continuums which amplify core impact.

BELIEF MAXIMIZATION EXERCISES
for core congruence

Belief Template Upgrade:
- beneficial belief determination:
  ideal talent-based and flow-based beliefs
  identity beliefs, reality creation beliefs
- problem belief determination:
  fear beliefs, toxic beliefs, conflicting beliefs
- event-driven template upgrade process
- quantum leap template exchange process:
  goal-packaging identities, reincarnation

Action Learning Experimentation
- proving beliefs create reality
- improving belief engineering in your own and other systems
- improving template determination / design
- quantum leap experimentation

YOUR BELIEF TEMPLATE

Your belief template governs both you and your reality as a single system

Beliefs are information storage units like genes

---

3. **IMMUTABLE BELIEFS**
   (innate gene-based beliefs)
   These define the essence of your system and why it came together in the first place. These beliefs are genetically based and inherent to the built-in creative expression of your system. See *Note above.

4. **CHANGEABLE BELIEFS**
   ideally designed to support the key talents, addictive drives, and immutable beliefs to maximize your performance, development, and survival in biological terms. The goal is core congruence.

---

im·mu·ta·ble: unchanging or unchangeable: not changing or not able to be changed

© 2006 Lauren Holmes

Recording20: Natural Identity Quantum Leaps

LEADERING™ SYSTEMS MAXIMIZATION TOOLKIT

FLOW MAXIMIZATION TOOLS:

YOUR FLOW ENGINE: Capitalizing on the flow to flow or natural forces inside and outside of you act on your core for maximum performance and advancement
- **Quantum leaps** harnessing the power of the flow to flow
- **Partnering with internal and reality dynamics:** 15 dynamics
- **Key talents and their addictive drives** (immutable beliefs)

BELIEF MAXIMIZATION TOOLS:

YOUR BELIEF TEMPLATE: Your belief template governs both you and your reality as a single system. Beliefs are information storage units like genes
- **Quantum leaps** or paradigm shifts or belief template exchanges
- **Partnering with reality events:** reality is a self-correcting feedback system
- **Changeable beliefs** in partnership with your immutable beliefs (innate gene-based beliefs associated with your key talents and their addictive drives)

Byproduct: THE META-COMPETENCIES OF LEADERS, ENTREPRENEURS, INNOVATORS AND HIGH ACHIEVERS

20-2E   © 2006 Lauren Holmes

Dynamics of a Quantum Leap

PRE-LEAP
Integrated Stable State or internal congruence

POST-LEAP
Integrated Stable State or internal congruence.

OLD BELIEF TEMPLATE

OLD REALITY

PLUS
NEW INFO

Emergence

Direction congruent with the generative flow of the contextual system: external congruence

NEW BELIEF TEMPLATE

NEW REALITY

INTERNAL CONGRUENCE
A naturality-based state. Discernible through patterns of naturality expansion, talent-based flow, expressions of one's art, and spontaneous knowledge.

EXTERNAL CONGRUENCE
Discernible through patterns of coincidences, flow events, and the following drives which are a subsystem's links to the flow to congruence of its contextual system: drives for creativity, growth, frontiering, resonance, flow state, emotional highs, knowledge.

A QUANTUM LEAP IS A TEMPLATE EXCHANGE CAUSING A REALITY EXCHANGE

It is a system reincarnation at a more advanced state

20-3A © 2006 Lauren Holmes

THE LEADERING™ QUANTUM LEAP PROCESS

Design it!   Feel it!   Be it!

PRE-LEAP
1. Choose the right quantum leap or post-leap state
5. Define the post-leap state with clarity
3. Define the post-leap state without previous limitations or toxicity
4. Emotionally template the post-leap state
5. Add the information to fuel emergence
6. Expect the unexpected post-leap

LEAP
1. Release the linear connection to the past
2. Feel yourself 100% fluid
3. Feel the post-leap state
4. Feel who the "post-leap you" will be
5. Commit to the quantum leap
6. Make an abrupt, no-return, reincarnation
7. Trigger spontaneous self-organization by intent

POST-LEAP
1. Operate as if the quantum leap was successful
2. Walk around as the person with the post-leap reality
3. Hold this new identity until reality restructures
4. Ignore evidence of events created by the old template
5. Trigger cascading quantum leaps by intent
6. Establish quantum leaping as a way of life
7. Consolidate your new quantum leap expert beliefs

20-3B   © 1998 Lauren Holmes

15 LEADERING™ DYNAMICS
for advancing systems within the Flow to Flow

1. **SYSTEMS MINDSET:**
   - Systems-based dynamic
   - Expanding consciousness to systems mindset

2. **ADVANCEMENT MECHANICS**
   - quantum leap dynamic
   - templating dynamic
   - self-organization dynamic
   - emergence dynamic

3. **ADVANCEMENT DIRECTIONS**
   - knowledge pursuit dynamic (talent-based)
   - adaptation dynamic
   - evolution dynamic
   - co-evolution dynamic
   - talent-based flow dynamic
   - flow-within-flow dynamic
   - expanding consciousness dynamic

4. **DYNAMICS FOR THE UNKNOWN**
   the essence or definition of leadership, entrepreneurship, innovation, and career creation
   - frontiering dynamic™: penetrate unknown systems
   - creation/creativity dynamic: bring unknown systems into existence

© 2006 Lauren Holmes

Systems Management used by Nature and Natural Leaders

FLOW to GENERATIVE CONGRUENCE DRIVE → →

FLOW to FLOW DRIVE — THE FLOW ENGINE → →

Nature pressures all human systems into generative congruence internally and externally. Successful leaders do the same thing.

The 14 paradigm dynamics or leader drives below promote the 15th drive:
the flow of systems to generative congruence internally and externally.
Congruence is the driving force of the target paradigm of Leading™.

SYSTEMS MINDSET

A systems-based drive
Everything in the paradigm is a system, including individuals, organizations, and processes.

An expanding consciousness drive to oneness. Consciousness expands due to operating in the flow to congruence and stretching to view interacting systems.

ADVANCEMENT MECHANICS

A quantum leap drive
A templating drive
A self-organizing drive
An emergence drive
Leaders orchestrate abrupt nonlinear system advancements, adaptations, co-evolutions, and re-optimizations using mechanisms available in the flow to congruence. They operate as belief engineers, cultural engineers, reality architects, quantum leap leaders, and emergence leaders:
NONLINEAR UPGRADE MECHANISMS

ADVANCEMENT DIRECTIONS

A knowledge-pursuit drive*
Leaders harness a system's innate drives for advancing its talent-based expression in order to achieve multi-system goals and maximization:
EVOLUTIONARY PATH DETERMINANT

An adaptation drive*
Externally driven adjustment to advances in the shared contextual system caused by the adaptation / evolution of other subsystems:
CHAIN REACTION: THE DANCE

An evolution drive*
'Growth' and 'Learning' help human systems achieve their existing potential. 'Evolution' advances that potential. Human systems advance by (1) quantum-leap intensifications of their natural core and (2) belief template upgrades: UPGRADED POTENTIAL / FUNCTIONALITY

A co-evolution drive*
Internally driven system upgrade achieved by capitalizing on external upgrading systems: OPPORTUNISTIC SYNERGY + LOCKSTEP ADVANCEMENT

A talent-based flow drive* (internal)
A flow-within-flow drive* (hierarchical)
The flow to internal/external congruence:
PEAK-PERFORMING / PEAK-EVOLVING STATE

DRIVES FOR THE UNKNOWN:
the essence of leadership, entrepreneurship, innovation, and career creation

1. **A frontier-pursuit drive*:** Penetrate unknown systems.
2. **A creation / creativity-pursuit drive*:** Bring unknown into existence.
   NATURE IS ENDLESS MULTI-SYSTEM CREATIVITY - LEADERSHIP IS AN EXTENSION

These dynamics form the toolkit for maximizing any human system in the paradigm whether the system is an individual, organization, market, civilization, or process such as leadership development, career management, or organizational change.

15-2 upgraded   © 2006 Lauren Holmes   * addicting talent-based drives

EVENT PATTERNS TRACKED FOR THEMES
These patterns are indicative of the flow to internal and external congruence

In the target paradigm, the life-long patterns of the following 'talent-based' or 'work' events are analyzed for themes indicating the flow to generative congruence or flow internally or externally:

- **an unpaid work theme** based on patterns of events in which you freely give away "work" that others would charge for or that you are so passionate about that you would pay for the opportunity to do.
- **a talent-based knowledge-pursuit or learning-pursuit theme** based on patterns of events of seeking knowledge passionately and willingly for the application of key talents (learning-pursuit theme)
- **a talent-based spontaneous knowledge theme** based on patterns of events in which spontaneous knowledge emerged to support the application of key talents
- **a talent-based frontier-pursuit theme** based on patterns of events of new territories of growth, learning and achievement the system was drawn to pursue for the application of key talents
- **a talent-based creativity-pursuit theme** based on patterns of events of preferred creative expression or creative expression which you or system was drawn to pursue for the application of key talents along with events in which creativity or creative invention or innovation spontaneously emerged for the application of key talents
- **a talent-based creative expression theme** based on patterns of events of creative expression in which your passion and enthusiasm were inflamed
- **a talent-based meaning-pursuit theme** based on patterns of events of work or achievements or contributions considered a meaningful application of key talents
- **the theme(s) of talent-based flow states** indicated by patterns of events whereby you went into flow state during the application of key talents
- **a talent-based flow-to-flow theme, theme(s) of projects** requiring the application of key talents which were supported by lots of coincidences, flows, spontaneous knowledge / creativity
- **talent-based naturality expansion theme** indicated by patterns of expansions or intensifications of your system around its core to greater impact on reality - the key direction of growth and advancement of any system in the Leadering™ paradigm.
- **a talent-based resonance theme** based on patterns of subjects or activities for the application of key talents with which you resonated
- **a talent-based positive emotion theme** based on patterns of events in which passion, excitement, and enthusiasm emerged during the application of key talents

All of the above themes indicate when a system is integrated into the flow to congruence.

5 PERSONAL FORMULAS
for operating in the target Leadering™ paradigm

Based on the themes of the event patterns tracked in the paradigm, the following 5 formulas will emerge to help participants determine how to capitalize on the flow to flow of all human systems.

Your key talents are a system of your strongest capabilities which you are passionate about using and improving which advance reality in some way. This system is what is being acted upon by the flow to flow and your addictive drives.

ADVANCING YOUR SYSTEM

1. **Talent-based lifetime development formula** or personal evolution formula

2. **Greatest lifetime level of talent-based operation**: the culmination of living one's lifetime development formula.

ADVANCING YOUR SYSTEM BY ADVANCING OTHER SYSTEMS

3. **Talent-based leadership formula**: leadership as an expression of one's lifetime development formula

4. **Talent-based leadership development formula**: merging one's lifetime development formula with one's talent-based leadership formula.

5. **Greatest lifetime level of operation as a leader**: based on the previous 4 formulas.

OUR FLOW ENGINE

OUR CORE FLOW DRIVE COMPLEX:

Your flow engine consists of addictive drives associated with your key talents

Flow is addicting because each of its component drives are addicting: the more you use them the more you want to use them

Our key talent-based drives: our flow engine
- flow-pursuit drive
- creativity-pursuit drive
- creative-expression or self-expression drive
- frontier-pursuit drive
- knowledge-pursuit drive
- meaning-pursuit drive

Our secondary talent-based drives:
- quantum leap drive
- evolution drive
- co-evolution drive
- self-organization drive

These addictive drives form a unique synergistic thrust within each of us: our flow engine

Your 5 talent-based operating formulas for top performance in the Leadering paradigm

Lifetime development formula →

Greatest personal performance →

Natural leader formula →

Natural leadership development formula →

Greatest leader performance →

20-6A

© 2006 Lauren Holmes

YOUR FIVE PERSONALIZED OPERATING FORMULAS
for maximizing in the Leadering™ paradigm

Key talents being acted on by the flow to flow

Your key talents are a system of your strongest capabilities which you are addicted to using and improving. When used, they advance reality in some way. All 5 formulas are operating strategies for capitalizing on your key talents. Therefore they are interlinked. Your key talents are also interlinked into a system of addictive drives which form your flow engine. The flow engine promotes operating in a peak performance flow state in which you are using your key talents. The key talents being acted on by the flow engine need to be known in order to determine one's 5 operating formulas for the Leadering™ paradigm.

Advancing your system

1. Your talent-based lifetime development formula:
If natural forces continuously pressure you to expand or intensify your ability to use your key talents for creation - to advance reality - what will be the development path or theme of that intensification process underpinning your life?

2. Your greatest talent-based performance as an individual:
If you were to pursue the continuous expansion of your key talents over a lifetime and at top speeds, what is the highest level of creative impact or reality creation that you would likely achieve. What is the highest possible culmination of living your lifetime development formula? What is your maximum attainment based on a lifetime of accelerating development of your key talents?

Advancing other systems to advance your system

3. Your talent-based leadership formula:
If you complied with the addictive drives pulling you to the continuous expansion of your key talents, what would be the territory and form of your leadership? How would formulas 1 and 2 define you as a leader by logical extension? What would your leadership formula look like if it was 100% based on your greatest performance with your key talents and their continuous expansion?

4. Your talent-based leadership development formula:
Your leadership development formula just allows you a more specialized lens with which to examine and strategize your personal development. The continuous expansion of the intensity and impact of your key talents define both your development as an individual and a leader. Therefore, leadership development and lifetime development form the same single continuum. The advancement of your key talents increases your strength, impact, and creativity as a leader. How would the previous 3 formulas define a leadership development formula? For those on the Leadering™ program who assume they will never be a leader, it is built in.

5. Your greatest talent-based performance as a leader:
Based on your 4 previous formulas, determine your greatest lifetime level of performance as a leader. Given your advancement as an individual and a leader based on the continuous intensification of your key talents, and given the formula for your greatest performance as an individual, what would be the dimensions of your ultimate performance level as a leader: generically, what will be your greatest levels of capability for causing reality advances?

The advantage of operating in talent-based flow within the talent-based flow of the contextual system

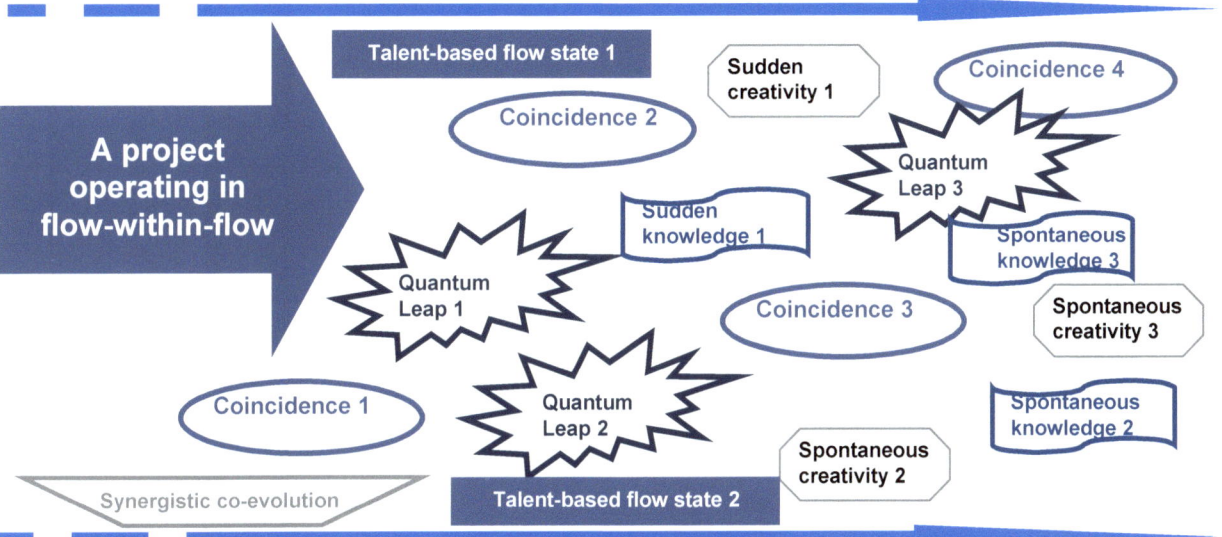

Increasing functionality with each flow experience:
- expanding consciousness and conceptual capacity
- peak performance
- peak evolution
- increasing creative capability
- expansion / intensification / enlargement of the system's natural creative expression

Proof of the Leadering™ paradigm – Proof of the accuracy of your 5 formulas
If you are operating in talent-based flow and the clustering of natural quantum leaps above emerge in your reality, then you have proof that the Leadering paradigm™ and nature's machinery inside and outside of you do indeed operate in the way Leadering™ describes.

META-COMPETENCIES and DRIVES targeted by Leadering™
Shared by leaders, entrepreneurs, innovators, and high achievers

Systems-Based and Core-Based Operation
systems thinking, relational thinking, big-picture thinking, conceptual skills, belief system management, model development and application, system co-evolution and adaptation, leadership (advancing human systems in opportunistic synergy)

Accelerating and Continuous Development
- conditioned reflexes installed to trigger multi-front, life-long advancement and leadership development.
- addictive drives installed to pull one to growth.
- learning to learn, mental agility, adaptivity, expanding self-expression and self-awareness, belief engineering, expanding consciousness

Improved and Improving Cognitive Capabilities
- thinking: conceptual, inductive, deductive, abstract, big-picture, relational
- learning to learn, mental agility, pattern recognition, internally referenced, emotional intelligence, use of models, theories, and inferences

Expertise with Ambiguity and the Unknown
- **pioneering**: penetrating the unknown
- **creativity/innovation**: bringing unknown into being

systems thinking, informationless decision-making, abstract thinking, conceptual skills, pattern recognition, trend perception, change detection, environmental scanning, problem reframing, ambiguity resolution

Improved Performance
flow (our peak performance state), enhanced functionality, systems-based operation, accelerated implementation through quantum leap change management

Addictive Drives cultivated and capitalized upon by Leadering™
(the more you use them, the more you want to use them):
- Drives to: learning, pioneering, creativity, innovation, meaning, positive emotions, adaptivity, creativity, learning knowledge, achievement, flow, (the optimal experience), self-expression, self-knowledge, advancement, unity, growth
- Drives to using and improving your key talents - a must for operating at your full potential

---

Meta-competencies or enduring competencies are systems of knowledge, skills, and strategies which facilitate the acquisition and use of competencies.

Traditional leadership development addresses competencies and skills
Leadering™ addresses leader dynamics and meta-competencies.

Traditionally, leaders are developed bottom up skill by skill
Leadering™ uses a single paradigm shift to install an integrated system of meta-competencies, drives, reflexes, and beliefs.

Traditionally, senior leaders use different meta-competencies.
Leadering™ offers a single systems maximization toolkit for use by everyone on every human system thus unifying organizations around a single culture and modus operandi. Leadership becomes distributed.

Recording 20: Natural Identity Quantum Leaps

EXAMPLES OF CONDITIONED REFLEXES - 1
installed for the paradigm shift and operating in the Leadering™ paradigm

CONDITIONED REFLEX TRIGGER	CONDITIONED REFLEX RESPONSE
New goal to advance a system(s)	**SYSTEMS THINKING** Treat every relevant individual, groups of people, processes and bodies of knowledge as systems with a core template and flow engine. Treat every event as part of the patterns indicating the direction of the flow to flow of some system. A system and its reality are a single system with the same template. No events are separate. Upgrade the core of the system first - your or others - before taking action in compliance with the flow to flow. Expand consciousness to see the patterns and the interconnectedness of all systems in the flow to flow and to determine opportunities for synergy and co-evolution
Yearning for meaning	**KEY TALENTS** Continuously comply with addictive drives pressuring the use of your system of key talents
Need for achievement	Shift into talent-based flow state by applying your system of key talents
Every problem or advancement challenge	Translate into terms solvable by one's key talents and the flow to flow associated with your system and the system(s) to be advanced.
Unknown solution or change required with no idea how it will be achieved	**QUANTUM LEAPS** Emotionally blueprint the post-leap state and quantum leap. Take actions as if the quantum leap was successful.
New goal to advance a system(s)	Quantum leaps to advance systems from one stable state to the next. Bypass the need for unstable transitional state.
Desire to quantum leap	Several conditioned reflexes throughout the Leadering quantum leap process itself
A problem situation	Quantum leap to a post-leap reality without the problem.
Need for organizational change	Define the post-leap. Source the new information. Make the template changes. Use the Leadering™ quantum leap process to complete the quantum leap. Operate as if the quantum leap has been successful.

20-8A © 2006 Lauren Holmes

EXAMPLES OF CONDITIONED REFLEXES - 2
installed for the paradigm shift and operating in the Leading™ paradigm

CONDITIONED REFLEX TRIGGER	CONDITIONED REFLEX RESPONSE
Decision required with no information for making it.	**FLOW-TO-FLOW** Move into unknown territory in compliance with the flow to flow to collide with the information coincidences which will fuel the emergence process which will result in creative solutions beyond the potential of your system
Frontiering™: the need to penetrate unknown territory quickly and safely	Stop with the blocks and comply with the facilitating events, patterns, themes, natural quantum leaps and signposts of the flow-to-flow.
Creation/Innovation: the need to bring the unknown into existence	Immediately pursue the 3 to 7 information systems which will fuel the emergence process by stopping with the blocks and complying with the facilitating events, patterns, themes, natural quantum leaps and signposts of the flow-to-flow.
A craving for rapid growth in functionality and capabilities	Begin applying your system of key talents in talent-based flow state while complying with the life themes indicative of the flow-to-flow in your life system.
A problem situation	**CHALLENGES** Quantum leap to a post-leap state without the problem. Belief engineering to change the template to change the reality Expand around your core and key talents - expand beyond the problem - to have the capacity and functionality to deal with this challenge Solve the problem with the emergence, synergy, co-evolution, coincidences, facilitating events, spontaneous knowledge, and spontaneous creativity inherent in the flow to flow.

EXAMPLES OF CONDITIONED REFLEXES - 3
installed for the paradigm shift and operating in the Leading™ paradigm

CONDITIONED REFLEX TRIGGER	CONDITIONED REFLEX RESPONSE
Unpreferred event or situation in reality	**EVENT-DRIVEN TEMPLATE UPGRADE PROCESS** Make the necessary change to your belief template to change your reality
A craving for rapid growth in functionality and capabilities	**GROWTH IN CAPACITY** Quantum leap continuously through frontier after frontier of expansion of the application of your system of key talents or those of the system you wish to advance in order to increase your impact and functionality.
Unpreferred event or situation in reality	**REALITY CREATION** Make the necessary change to your belief template to change your reality
New reality desired	Visualize to the point of feeling the emotions associated with the new reality in order to change the beliefs to change the reality.

20-8C © 2006 Lauren Holmes

SAMPLE CATEGORIES OF LEADERING'S BUILT-IN GROWTH

CONTINUOUS DEVELOPMEMT
Addiction to continuous development:
- the continuous increase in drives which addict you to using and improving your system of core talents
- these addictive drives cause the continuous improvement of your system of core talents becomes the founding dynamic of your life to which the other segments of your life are integrated.
- an accelerating increase in speed of development of your system of core talents
- the continuous increase in the development of drives associated with meta-competencies such as frontiering™, creativity, learning to learn, and learning agility which promote continuous development
- addiction to peak performance and peak advancement flow states

CONTINUOUSLY IMPROVING PERFORMANCE
1. Continuous increase in time spent operating in peak performance and peak advancement flow states
2. Depth of your talent-based flow states increases with each experience thus increasing performance further
3. Event-driven belief upgrade process continually improves performance through more supportive beliefs

CONTINUOUSLY INCREASING IMPACT
1. Continuous increase in impact of creations
2. Reality creation precision
3. Continuous increase in creativity and innovation
4. Continuous increase in your impact on reality
5. An increase in the level of complexity handled from single system to multiple systems impact; from transactions to process; from process to quantum leaps; from linear to nonlinear; more impactful quantum leaps impacting more systems more quickly

CONTINUOUSLY INCREASING FUNCTIONALITY
1. Continuous increase in the specialization of your system of core talents
2. Accelerating improvement of abilities to use your core talents
3. Increasing ability to penetrate the unknown or bring the unknown into existence and a craving for both: frontiering™ and creativity.
4. Continuous improvement in your facility for nonlinear quantum leaps to speed advancement of your system and other systems
5. Systems-based modus operandi: single toolkit for advancing systems, continuous increase in your ability to advance systems and to create new systems
6. Continuous acquisition and improvement of meta-competencies associated with successful leaders, entrepreneurs, innovators and high achievers. (Meta-competencies improve the ability to assimilate and use competencies): continuous development, improved cognitive capabilities, improved performance. These allow you to move more quickly easily and safely into unknown territory and frontiers, increase your creativity and innovation, increase your knowledge-acquisition capabilities, increase your ability to court coincidences and facilitating events which will improve your performance of your art.
7. Continuous improvement to cognitive skills:
    - concept formation, conceptualization of complex ideas, abstract thinking, deductive and inductive logic, problem reframing, dealing with multiple perspectives and ambiguity, skillful formulation of ends, ways, means
    - frame of reference development: systems understanding, environmental scanning, pattern recognition
    - proactive thinking using critical, creative, and reflective thinking
    - analysis of complicated events, trend perception, change detection, creative and opportunistic problem-solving
    - deployment of models, theories and inferences
    - visualization, addressing, and capitalization of complex interrelationships: see the interaction of more systems and the opportunities for synergy and co-evolution; impact more systems, impact more complex systems, impact larger systems
    - big-picture thinking and see more patterns to have more information for decision-making and strategic and tactical planning

WHY GROWTH IS BUILT INTO LEADERING™

1. **TALENT-BASED FLOW STATE**
   - peak performance - only relevant portions of brain fire during flow state. Over time your accomplishments will become greater thus laying the foundation for operating at even higher levels of performance in future flow states
   - builds the creative application of your talents over time to with experience, talent-based flow state deepens over time and you progress along a flow continuum to greater impact and novelty in changing reality. More new frontiers. Exponential growth
   - must be stretched beyond your previous capabilities to sustain talent-based flow.
   - flow state is an addictive drive, the more you experience it, the more you want to experience it until you are operating 100% of your day in talent-based flow state or at least flow state
   - altered states of consciousness such as expanded and unity consciousness. Talent-based flow offers all of the growth benefits of meditation. Call it active meditation
   - toxic emotions and the beliefs behind them atrophy from disuse in flow

2. **ADDICTIVE DRIVES**
   - lead to penetrating new territory
   - bringing the 'new' into existence
   - frontiering™ and creation as a way of life resulting in the exponential advancement of your system
   - constantly frontiering™ new territories

3. **EVENT-DRIVEN BELIEF TEMPLATE UPGRADE PROCESS:**
   - automatic belief template upgrade process: clears problem or interfering beliefs
   - flow state: no negative emotions: they atrophy because the beliefs behind them atrophy
   - have better beliefs to support application of key talents

4. **MORE TIME PERFECTING THE SYSTEM OF YOUR KEY TALENTS**
   - less time on activities you think you need to do in order to have an opportunity to use your key talents or on totally non-key talent activities
   - changing your core to change reality nonlinearly instead of a whole bunch of linear activities to get from point A to B

WHY GROWTH IS BUILT INTO LEADING™

5. **BUILT-IN NATURAL QUANTUM LEAPS CATAPULTING YOUR SYSTEM AHEAD**
    - coincidences, spontaneous knowledge, spontaneous creativity
    - flow to congruence or flow to flow
    - in right place at right time for coincidences or opportunistic synergy, co-evolution or co-adaptation with other systems
    - with spontaneous knowledge and spontaneous creativity, exponential increase in your impact on reality and the advancement of the capacity and impact of your system of key talents.

6. **QUANTUM LEAP EXPERTISE**
    - a quantum leap to quantum leap expert who routinely advances himself/herself or the systems in their reality by wholes from one stable state to the next. A template change to each person to permit easier quantum leaps during and after the invention.
    - linear to nonlinear advancement so you do not have to keep a system stable during transition states which may also introduce new toxicity which slows down your system. release the belief in slow linear evolution
    - progression of your quantum leap expertise with each quantum leap: experiential learning, new beliefs, emotional memories, conditioned reflexes.
    - increasing quantum leap expert identity beliefs which create that reality
    - increased fluidity
    - increased congruence from which to orchestrate the quantum leap more cleanly
    - increased belief engineering expertise
    - increased pathfinding strength and comfort and expertise with the unknown
    - increased speed of quantum leaps
    - increased magnitude of quantum leap
    - increased ability to facilitate cascading quantum leaps
    - orchestrated to more information coincidences which expedite progress
    - improved template management
    - emergence expert: can hold the post-leap while orchestrating the emergence process
    - improved ability to capitalize on nature-initiated quantum leaps for self-initiated quantum leaps.
    - Improved systems thinking making it easier to advance by wholes

7. **YOUR CAPABILITIES ARE EXTENDED BY NATURE'S CAPABILITIES SO YOU CAN OPERATE BEYOND YOUR POTENTIAL: OVERDRIVE.**

LEADERING'S BUILT-IN KEY TALENT DEVELOPMENT

Use these to surmise the lifetime maximum possible impact of your key talents as an individual, a leader, an entrepreneur, and/or an innovator

Consider the following talent development processes built into the Leadering™ paradigm and this program when doing the core determination exercises:

If the below assumptions are true,
- **How would the art and science behind the use of your system of key talents develop over your lifetime?**
- **What could be the maximum possible impact of your key talents on reality?**
- **What would your five operating formulas or strategies be in the Leadering™ paradigm?**

1. Assume you have all of the money and resources and freedom to pursue the use of your key talents to the maximum.
2. Assume your system operates day after day in talent-based flow state within the talent-based flow state of the larger contextual system of which you are a part.
3. Assume your capabilities are extended by nature's capabilities.
4. Assume your drives merge with nature's drives to shift you into overdrive.

5. Assume you will be constantly breaking through new frontiers of the art and science behind applying your key talents.

6. Assume a constant increase in the impact on reality of your key talent system as you constantly expand or intensify around your core.

7. Assume years of side ventures which have increased your specialization in various aspects of your art or the creative expression of your key talents

8. Assume the depth of your talent-based flow states increases with each experience thus
   - speeding the increase of your functionality and performance
   - speeding the advancement of your art,
   - speeding the increase of your levels of peak performance
   - increasing the speed of your development exponentially.
   - allowing you to advance reality continuously in your peak performance state

9. Assume the addictive drives associated with using your key talents get stronger with each use and pull you to accomplish more without "work" or discipline. Assume the more you use them the more you want to use them.

20-9C © 2006 Lauren Holmes

LEADERING'S BUILT-IN KEY TALENT DEVELOPMENT

Use these to surmise the lifetime maximum possible impact of your key talents as an individual, a leader, an entrepreneur, and/or an innovator

10. Assume these addictive drives and the growth built into talent-based flow states pull you along the development continuum.

11. Assume a narrowing of your work to using your key talents more precisely and accurately with less baggage and encumbrances around them. You eliminate from your life the things you think you need to do in order to do your art or to be able to do your art but are not your art.

12. Assume that Leadering™ increases the meta-competencies of leaders, entrepreneurs, innovators, and high achievers which will allow you
    - To move more quickly easily and safely into unknown territory and frontiers,
    - To increase your creativity and innovation,
    - To increase your knowledge,
    - To increase your coincidences and facilitating events which will improve your performance of your art.

13. Assume an increase in the level of complexity that you are able to deal with and apply your key talents to
    - from single system to multiple system impact
    - from transactions to process. from process to quantum leaps
    - from linear to nonlinear
    - more impactful quantum leaps impacting more systems more quickly

14. Assume your consciousness, big picture thinking, and conceptual skills continue to increase and expand so that you can
    - see more patterns, have more information, for decision-making and strategic planning
    - see the flow of systems to congruence or the flow to flow
    - see the interaction of more systems and the opportunities for synergy and co-evolution
    - impact more systems, impact more complex systems, impact larger systems

15. Assume the adaptivity of your belief template is continuously improved by Leadering's event-driven belief template upgrade process so that your precision for reality creation is improving exponentially and benefiting from the creativity inherent in the flow to flow

LEADERING'S BUILT-IN KEY TALENT DEVELOPMENT

3

Use these to surmise the lifetime maximum possible impact of your key talents as an individual, a leader, an entrepreneur, and/or an innovator

Note: CONCEPTUAL COMPETENCIES CONSIST OF THE APPROPRIATE PARADIGMS, MINDSETS, AND CONCEPTUAL SKILLS NECESSARY TO:
   assess the environment
   see the long-range needs and implications of a situation and to build a plan for meeting these needs and
   visualize, address, and capitalize on the complex interrelationships that exist in a workplace in order to set priorities, make decisions, anticipate the future, and formulate strategies and tactics, and
   comprehend the culture of historically developed values, beliefs, and norms in order to visualize its future.

Note: CONCEPTUAL SKILLS INCLUDE:
   concept formation which is the capacity to analyze relationships between objects
   abstraction or the ability to think symbolically
   deductive logic which is the application of general rules or concepts in making a decision for a specific set of stimuli and/or
   inductive logic which is the analysis of feedback or identification of relevant details in formulating a concept to use in decision making,
   problem reframing to enhance creativity
   dealing with multiple perspectives and ambiguity
   frame of reference development including systems understanding, environmental scanning, pattern recognition
   idea and concept development and use to solve complex problems
   envisioning to anticipate the future
   proactive thinking using critical, creative, reflective thinking
   skillful formulation of ends, ways, means
   analysis of complicated events
   trend perception
   change detection
   creative and opportunistic problem-solving
   ability to conceptualize complex ideas
   deployment of models, theories and inferences, and
   pattern recognition.

© 2006 Lauren Holmes

Natural Identity Quantum Leaps
Install belief systems using identities as the post leap

A. YOUR NATURAL IDENTITY QUANTUM LEAP:

Leadering™ re-centres your system onto its natural core and then expands that core.

- Quantum leap to the talent-based core defined by the 5 Leadering™ operating formulas
  Quantum leap to talent-based living and talent-based flow state.

- Quantum leap from externally referenced and created by your reality to internally referenced and creating your reality.
  Quantum leap from reality-driven to core-driven.

- Quantum leap to the core-driven approach required to drive the Leadering™ machinery.
  Re-boot your system into the driver's seat of your personalized Leadering™ machinery

- Re-boot your system onto its core consistent with pressures by natural forces and built-in growth continuums

- Apply natural identity quantum leaps to other systems to facilitate the achievement of their goals and yours.

IDENTITY QUANTUM LEAP BASICS:

1. Identities are integrated systems of beliefs.

2. Beliefs, like genes in the nucleus of a cell, are information storage units which define the core of any human system.

3. All advancement of human systems in the Leadering™ paradigm requires a change of beliefs. Leaders are therefore belief engineers.

4. Internalize the 'feel' or emotional template of your desired post-leap identity to lock in the belief upgrades which will change reality to coincide with those new beliefs.

5. Assume you or systems you lead have operated with the proposed post-leap identity successfully for 10 years.

6. Your selected post leap must be consistent with the direction of the flow to flow for natural forces to energize the leap.

The **REALITY-DRIVEN** to **CORE-DRIVEN** Quantum Leap

- the quantum leap from externally to internally referenced
- a quantum leap to the core-driven advancement of systems in the Leadering™ paradigm

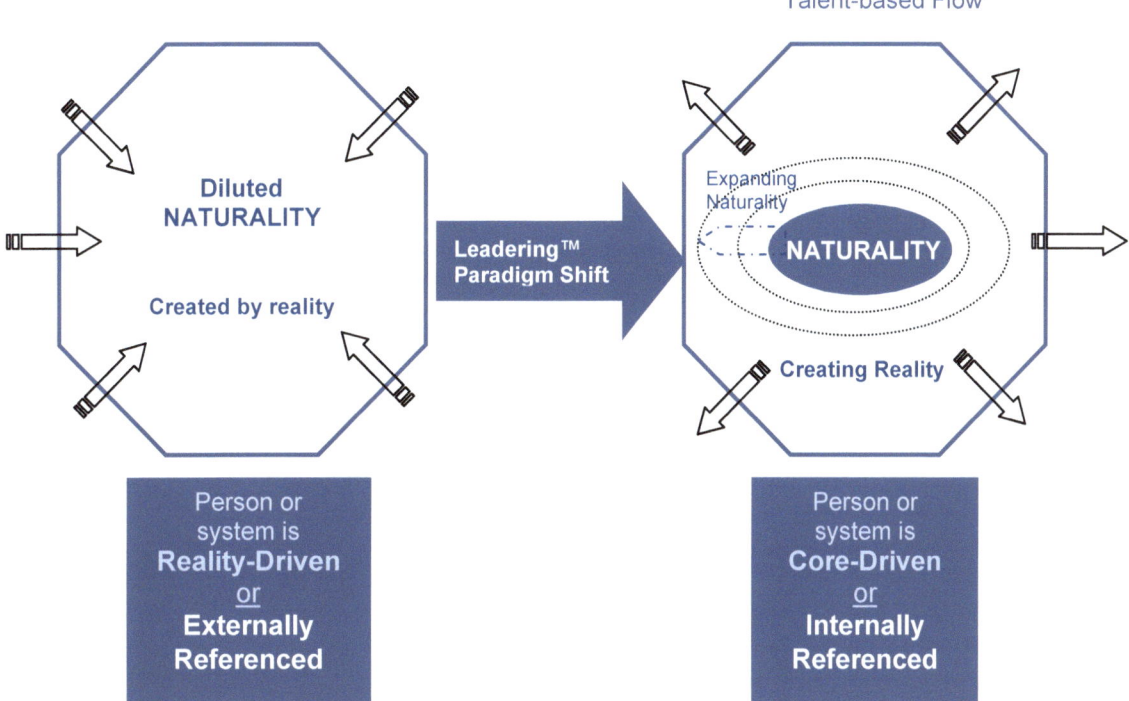

Re-boot your system onto its natural core to drive the Leadering™ machinery

In the Leadering™ paradigm, beliefs create reality. You and your reality are a single system created and run by a single belief template. Therefore, the quantum leap from externally referenced and created by the people and events in your reality to internally referenced and creating your reality is critical to leadership, entrepreneurship, innovation, peak performance and precise reality creation. This is a quantum leap from reality-driven to core-driven. It is the pivotal quantum leap to operating in the driver's seat of the Leadering™ machinery in a paradigm which must be personalized to your system.

The natural forces, mechanisms and dynamics which compose the Leadering™ machinery are acting on your natural core. To use them, you need your system to be centred on that core.

The advantage of operating in talent-based flow within the talent-based flow of the contextual system

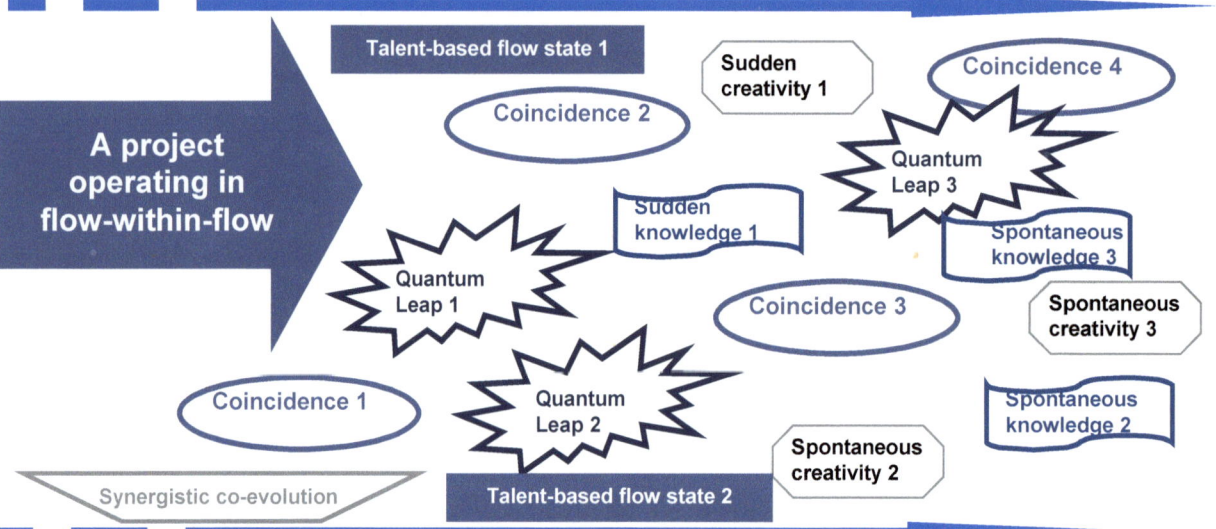

Increasing functionality with each flow experience:
- expanding consciousness and conceptual capacity
- peak performance
- peak evolution
- increasing creative capability
- expansion / intensification / enlargement of the system's natural creative expression

Proof of the Leadering™ paradigm – Proof of the accuracy of your 5 formulas
If you are operating in talent-based flow and the clustering of natural quantum leaps above emerge in your reality, then you have proof that the Leadering paradigm™ and nature's machinery inside and outside of you do indeed operate in the way Leadering™ describes.

QUANTUM LEAP FROM
- **REALITY-DRIVEN TO CORE-DRIVEN**
- **EXTERNALLY TO INTERNALLY REFERENCED**

If we are internally referenced, *we* create our realities. If we are externally referenced, our realities create us. Most of us are trained from childhood to be externally referenced - to take our identities and our other beliefs from outside of us. Rather, to achieve the full power of identity, we will want to move inside to listen to our own resonance and naturality.

INTERNALLY REFERENCED or CORE-DRIVEN
Internally referenced means you are expressing the "true you," from the inside out, regardless of reality's reaction. It is your innate natural identity. It is about expressing your core. It is about listening to your inner voice or your own drum. Alignment with your natural core happens at the moment you become internally referenced. Therefore, operating internally referenced moment after moment after moment, is the driving dynamic of core-based operation in the Leadering paradigm.

EXTERNALLY REFERENCED or REALITY-DRIVEN
To be externally referenced, we would decide who we were, or what to think of ourselves, or how to feel, or what actions to take based on the opinions of others or based on symbols or events external to us. Letting your identity be determined by how much money you have or by what others call you are examples of being externally referenced. An externally referenced identity is a "borrowed identity" based on the people, things and events in your reality. Externally referenced power is "borrowed power." If your power is given to you by something or someone outside of you, it is transient. If power is based on money or possessions or position, these things can be lost. Your identity and power will also be lost as a result.

If you are externally referenced, you are simply whatever reality creates you to be at any moment in time. You will not have the power of a clear identity emitting pure instructions to reality. Here is a way to look at the problem. Imagine you are emitting a single beam of light with instructions to reality. Now imagine you are a leaf being swirled around endlessly by rapids on a river and try to emit the beam-of-light instructions. This light stream of instructions is now being emitted in all different directions as a result of your being buffeted about. Chunks of all sorts of realities are springing up all over the place and, just as rapidly, disappearing.

If multiple identities and conflicting beliefs are creating your reality, then your power will be dissipated by its division. You will not have your full force working to create your new goal reality or that of a system you choose to lead. The moment you become internally referenced is the moment your power over what you will experience increases dramatically. It "quantum leaps." When you become internally referenced, you allow your well-ordered and integrated core identity beliefs to send clear, concise instructions to your reality to create what is absolutely reflective of the true you. As a result, you will find that physical materialization of your goals becomes rapid and effortless.

20-10E   © 2006 Lauren Holmes
Excerpted from *Peak Evolution* (Lauren Holmes, 2001)

QUANTUM LEAP FROM
- **REALITY-DRIVEN TO CORE-DRIVEN**
- **EXTERNALLY TO INTERNALLY REFERENCED**

OVERCOMING EXTERNAL REFERENCING FOR THE LEADERING™ PARADIGM

You can more easily visualize why those who have lived externally referenced or have been living life responding to unnatural demands of others or their environment. will have a harder time of the core determination exercises to identify their naturality or natural core of their flow engine or their addictive drives indicative of their key talents. They have been overruling those internal guidance systems to serve external rules. Just as those addictive drives associated with our key talents strengthen every time you use them, they atrophy every time you overrule them.

Hopefully there is a time in your childhood or some time in your past when you were not overruling them so you can figure out the themes. Depending on the degree of living externally referenced, some may need to begin operating consistent with the 15 dynamics in their life, to begin doing things they love, the thing they are most enthusiastic about doing moment by moment in order to see the flow to flow in action and begin now to collect the patterns of events from which one can deduce themes. Then they will be able to figure out their key talents in order to get nature's machinery working for them.

THE INTERNALLY REFERENCED ORGANIZATION

It is the same with other human systems such as organizations or companies or societies.

Organizational systems and other human systems create their realities in the same way. Every human system can be advanced in the same way as we are doing to your systems in the Leadering paradigm. There is a single systems management toolkit. That is why core-based leadership promotes the quantum leap process of exchanging the belief template for a new template in order to advance the system and its reality: a more effective change management process. This is why cultural management is critical to leadership. It is the system of beliefs or belief template of the organizational system which creates both the organization and its reality in the same what that your does.

20-10F © 2006 Lauren Holmes
Adapted from *Peak Evolution* (Lauren Holmes, 2001)

QUANTUM LEAP TO FULL POWER IN THE LEADERING™ PARADIGM

INTERNAL POWER versus REFLECTED POWER

Let me oversimplify for a moment to extend our investigation of power in the Leadering™ paradigm. Think of power in our old worldview as being *externally referenced* and conferred from outside of us by our positions, possessions, and associations with people or things. We receive *reflected power* based on things or events *external* to us. In the self-created realities of the Leadering™ paradigm, we have 100% *internally referenced* power. This is power based on our ability to create what we want when we want it by the reflection of our beliefs out into reality. This is a new distinction for many in our understanding of power. Yet, in the Leadering™ paradigm, it is a power so great it needs only a whisper to express itself. The Leadering™ paradigm shift will induce internally referenced power in you even if power is not your goal. It is built-in.

THE POWERLESSNESS OF EXTERNALLY REFERENCED POWER

What we are really seeking is *the power and freedom to be who we truly are*. This is healthy. As a society, however, we have been taught to pursue this power by specific channels. We are incited to pursue reflected power - titles, possessions or associations with people or things that will give us power over others. The peak evolution science offers an alternate route to our goal.

To most people, the pursuit of externally referenced power is a recipe for powerlessness. As we pursue reflected power, we will actually become drained of our personal power, making us feel powerless. Think of yourself trying for the next job title up the hierarchy. Think about asking for a raise. Think about trying to get your superiors to like you so they will give you a promotion or a raise without you having to ask for it. Do you *feel* the powerlessness? Now think of a situation where someone threatens your child. Your power quotient can go off the scale as you do whatever it takes to protect your child. You will move mountains, fight incredible demons, and take action with internal stores of power you never knew you had. In emergencies, we get a glimpse of our true power. The challenge is how to release yourself to full power and peak performance at all times. How do we make our emergency power structure available to us in our everyday living?

20-10G © 2006 Lauren Holmes
Adapted from *Peak Evolution* (Lauren Holmes, 2001)

QUANTUM LEAP TO FULL POWER IN THE LEADING™ PARADIGM

RELEASING INTERNAL POWER

Now think for a moment of times when power emerged spontaneously from inside of you. Imagine a time, for example, when you have found a critical solution to a problem. You *know* in every fibre of your being you have discovered something truly of benefit to others. You would then feel totally empowered, for example, to bring onside those same superiors who would invoke powerlessness if you had to approach for a raise or promotion. *Power of purpose empowers*. Benjamin Disraeli once said, "Nothing can resist the human will that will stake even its existence on its stated purpose." We are rallied to peak engagement around causes that seem to be driven from our deepest authentic core.

Let's look at what else invokes our full power. *Doing your art empowers. Talent-based creativity and creation empowers*. Would you not work nights and weekends, go without food and sleep and money, endure whatever it took, to be able to use and improve your key talents? We have great power when we are passionately pursuing our *art*. The musician will find the courage, tenacity and strength to do whatever is necessary to play his music. The same can be said of artists and actors willing to starve for the opportunity to creatively express their natural core. How many of us have worked overtime without pay to finish a work assignment we loved? Doing one's *art* leads one to shift into *flow* which, by definition, incites one to peak performance and power.

Identity empowers. If individuals view themselves with a particular identity, they will again be highly empowered to sustain that identity. A person with the identity of leader will lead in any territory. A doctor who views himself as a healer will seek to cause healing no matter what the circumstance . . . whether paid or not. A teacher will seek to teach. A coach will seek to coach.

What I am defining as the source of internal power is, in fact, the expression of our natural core - the interlinkage of our true identity, meaning, and *art*. The very foundations of Leadering, the natural flow of our system to its optimization around our natural core, are the means of moving to our greatest power. *Naturality empowers*. The natural growth path to the increasing expression of our key talents is the route to maximum power and peak performance. This is the reason I discovered that the most successful leaders were moving with the built-in growth continuums in the Leadering paradigm. The Emerson quote from "Power," *the Conduct of Life* (1860) is so appropriate: "All power is of one kind, a sharing of the nature of the world. The mind that is parallel with the laws of nature will be in the current of events, and strong with their strength."

QUANTUM LEAP TO FULL POWER IN THE LEADERING™ PARADIGM

UNEXPECTED POWER

Now here is the exciting thing. *Pursuing the expression of our naturality is not only the fastest route to internally based power but to externally based power.* For most people, the direct pursuit of externally based power makes us feel powerless. This powerlessness is reflected into the symbols and events of our reality. These serve to strengthen our belief in our powerlessness. The stronger our belief in our powerlessness, the faster and more effectively we will create a reality perfectly reflective of that powerlessness. As a result, we will not have the externally based power we are seeking but we may even have eroded our internal power.

Alignment with our core and the flow to flow is the only possible foundation for moving to our greatest personal power. A self-created reality would automatically reflect internally based power. Symbols of power would spontaneously materialize once internally referenced power emerges. These, of course, would include the symbols of externally based power - position, associations, and possessions. For those who are specifically seeking power, you now have the formula. The pursuit of internal power is the means to attain the external trappings of power. With both, you are in a position to stretch your being to the fullest. What is the maximum expression of your key talents possible? What is the ultimate peak performance of your system? What are the greatest contributions you can make to the world? What will be your legacy? Enjoy your new-found freedom.

20-10I © 2006 Lauren Holmes
Adapted from *Peak Evolution* (Lauren Holmes, 2001)

Expansion Identity Quantum Leaps

Natural Identity Quantum Leaps
Install belief systems using identities as the post leap

AA: GROWTH OR EXPANSION IDENTITY QUANTUM LEAPS

Once your system has been re-centred onto its natural core, establish one post-leap identity after the next for the next expansion of your core. Use your 5 Leadering operating formulas and especially formulas 2 and 5 to keep your growth identities consistent with the flow to flow.

Assume you have successfully been each of these identities for 10 years. Each identity penetrates the next frontier of applying your key talents in compliance with the built-in growth continuums operating in the Leadering™ paradigm. You can think of these post-leap growth identities as talent-based identities. They relate to the advancement of your key talents

IDENTITY QUANTUM LEAP BASICS:

1. Identities are integrated systems of beliefs.

2. Beliefs, like genes in the nucleus of a cell, are information storage units which define the core of any human system.

3. All advancement of human systems in the Leadering™ paradigm requires a change of beliefs. Leaders are therefore belief engineers.

4. Internalize the 'feel' or emotional template of your desired post-leap identity to lock in the belief upgrades which will change reality to coincide with those new beliefs.

5. Assume you or systems you lead have operated with the proposed post-leap identity successfully for 10 years.

6. Your selected post leap must be consistent with the direction of the flow to flow for natural forces to energize the leap.

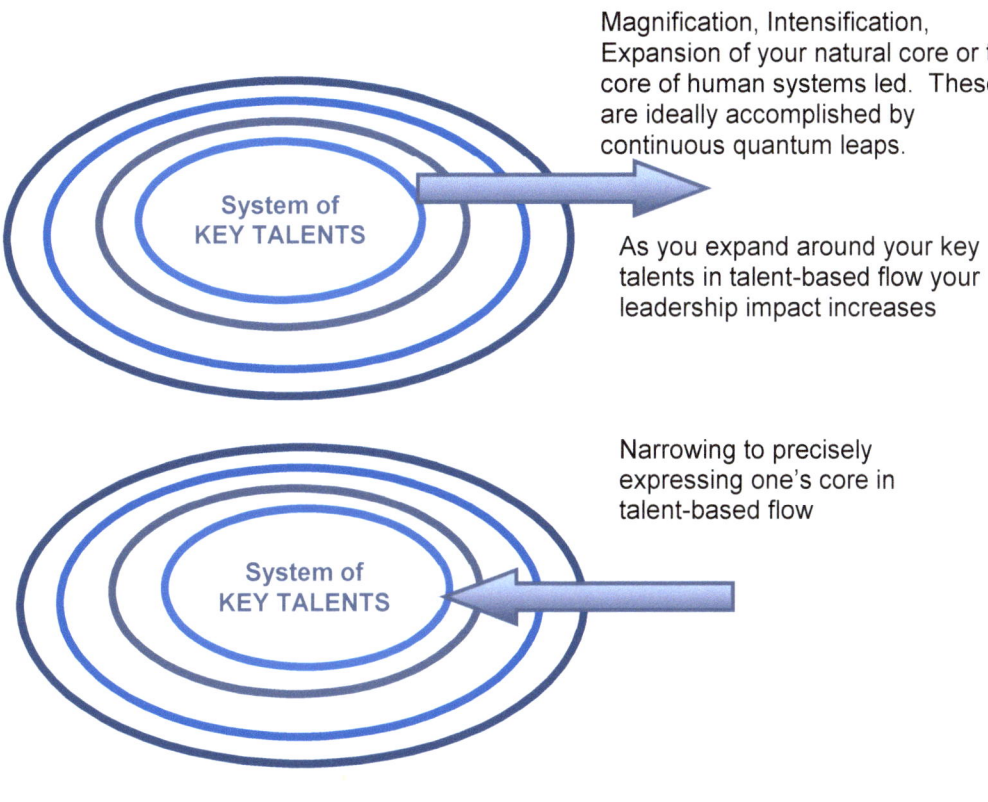

Nonlinear continuum direction

Amplification, Intensification, Expansion of your system's innate core. Core expansions in the Leadering™ paradigm are achieved by quantum leap - a method for core replacement.

As your key talents expand as a result of operating in talent-based flow state and the flow to flow, your impact on reality increases. The magnitude of change you cause in reality increases. Your creative impact increases.

Amplification of the strength and impact of your system of KEY TALENTS

20-11B2 © 2006 Lauren Holmes

Nonlinear reality advancement

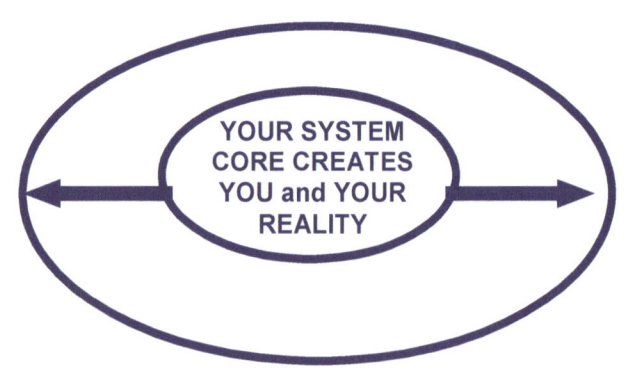

YOUR SYSTEM CORE CREATES YOU and YOUR REALITY

You and your reality are a single system in the Leadering™ paradigm. Realities are self-created by your system core.

Change your core to change your reality: the situations and events you will experience.

Formulas 1 and 2 not only advance your core but your reality or experience by reflection.

20-11B3 © 2006 Lauren Holmes

Increasing Magnitude of Impact on Belief Systems

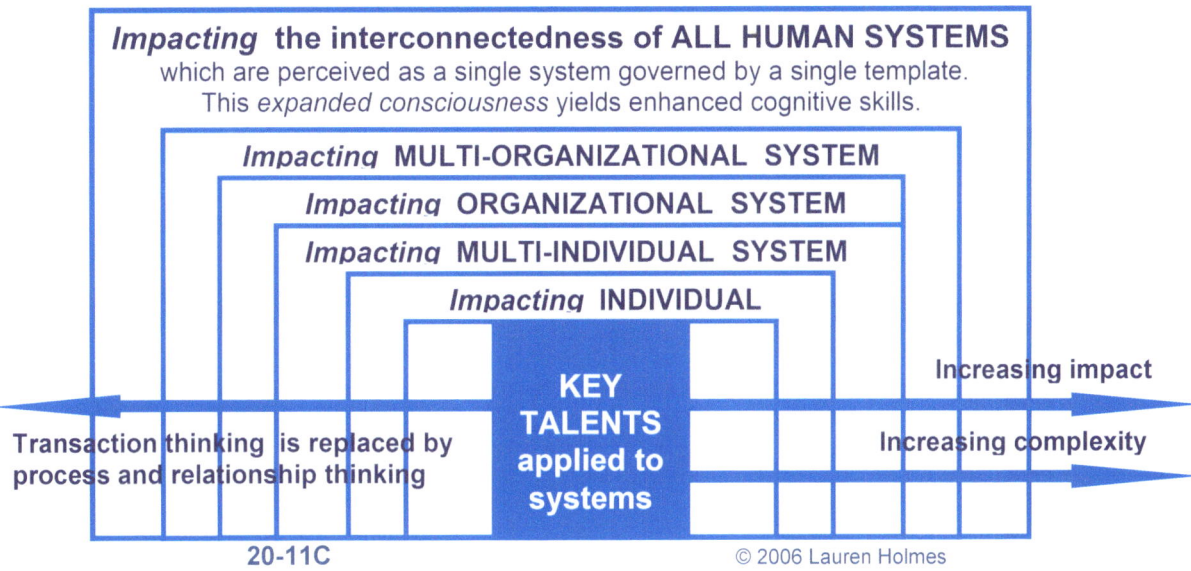

CREATING WORLD LEADERS

YOUR REALITY → ORGANIZATION → INDUSTRY → BUSINESS ECOSYSTEM → CIVILIZATION

POWER MUST INCREASE TO:

> Imprint **Beliefs** > Unify **Identities** > Increase **Creations** >

20-11D

© 1995 Lauren Holmes

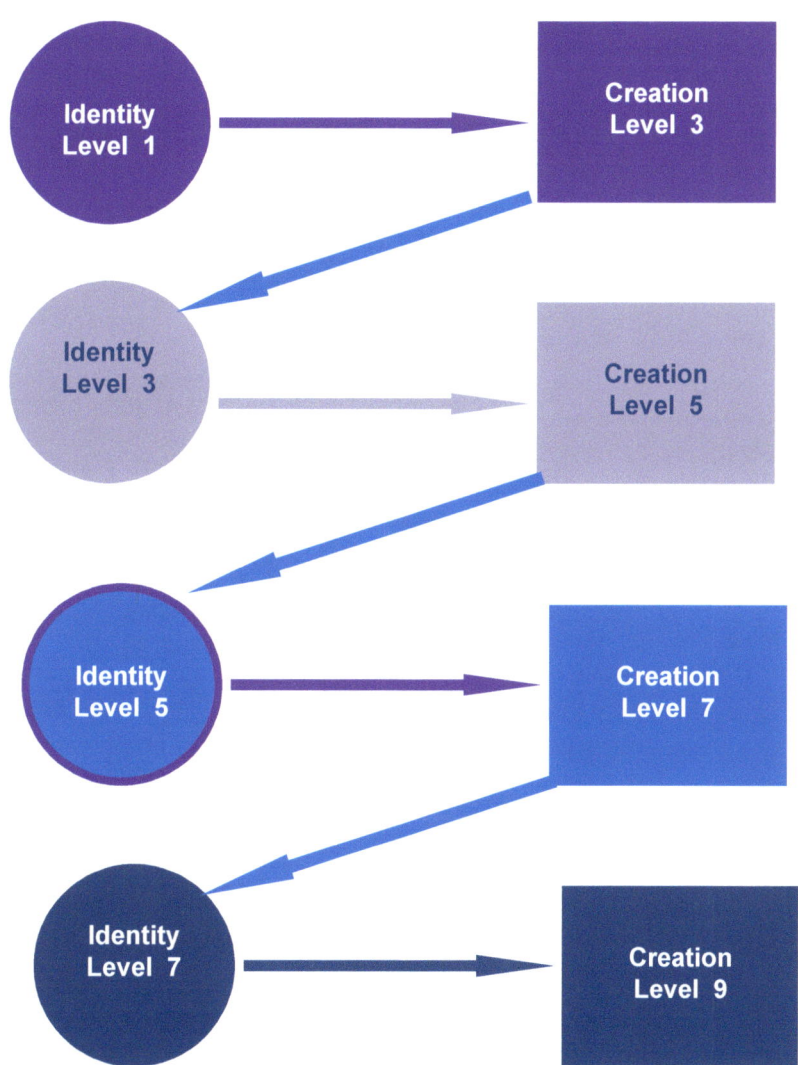

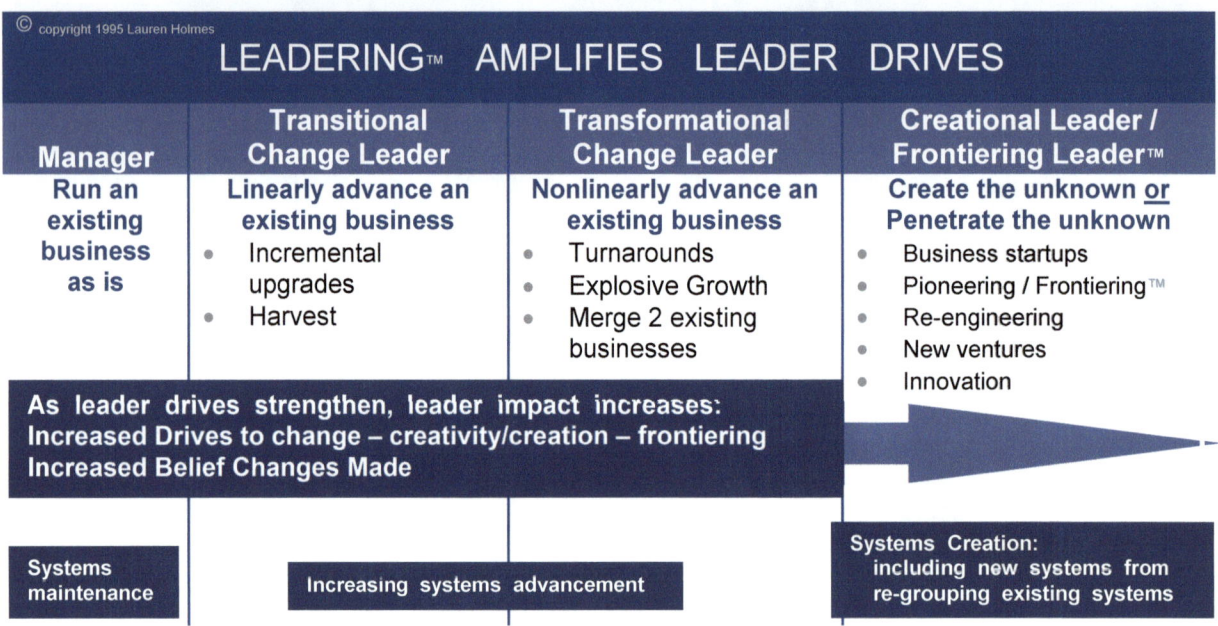

RECORDING 21

"There were moments of epiphany in Leadering™ that brought tears to my eyes and left me forever changed, forever elevated by a more expansive vision, a greater truth that, once experienced, can never be forgotten or reversed."

10 OPERATIONALIZING THE PARADIGM

Growth or expansion identity quantum leaps
The transition from completing the paradigm shift to operating in the paradigm is made within this recording

21. Goal-driven Identity quantum leaps — 35 minutes — 20 figures
    Subset: Flow-driven identity quantum leaps
    Subset: Corporate identity quantum Leaps
22. Identity quantum leaps to replace maladaptive beliefs — 18 minutes — 9 figures
23. Multi-System Identity quantum leaps — 41 minutes — 23 figures
    Leadering™ toolkit identity quantum leaps
    Subset: Leadering™ meta-competency identity quantum leaps
    Quantum leaps to goal 'states of being' rather than goal 'states':
    Subset: Assimilated Expert Identity quantum leaps
    Subset: Projected Expert Identity quantum leaps
24. Driving a Multi-System Paradigm — 57 minutes — 1 figure

21. Goal-driven Identity quantum leaps (*changeable beliefs*)
— 35 minutes — 20 figures

Subset: Flow-driven identity quantum leaps
Subset: Corporate identity quantum Leaps

Some exercises and action learning experiments are presented to install a system of beliefs, emotions, knowledge, and experiential learning to generate expertise for using this goal-driven identity quantum leap tool in the Leadering™ paradigm to quickly change beliefs to change reality.

The solution to 'new goal syndrome' is presented. The solution is one of belief clearing as a conditioned reflex after setting a new goal-driven identity.

Identity Quantum Leap Categories

Install belief systems using identities as the post leap

8 Identity Quantum Leap Tool Categories

PARADIGM SHIFT
1. Natural identity quantum leaps (*immutable beliefs*)

PARADIGM OPERATION
2. *Subset:* Growth or expansion identity quantum leaps
3. Goal-driven identity quantum leaps
4. *Subset:* Flow-driven identity quantum leaps
5. Corporate identity quantum Leaps
6. Identity quantum leaps to replace problem beliefs
7. Leadering™ toolkit identity quantum leaps
8. *Subset:* Leadering™ meta-competency identity quantum leaps
   Quantum leaps to goal 'states of being' *rather than goal* 'states':
   Subset: Assimilated Expert Identity quantum leaps
   Subset: Projected Expert Identity quantum leaps

IDENTITY QUANTUM LEAP BASICS:

1. Identities are integrated systems of beliefs.

2. Beliefs, like genes in the nucleus of a cell, are information storage units which define the core of any human system.

3. All advancement of human systems in the Leadering™ paradigm requires a change of beliefs. Leaders are therefore belief engineers.

4. Internalize the 'feel' or emotional template of your desired post-leap identity to lock in the belief upgrades which will change reality to coincide with those new beliefs. (figure 21-7A)

5. Assume you or systems you lead have operated with the proposed post-leap identity successfully for 10 years.

6. Your selected post leap must be consistent with the direction of the flow to flow for natural forces to energize the leap.

Goal-Driven Identity Quantum Leaps

Install belief systems using identities as the post leap

B. GOAL-DRIVEN IDENTITY QUANTUM LEAPS

Partner adaptive "goal-driven identities" with your "natural identity"
You can use quantum leaps as a form of reincarnation to package your natural identity in such a way that it will help you to achieve immediate goals by quickly changing reality.

For the best results you still need to honour the direction of the flow to flow and your natural core with its key talents and drives and immutable beliefs. Goals and quantum leaps will only be supported by natural forces when you are being true to the system and its contextual system.

Both your natural identity and any goal-driven identities with which you choose to package yourself are massive systems of beliefs which will therefore impact reality more dramatically than changing one belief at a time. As a result, goals are achieved more quickly.

BB. FLOW-DRIVEN IDENTITY QUANTUM LEAPS

Flow-driven identities arise opportunistically from the flow to flow when you set a new goal. **These flow-driven post-leap identities are absorbed from models, information systems, and people and events flowing in to you as part of the flow to flow when you set goals consistent with that flow.**

Once you set a goal which complies with the flow to flow and the advancement of your key talents through new frontiers, you have launched the support of natural forces, natural quantum leaps like coincidences, spontaneous knowledge, spontaneous creativity, and facilitative events, and the flow of supportive information systems. All of these could cumulatively suggest all or part of your post-leap identity or the ultimate solution to your immediate goal.

The flow to flow always orchestrates synergy and co-evolution and co-adaptation. It is only logical then that co-evolving systems will move into your vicinity which will support the goal for your system that you have selected consistent with the flow to flow.

Goal-Driven Identity Quantum Leap Exercises

EXERCISE 1: Generic Goal-Driven Identity quantum leaps

Figure 19-3B offers 4 generic examples for you to use to develop your ability to feel the emotions of being that identity so that beliefs and information are internalized into your belief template to change it from a pre-leap template to a post-leap template.

Develop the ability to quickly feel the whole system of emotions associated with the identity of a person who has successfully operated your desired goal reality for 10 years.

Build a conditioned reflex to assume the identity of a person with the goal reality

The identity is the means to install in your belief template a whole system of new beliefs quickly. You must change the template in order to change your reality. The change of the template IS the quantum leap.

It is easier to associate the emotional feel of an identity than a neutral system of beliefs that you have had to develop one by one or, worse, individual beliefs that have to be integrated.

This exercise serves as a work out of your muscles for changing your emotions and beliefs in a gym.

Notice how each "sub-identity" invokes whole systems of beliefs and emotions in a very concise way. Identity shorthand can provide an immense number of detailed instructions to rapidly change any reality. That's the kind of latent power we all have through the use of identity. The real challenge is whether you can release your linear connection to the past to incorporate the new identity. Can you move to a future state that is not a linear extension of everything that you have experienced in your life to this point? Can you quantum leap? Then, can you hold that change for a period of time until reality restructures?

21-3A © 2006 Lauren Holmes

An Action Learning Experiment

Goal-Driven Identity Test Drives:

Belief upgrades using goal-based identities

EXERCISE 1: Continued

GENERIC IDENTITY EXPERIMENTS

Take a few moments to "wear" each of these goal-based identities emotionally. While you're doing so, think about how many instructions or belief changes I've been able to communicate to you if I asked you to reincarnate as the following while still remaining true to your naturality.

1. **A world leader in your field** for the last 10 years

2. **A Nobel Prize winner** - the peace prize, for example. Notice how this goal-based identity suddenly shapes how you behave and what you would be doing out in the world. It communicates, in a precise package, a plethora of beliefs, feelings, emotions, historical accomplishments, modi operandi, and the kind of people in your world. You are instantly wearing an entirely different life than you are used to. You are internalizing new beliefs and those beliefs are actually communicating all of those instructions to reality. This is the basic power of goal-based identity. It is a short-form for communicating immense change to your reality. Try this one:

3. **A person with the Midas touch** who can create money effortlessly for yourself, for others, for your company, or for any cause. Assume that no matter what you did, you would generate wealth. Money will just roll in - much too much to ever worry about money again. Notice how, just by using the identity of the Midas touch, I have communicated much more than the words I've given you. Notice the emotional tapestry that you experience and all of the secondary concepts associated with the identity. You can begin to see the power of a goal-based identity as a short-form for communicating belief changes to transform yourself and then your reality.

4. **"Entrepreneur of the Year"** with your own successful company around your natural art, your key talents and their associated addictive drives, your knowledge-pursuit drive, your frontier-pursuit drive, and your creation/creativity-pursuit drives.

21-3B © 2006 Lauren Holmes
Adapted from *Peak Evolution* (Lauren Holmes, 2001)

Historical Evidence of
Goal-Driven Identity Quantum Leaps at Work

GOAL EVENT CLUSTERING:

Think of a past goal that you pursued which eluded you for a long time but was eventually achieved. Examples:
- sale of your house
- finding a job
- getting a specified promotion or raise
- finding a significant other

With 20:20 hindsight:

1. What were your beliefs during the pursuit of this past goal which prevented you from creating the goal reality, or, created the unpreferred reality?

2. What beliefs or belief systems changed to make the elusive goal reality now possible in a belief-created reality?
   For example,
   - Did you resolve one of more conflicting beliefs such as in Figure 21-7J by choosing the positive belief of the pair and letting the other go?
   - Did you quantum leap to a post-leap reality that did not include the interfering belief(s)?
   - Did you clear fears associated with either achieving the goal reality or realities you felt would result from achieving this goal reality
   - Did you learn new information or experience information coincidences which caused the requisite belief changes?

3. Were there multiple indicators or multiple opportunities or multiple options that occurred with respect to having the goal reality once you made the changes to your beliefs?
   For example,
   - Was there a bidding war for buying your home? or
   - Were their multiple job offers after many months of no job offers?

   This clustering would confirm that you had changed your beliefs which were now emphatically changing your reality.

4. From this exercise and others, what problem beliefs do you think have to be cleared to maximize your systems through core congruence and talent-based flow state, and flow to flow and to achieve all of the built-in growth continuums underlying the Leadering™ paradigm?

5. What problem beliefs need to be cleared in order to pursue your 5 Leadering operating formulas?

Event Clustering
in the Leadering™ Paradigm and Nature

Event "clustering" or "clumping" is a common occurrence in the Leadering™ paradigm and in nature (planets around a sun, for example). Clusters provide information for driving the Leadering™ machinery.

Event Clustering in the Leadering™ paradigm includes:

- the clustering of negative events created by a negative belief system interfering with your progress along Leadering's built-in growth continuums (Fig 21- 7I)

- the clustering of natural quantum leaps such as coincidences, facilitating events, spontaneous knowledge, spontaneous creativity and positive emotions when one is moving with the flow-to-flow.

- coincidences themselves are a clustering or synergy or opportunistic partnering or co-adaptation of multiple co-evolving systems within the flow-to-flow.

- the historical patterns of events we used to determine your life themes are indicators of the clustering of key talent development around the flow-to-flow - so much so that you can tell your lifetime key talent development continuum or formula 1 from the clustering and you can use the clustering to identify and capitalize on the flow-to-flow going forward.

Goal-Driven Identity Quantum Leap Exercises

EXERCISE 2A: Personal Goal-Driven Identity quantum leaps
1. Determine 5 current goals to use for this exercise
   a. Ensure that these 5 goals are consistent with the direction your system will be advancing:
      - your talent based life themes indicating the flow to flow,
      - your 5 operating formulas based on the flow to flow,
      - the Leadering™ built-in growth continuums based on the flow to flow,
      - clusters of facilitating events and natural quantum leaps occurring your reality currently (coincidences events, spontaneous knowledge events, spontaneous creativity events)
   b. Eliminate those with a negative emotional charge or which you have been been pursuing for a long time unsuccessfully. In addition, those with a positive emotional charge and even passion would be better. Those with a positive emotional charge, and even passion, would be better.
2. Determine intellectually an identity for each of the 5 goals of a person who has successfully operated for 10 years with that goal reality.
3. Internalize an emotional blueprint of that identity so it will add new information and new beliefs to your pre-leap template in order to transform it to your goal post-leap identity and reality.

EXERCISE 2B: Goal-Related Flow-Driven Identity quantum leaps
4. Allow yourself to be orchestrated by the flow to flow to all 5 goal identities/realities simultaneously in an interleaving fashion. If models in the form of individuals, or situations, or information emerge, internalize these as dimensions of the relevant goal-driven identity blueprinting your post-leap goal reality.

EXERCISE 2C:
New-Goal Syndrome Solutions using Goal-Driven Identity quantum leaps
5. If clusters of problem events emerge immediately after goal-setting, quantum leap to an identity without the problem beliefs which would have created such events. This cleanup should routinely be part of your quantum leap cycle.
6. Proceed as if the quantum leap has been successful and you already have the goal reality. Expect to find that people and events in reality respond differently than they did in your pre-leap reality.
7. Look for and capitalize on indicators of the flow to flow supporting your quantum leap: models, information systems, coincidences, spontaneous knowledge, spontaneous creativity, facilitating events
8. Lock in your experiential learning and quantum leap expertise to be able to increase the magnitude and complexity of similar goal quantum leaps in the future: If you find that people and events in your goal reality are responding differently from the pre-leap reality, diarize your findings to reinforce your quantum leap expertise belief systems.

Goal-Driven Identity Quantum Leap Exercises

EXERCISE 3: Group or Organizational Goal-Driven Identity quantum leaps

1. Select 5 goals for groups or organizations or other human systems to use for this exercise: your family, social or charitable organizations, work organizations or teams or whole companies, for example.

2. Ensure that these 5 goals are consistent with the direction your system will be advancing and with the direction of advancement for the systems involved as much as you are able at your current level of conceptual skills and expanded consciousness (these will advance with practice):
   - your life themes indicating the flow to flow,
   - your 5 operating formulas based on the flow to flow,
   - the Leadering built-in growth continuums based on the flow to flow, and/or
   - clusters of facilitating events and natural quantum leaps occurring your reality currently (coincidences events, spontaneous knowledge events, spontaneous creativity events)

3. Determine intellectually an identity for each of the 5 goals of an organization or group who has successfully operated for 10 years with that goal reality.

4. Internalize an emotional blueprint of that identity so it will add new information and new beliefs to the group system's pre-leap template in order to transform it to your proposed goal post-leap identity and reality.

5. Use any levers you can think of to cause the same new beliefs and information to integrate into the pre-leap template of each individual member of the group system to facilitate the proposed pre-leap to post-leap exchange of the entire human system.

6. Proceed as if the quantum leap has been successful and you already have the goal reality.

7. Look for and capitalize on indicators of the flow to flow supporting your quantum leap: models, information systems, coincidences, spontaneous knowledge, spontaneous creativity, facilitating events.

8. Lock in your experiential learning and quantum leap expertise to be able to increase the magnitude and complexity of similar goal quantum leaps in the future.

Corporate Goal-Driven Identity Quantum Leaps

Install belief systems using identities as the post leap

E. CORPORATE GOAL-DRIVEN IDENTITY QUANTUM LEAPS

Capitalize on existing corporate identities and identity uses to empower your corporate goal-driven identity quantum leap tool:

Historically, corporations have used identities
- **to unify**: individuals, teams, departments, companies, customer relationships, marketplaces around a product or company or cause or project or marketing campaign
- **as goals to be pursued by linear process**

Capitalize on existing corporate levers. The below can thus be adapted for use in the Leadering™ paradigm:

GENERIC CORPORATE IDENTITY EXAMPLES

Belief systems usable for advancing corporate goals or realities include:
- vision
- branding
- cultural imprinting
- corporate image management
- organizational identity
- logo
- marketing campaign slogans

SPECIFIC CORPORATE IDENTITY EXAMPLES:

1. Corporate identity of :
   - best company in the industry: best in class
   - a top performance company
   - best employer
   - innovative company
   - our employees are a community

2. Individual identity of:
   - the top performing team
   - change leader
   - entrepreneur
   - intrapreneur
   - leader
   - job titles

21-6B © 2006 Lauren Holmes

Corporate Goal-Driven Identity Quantum Leaps

Install belief systems using identities as the post leap

Using Corporate identities as a way of life

1. Allow each person to choose a job title which reflects their natural identity and key talents. But let that evolve over time as the individual expands around their core and narrows to greater precision of using their key talents as in figures 21-17B and 21-7C.

2. Allow each person to be benevolently labeled by an identity which reflects their key talents.

3. Promote informal and formal social or business meetings or teleconferences in which those with similar talents can congregate to reinforce and advance their talents.

4. Create Leadering peer advisory groups who meet regularly in person or by teleconference to accelerate advancement along their built-in growth continuums. Groups could be talent-based or work-based or based on their degree of advancement in the Leadering™ paradigm.

5. Ensure every team is labeled with a natural identity reflective of the key talents and natural core of the combined members. Figure out what core, natural forces will be acting on and label the team accordingly so that whatever goal they are pursuing they will know where the natural forces will be pressuring the system and capitalize on it for the goal.

6. Define the corporate culture with clarity using one or more synergistic identities as a short-form means of communicating a massive number of systems of beliefs to change the core of the corporate system in order to change its reality.

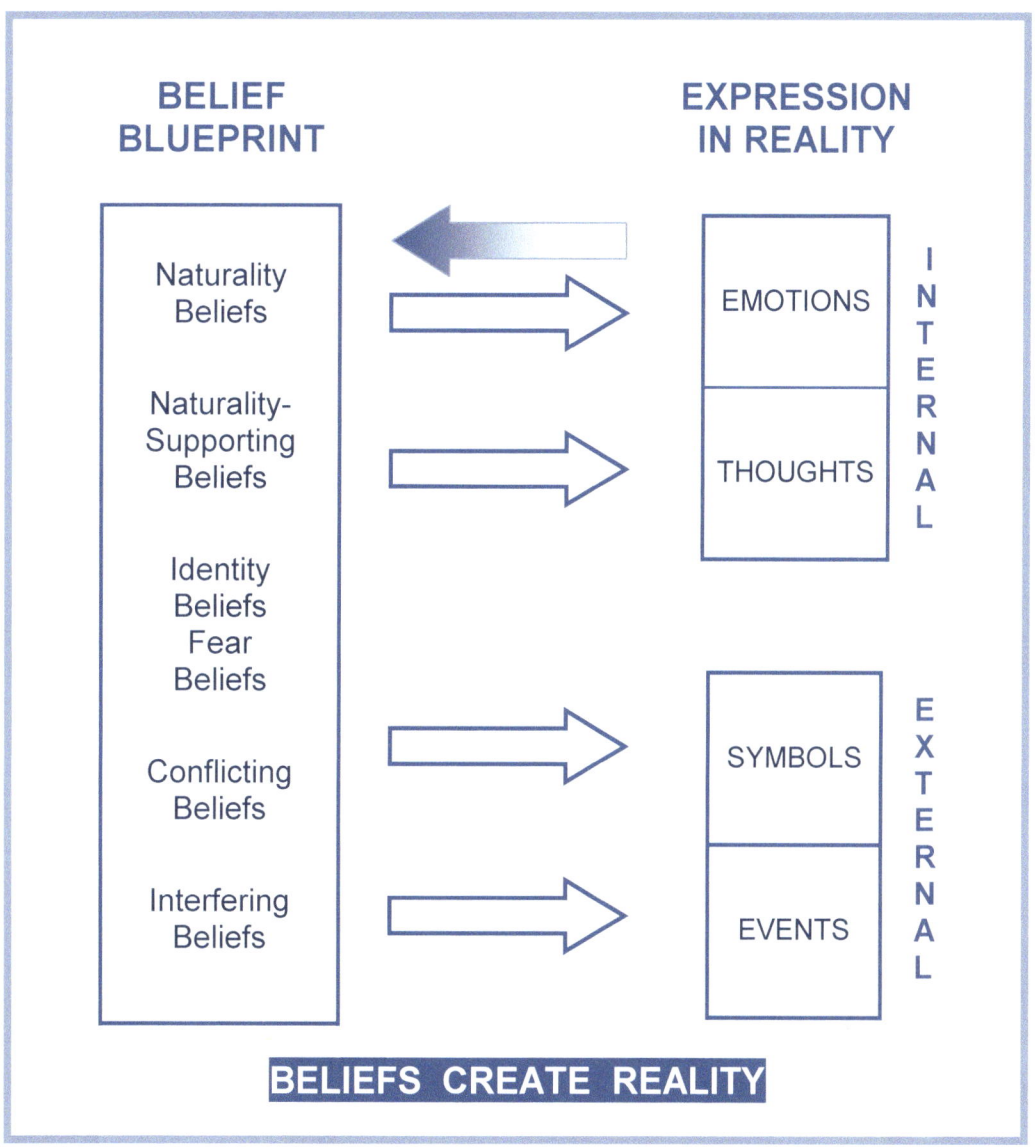

21-7A © 1993 Lauren Holmes
Excerpted from *Peak Evolution* (Lauren Holmes, 2001)

Nonlinear continuum direction

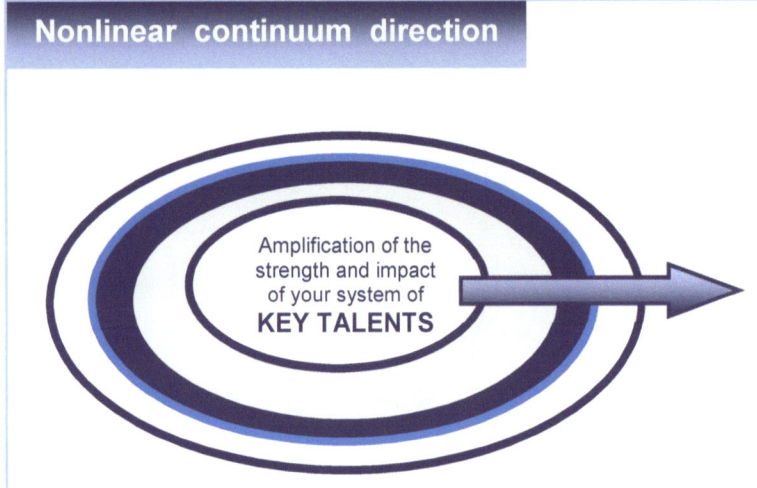

Amplification, Intensification, Expansion of your system's innate core. Core expansions in the Leadering™ paradigm are achieved by quantum leap - a method for core replacement.

As your key talents expand as a result of operating in talent-based flow state and the flow to flow, your impact on reality increases. The magnitude of change you cause in reality increases. Your creative impact increases.

21-7B   © 2006 Lauren Holmes

Nonlinear reality advancement

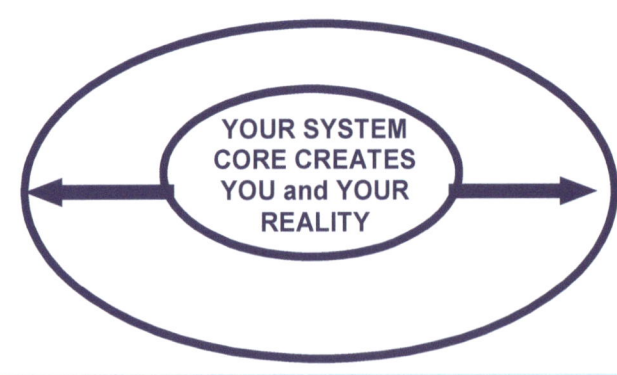

You and your reality are a single system in the Leadering™ paradigm. Realities are self-created by your system core.

Change your core to change your reality: the situations and events you will experience.

Formulas 1 and 2 not only advance your core but your reality or experience by reflection.

21-7C   © 2006 Lauren Holmes

CORE CONGRUENCE: The Changeable Beliefs

AUTOMATIC REALITY CREATION

IMMUTABLE or GENE-BASED BELIEFS

The beliefs behind the key talents and drives innate to your system core and flow engine.

Consistent with the Flow-to-flow.

Adaptive realities are created automatically and continuously to amplify core through Leadering's built-in growth continuums.

Life Themes, Key Talent, and 5 Formula

CHANGEABLE

1. SUPPORTIVE

Promote flow to flow and Leadering's built-in growth continuums which amplify core expression and advancement for your system core.

Belief Upgrade Exercises

2. INTERFERING

Block flow to flow and built-in growth continuums required to maximize and advance core talents and drives

Belief Clearing Exercises

Leadering's single systems management toolkit can also be applied to belief systems.

Belief changes are achieved by quantum leap. It is easier to exchange a belief template than to try to change beliefs already logically integrated and interlinked into systems.

Goal-Driven Identity Quantum Leaps

Internalize the identity belief system of a person who has achieved a goal to make it a reality

BELIEF-CREATED REALITY

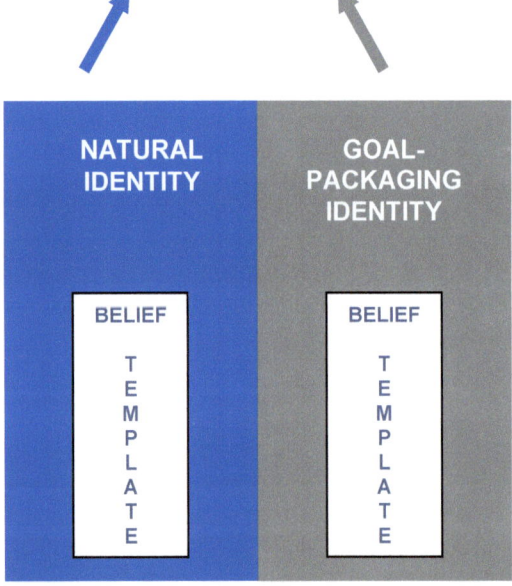

Both systems of beliefs are creating your reality. Core congruence is therefore essential for precise reality creation.

Immutable Beliefs

A system of **Changeable Beliefs** which support the <u>Immutable Beliefs</u> to achieve a specific goal reality consistent with the flow to flow.

Identities are systems of beliefs. Beliefs create reality in the Leadering™ paradigm. Therefore belief congruence ensures the greatest power and precision of reality creation. Since your natural identity, key talents and drives are predetermined, you will want changeable beliefs associated with the achievement of specific goals to be synergistic with your existing core.

© 2006 Lauren Holmes

Natural + Goal Identity Belief Systems

Goal-Driven Identity Quantum Leaps

GOAL REALITY A

GOAL-PACKAGING IDENTITY

a system of synergistic beliefs designed to create a goal reality

NATURAL IDENTITY

the system of beliefs, key talents, and drives upon which your system is founded

GOAL REALITY A

A system of beliefs is added to your natural identity beliefs to assist with the achievement of goals. These new beliefs are consistent with the creative expression and advancement of this natural identity with its system of beliefs, talents, and drives. Synergy or core congruence is requisite to effective creation of the goal reality.

Dynamics of a Quantum Leap

PRE-LEAP
Integrated Stable State or internal congruence

POST-LEAP
Integrated Stable State or internal congruence.

OLD BELIEF TEMPLATE

OLD REALITY

PLUS **NEW INFO**

Emergence

Direction congruent with the generative flow of the contextual system: external congruence

NEW BELIEF TEMPLATE

NEW REALITY

INTERNAL CONGRUENCE
A naturality-based state. Discernible through patterns of naturality expansion, talent-based flow, expressions of one's art, and spontaneous knowledge.

EXTERNAL CONGRUENCE
Discernible through patterns of coincidences, flow events, and the following drives which are a subsystem's links to the flow to congruence of its contextual system: drives for creativity, growth, frontiering, resonance, flow state, emotional highs, knowledge.

A QUANTUM LEAP IS A TEMPLATE EXCHANGE CAUSING A REALITY EXCHANGE

It is a system reincarnation at a more advanced state

21-7G © 2006 Lauren Holmes

THE LEADERING™ QUANTUM LEAP PROCESS

Design it!   Feel it!   Be it!

PRE-LEAP
1. Choose the right quantum leap or post-leap state
2. Define the post-leap state with clarity
3. Define the post-leap state without previous limitations or toxicity
4. Emotionally template the post-leap state
5. Add the information to fuel emergence
6. Expect the unexpected post-leap

LEAP
1. Release the linear connection to the past
2. Feel yourself 100% fluid
3. Feel the post-leap state
4. Feel who the "post-leap you" will be
5. Commit to the quantum leap
6. Make an abrupt, no-return, reincarnation
7. Trigger spontaneous self-organization by intent

POST-LEAP
1. Operate as if the quantum leap was successful
2. Walk around as the person with the post-leap reality
3. Hold this new identity until reality restructures
4. Ignore evidence of events created by the old template
5. Trigger cascading quantum leaps by intent
6. Establish quantum leaping as a way of life
7. Consolidate your new quantum leap expert beliefs

21-7H   © 1998 Lauren Holmes

Prioritized Problem Belief Clustering:

Reality systematically clears interfering beliefs

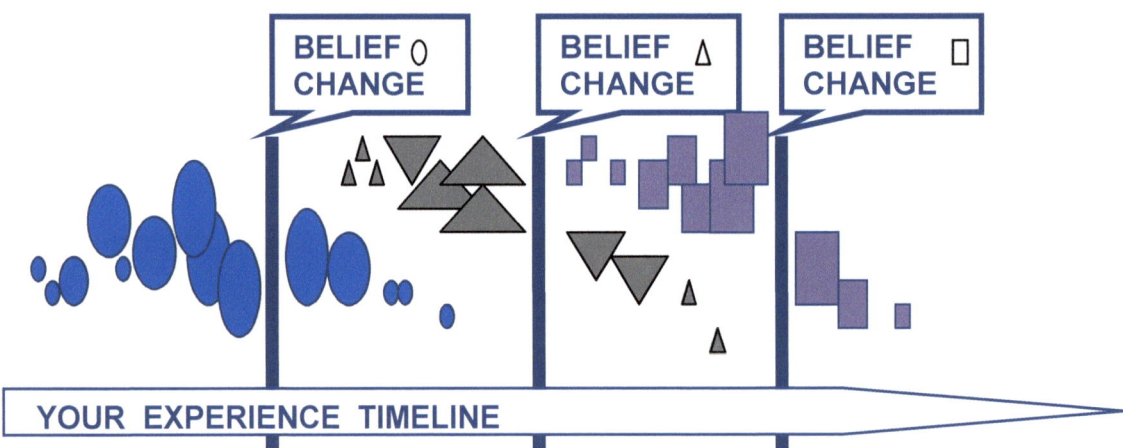

Clusters of belief-created problem events increase over time until the problem belief is replaced. With no problem belief to create events the associated events will gradually disappear. Then the next problem belief begins creating problem events . . .

Problem beliefs become evident in events in reality in a priority order which is determined by the strength of the belief to interfere with all of the forces promoting the flow to flow

The degree of blocks, resistance and toxicity increases as one conflicts with the flow to flow - including problem beliefs.

If one has beliefs creating reality which is in conflict with the immutable beliefs defining the core of your system which are also sending instructions to reality, the two realities will collide to create struggle events and blocks to your progress

If there is a conflict of systems of beliefs inside of you, that conflict will be perfectly dumped into reality as maladaptive events.

© 2006 Lauren Holmes

A COMMON SYSTEM OF CONFLICTING BELIEFS

Exchange the 'powerless' belief system for the 'powerful' belief system in a single quantum leap

Individual belief replacements fail because the interlinks within the system of beliefs cause eliminated beliefs to be reinstated. This sustains problem beliefs and their reflected problem realities.

POWERFUL: *Can have what you want		POWERLESS: *Cannot have what you want
Work / Life has meaning	vs	No power to do meaningful things.
Valuable Contribution		No power to achieve significantly
Safe - *World is benevolent*	vs	Not Safe - *World is malevolent*
Effortlessness	vs	Struggle / Force
		- *Expect conflict or resistance*
	vs	- *World blocks your progress*
Supported - *By everyone / world*		Not Supported - *Alone*
Free to be you		Controlled by Others
- *Internally referenced*	vs	- *Externally referenced*
Free to do what you want		Controlled by others or rules
Worthy:	vs	**Unworthy:**
Deserve to have what you want	vs	*Do not deserve to have what you want*
Valued / Valuable	vs	**Not Valued / Not Valuable**
Respected	vs	Not Respected
Capable	vs	Not Capable
Successful	vs	Not Successful
Included / Accepted	vs	Excluded / Isolated / Judged
Trusting	vs	Not Trusting
Abundance	vs	Scarcity - *Time, money, friends, opportunities, etc.*

- Conflicting and dysfunctional beliefs make core congruence difficult to achieve.
- Clarity of beliefs is a critical element of leadership especially for imprinting both culture and the vision of future realities the leader wants to create.
- Strength and consistency of beliefs is critical to the consistency of leadership required to achieve any new reality.

21-7J © 1998 Lauren Holmes
Adapted from *Peak Evolution* (Lauren Holmes, 2001)

Interfering Belief Replacement Identity Quantum Leaps
Install belief systems using identities as the post leap

D. IDENTITY QUANTUM LEAPS FOR PROBLEM BELIEF REPLACEMENT

Only activated problem beliefs which are creating unpreferred realities right now in the present need to be cleared. Old inactive problem beliefs will eventually atrophy from disuse and no longer create unpreferred realities - especially as you spend time in talent-based flow state. Only supportive beliefs and positive emotions are activated in talent-based flow.

1. **Post-leap identities without the pre-leap problems:** Quantum leap to a post-leap identity without the problem beliefs creating the problem reality. (figure 21-2B)

2. **Event-driven belief upgrade tool**: Use unpreferred events in reality to instantly trigger a conditioned reflex to have you quantum leap to an identity without the problem beliefs creating these events. (figure 21-12)

3. **Clear problem beliefs by *systems*:** Beliefs travel in packs or schools. Use identity belief systems to quantum leap to eliminate whole systems of interconnected problem beliefs. You need to clear them as a system or they keep resurrecting themselves from the remnants of the interconnections. Quantum leap to **jettison a key culturally induced conflicting belief complex,** the only belief clearing that has to be done right now before the ongoing cleanup.

4. **New goal syndrome:** Belief clearing as a conditioned reflex after setting a new goal-driven identity. New goals activate all relevant beliefs in your belief template. As a result, new goals may activate beliefs you have not yet cleared which create unpreferred realities. Use the problem realities to trigger a conditioned reflex to routinely reinforce your post leap to facilitate belief clearings of the problem beliefs that are activated by goal setting.

   On the positive front, new goals also trigger the flow-driven identity quantum leaps and natural quantum leaps and facilitative events.

5. **Identifying interfering beliefs from problem event clusters:** The belief most interfering with your immediate advancement along Leadering's built-in growth continuums creates a cluster of problem events which will increase in number and severity over time. Use the clustering to trigger a conditioned reflex to reinforce your quantum leaps to natural and goal-driven identities which do not include the offending belief.

Leadering™ complies with and capitalizes on natural growth mechanisms which are trying to expand or intensify one's system around its core system of key talents and drives.

10 OPERATIONALIZING THE PARADIGM continued

22. **Belief Clearing with Identity quantum leaps**   18 minutes   9 figures
    NOTE: Only activated problem beliefs which are creating unpreferred realities right now in the present need to be cleared. Old inactive problem beliefs will eventually atrophy from disuse and no longer create unpreferred realities - especially as you spend time in talent-based flow state. Only supportive beliefs and positive emotions are activated in talent-based flow.

    Clearing problem beliefs was begun in the previous recording (new goal syndrome). Two exercises for clearing problem beliefs are provided here:
    - An identity quantum leap to clear a whole system of integrated conflicting beliefs which tend to be inherent in our culture.
    - Action learning experiments to help you to investigate your historical problem beliefs in order to clear them. These experiments will
        - not only identify problem beliefs to be cleared, but simultaneously
        - install conditioned reflexes to problem beliefs for future ongoing clearing and
        - prove that beliefs create reality so you have those new beliefs to improve your performance in creating goal realities in the future.

    In addition, the following *Identity Quantum Leaps for Problem Belief Replacement* are discussed:
    - post-leap identities without the pre-leap problems
    - event-driven belief upgrade tool
    - clearing problem beliefs by *systems*
    - new goal syndrome
    - identifying interfering beliefs from problem event clusters

Identity Quantum Leap Tool Categories

Install belief systems using identities as the post leap

8 Identity Quantum Leap Tool Categories

PARADIGM SHIFT
1. Natural identity quantum leaps (*immutable beliefs*)

PARADIGM OPERATION
2.   *Subset:* Growth or expansion identity quantum leaps
3. Goal-driven identity quantum leaps
4.   *Subset:* Flow-driven identity quantum leaps
5. Corporate Identity Quantum Leaps
6. Identity quantum leaps to replace problem beliefs
7. Leadering™ toolkit identity quantum leaps
8.   *Subset:* Leadering™ meta-competency identity quantum leaps
      Quantum leaps to goal 'states of being' *rather than goal* 'states':
         Subset: Assimilated Expert Identity quantum leaps
         Subset: Projected Expert Identity quantum leaps

IDENTITY QUANTUM LEAP BASICS:

1. Identities are integrated systems of beliefs.

2. Beliefs, like genes in the nucleus of a cell, are information storage units which define the core of any human system.

3. All advancement of human systems in the Leadering™ paradigm requires a change of beliefs. Leaders are therefore belief engineers.

4. Internalize the 'feel' or emotional template of your desired post-leap identity to lock in the belief upgrades which will change reality to coincide with those new beliefs.
   (figure 21-7A)

5. Assume you or systems you lead have operated with the proposed post-leap identity successfully for 10 years.

6. Your selected post leap must be consistent with the direction of the flow to flow for natural forces to energize the leap.

Leadering™ Belief Engineering Tools

Tools for the '*Changeable Core Beliefs*' requisite to core maximization

THREE CATEGORIES OF BELIEF UPGRADE TOOLS to

- upgrade your "*Changeable Core Beliefs*" to support the maximum performance and advancement of your core. (figure 22-7)
- clear the interfering beliefs which are creating unpreferred realities: problem beliefs, conflicting beliefs, fear beliefs, and beliefs interfering with the built-in growth continuums. (figure 22-7)
- add layers of advantageous beliefs such as goal-driven identities and core-expansion identities

1. QUANTUM LEAPS
Quantum leaps are belief system exchanges. Changed beliefs result in a changed reality. Quantum leaps are power tools in Leadering's single systems management toolkit. There are no quantum leaps without a change in beliefs.

2. REALITY PARTNERING:
Belief determination, reinforcement and upgrade:
- Event-driven belief upgrades: events in reality serve as triggers for a conditioned reflex to quantum leap to upgrade your beliefs (figure 22-8)
- Reality is a self-correcting feedback system
- Action learning experimentation

3. LEADERING™ SYSTEMS MAXIMIZATION TOOLKIT AND MACHINERY
Talent-based flow state merged with the flow to flow and the Leadering™ machinery:
- Installs and strengthens beliefs supportive of the maximum advancement and performance of your system
- Activates the belief systems supporting your key talents and core to create adaptive realities promoting the built-in growth continuums
- De-activates interfering beliefs allowing them to atrophy from disuse over time.

© 2006 Lauren Holmes

Belief Clearing Identity Quantum Leaps

Install belief systems using identities as the post leap

D. IDENTITY QUANTUM LEAPS FOR PROBLEM BELIEF REPLACEMENT

Only activated problem beliefs which are creating unpreferred realities right now in the present need to be cleared. Old inactive problem beliefs will eventually atrophy from disuse and no longer create unpreferred realities - especially as you spend time in talent-based flow state. Only supportive beliefs and positive emotions are activated in talent-based flow.

1. **Post-leap identities without the pre-leap problems:** Quantum leap to a post-leap identity without the problem beliefs creating the problem reality. (figure 22-7)

2. **Event-driven belief upgrade tool**: Use unpreferred events in reality to instantly trigger a conditioned reflex to have you quantum leap to an identity without the problem beliefs creating these events. (figure 22-8)

3. **Clear problem beliefs by *systems*:** Beliefs travel in packs or schools. Use identity belief systems to quantum leap to eliminate whole systems of interconnected problem beliefs. You need to clear them as a system or they keep resurrecting themselves from the remnants of the interconnections. Quantum leap to **jettison a key culturally induced conflicting belief complex,** the only belief clearing that has to be done right now before the ongoing cleanup.

4. **New goal syndrome:** Belief clearing as a conditioned reflex after setting a new goal-based identity. New goals activate all relevant beliefs in your belief template. As a result, new goals may activate beliefs you have not yet cleared which create unpreferred realities. Use the problem realities to trigger a conditioned reflex to routinely reinforce your post leap to facilitate belief clearings of the problem beliefs that are activated by goal setting. On the positive front, new goals also trigger the flow-driven identity quantum leaps and natural quantum leaps and facilitative events.

5. **Identifying interfering beliefs from problem event clusters:** The belief most interfering with your immediate advancement along Leadering's built-in growth continuums creates a cluster of problem events which will increase in number and severity over time. Use the clustering to trigger a conditioned reflex to reinforce your quantum leaps to natural and goal-driven identities which do not include the offending belief. (figure 22-6)

Clear A Common System of Conflicting Beliefs
Quantum Leap to a Powerful-and-Valued Identity

Exchange the 'powerless' belief system for the 'powerful' belief system in a single quantum leap

Individual belief replacements fail because the interlinks within the system of beliefs cause eliminated beliefs to be reinstated. This sustains problem beliefs and their reflected problem realities.

POWERFUL: *Can have what you want		POWERLESS: *Cannot have what you want
Work / Life has meaning	vs	No power to do meaningful things.
Valuable Contribution	vs	No power to achieve significantly
Safe - *World is benevolent*	vs	Not Safe - *World is malevolent*
Effortlessness	vs	Struggle / Force - *Expect conflict or resistance* - *World blocks your progress*
Supported - *By everyone / world*	vs	Not Supported - *Alone*
Free to be you: - *Internally referenced*	vs	Controlled by Others - *Externally referenced*
Free to do what you want	vs	Controlled by others or rules
Worthy: *Deserve to have what you want*	vs	**Unworthy:** *Do not deserve to have what you want*
Valued / Valuable	vs	**Not Valued / Not Valuable**
Respected	vs	Not Respected
Capable	vs	Not Capable
Successful	vs	Not Successful
Included / Accepted	vs	Excluded / Isolated / Judged
Trusting	vs	Not Trusting
Abundance	**vs**	Scarcity - *Time, money, friends, opportunities*

- Conflicting and dysfunctional beliefs make core congruence difficult to achieve.
- Clarity of beliefs is a critical element of leadership especially for imprinting both culture and the vision of future realities the leader wants to create.
- Strength and consistency of beliefs is critical to the consistency of leadership required to achieve any new reality.

© 1998 Lauren Holmes
Adapted from *Peak Evolution* (Lauren Holmes, 2001)

Recording 22: Belief Clearing 182

- **Clear Problem Beliefs**
- **Prove Beliefs Create Reality**

INVENTORY RECENT NEGATIVE EVENTS

Prepare an inventory of recent negative events to determine maladaptive beliefs interfering with core congruence and your maximization

Specifically, make a list of events in the last 3 to 6 months which you would consider negative events. Events which:
- invoked negative emotions such as fear, anger, frustration, sadness
- may not have been emotionally charged but which blocked you from proceeding to your goal or were setbacks
- were conflicts or struggle events

This list will be used for all of the belief-clearing exercises.

EXPERIMENT TO TEST THE BELOW HYPOTHESES

HYPOTHESIS 1: Beliefs create reality in the Leading™ paradigm.

Reality is a therefore a self-correcting feedback system with all of the checks and balances and redundancy that we observe with systems inside of the human body.

HYPOTHESIS 2: If beliefs create reality, recent unpreferred events will indicate beliefs in your belief template which are interfering with maximizing you through core congruence

1. Examine past significant negative events from you inventory of recent events.

2. If beliefs create reality, what beliefs would you have had to have to create these events? Determine the beliefs that must be in your belief template to create patterns of unpreferred events in your past.

3. Are these in fact your maladaptive beliefs that you know you have?

4. Did reality reflect interfering beliefs you know you have? Did your problem beliefs create problem realities?

5. Group these negative events by the beliefs that generated them? What do you know as a result of the pattern?

6. What are the beliefs you would prefer to have creating your reality from here on in, to prevent the negative events from recurring or to stop existing negative situations from persisting?

22-5A © 2006 Lauren Holmes
Adapted from *Peak Evolution* (Lauren Holmes, 2001)

- **Clear Problem Beliefs**
- **Prove Beliefs Create Reality**

HYPOTHESIS 3: If your interfering beliefs are not changed, the pattern of unpreferred events will persist.

If you choose not to change these interfering beliefs, do they continue to create the same pattern of problem events over the next 3 months as they have in the past? Document your experience so you internalize new beliefs about the relationship between beliefs and reality and improve your reality creation precision.

HYPOTHESIS 4: If you replace these interfering beliefs with better beliefs, your future experience will improve in predictable ways

7. Choose advantageous replacement beliefs for ones that created the unpreferred situations you examined in hypothesis 1. What are the beliefs that you want to have from here on in, to prevent the negative events from recurring or to stop negative situations from persisting?

8. See if the pattern of events in your life becomes more positive over the next 3 months to reflect these replacement beliefs.

9. See if the pattern of unpreferred events associated with the interfering beliefs you no longer have also disappears over the next 3 months.

> - **Clear Problem Beliefs**
> - **Prove Beliefs Create Reality**
>
> 3

THE CHALLENGE TO EXPERIMENT
Continue with your action learning experimentation:

10. Devise new ways to test these 4 hypotheses in your life and the lives of others. As you begin altering one belief system after another and find that the events you experience are being manipulated quite specifically by your experimentation, you will be internalizing some very powerful new beliefs about your ability to control what you will experience through your beliefs. These new beliefs will enhance the precision with which you can create goal realities in the future.

    In addition, over time, you will gradually eliminate all of the major problem beliefs creating unpreferred realities. As a result, any remaining significant challenges will be confined to those associated with scaling new frontiers with your key talents: the admission price to enter and sustain your talent-based flow state.

Install a conditioned reflex to upgrade your template in response to unpreferred events:

11. Launch an event-driven belief template upgrade process whereby you have a conditioned reflex to automatically trigger a quantum leap to change problem events in response to unpreferred events in your reality.

    Eventually, all events will become neutral information events from which you can determine the adjustments you would like to make to your internal belief structure. As proficiency and experience increase, the "*corrections*" in response to environmental stimuli become as automatic as those done unconsciously while driving a car.

NOTE:
If you are not seeing the orderliness of beliefs creating reality in your own life, it could be that you have been living externally referenced and being created by your reality rather than internally referenced and creating your reality. Find someone who is internally referenced and test the 4 hypotheses in his/her life in order to internalize the beliefs requisite to becoming a reality creation expert. Alternatively, begin operating in the flow-to-flow for a few weeks and then try these exercises again with the resulting feedback from reality which may be more meaningful.

Prioritized Problem Belief Clustering:

Reality systematically clears interfering beliefs

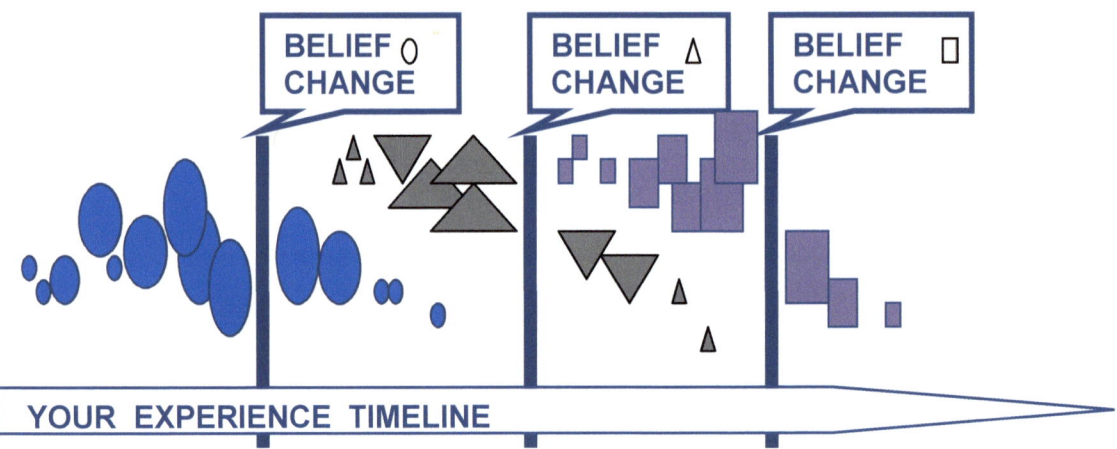

Clusters of belief-created problem events increase over time until the problem belief is replaced. With no problem belief to create events the associated events will gradually disappear. Then the next problem belief begins creating problem events . . .

Problem beliefs become evident in events in reality in a priority order which is determined by the strength of the belief to interfere with all of the forces promoting the flow to flow

The degree of blocks, resistance and toxicity increases as one conflicts with the flow to flow - including problem beliefs.

If one has beliefs creating reality which is in conflict with the immutable beliefs defining the core of your system which are also sending instructions to reality, the two realities will collide to create struggle events and blocks to your progress

If there is a conflict of systems of beliefs inside of you, that conflict will be perfectly dumped into reality as maladaptive events.

CORE CONGRUENCE: The Changeable Beliefs

AUTOMATIC REALITY CREATION

IMMUTABLE or GENE-BASED BELIEFS

The beliefs behind the key talents and drives innate to your system core and flow engine.

Consistent with the Flow-to-flow.

Adaptive realities are created automatically and continuously to amplify core through Leadering's built-in growth continuums.

Life Themes, Key Talent, and 5 Formula

CHANGEABLE BELIEFS

1. SUPPORTIVE	2. INTERFERING
Promote flow to flow and Leadering's built-in growth continuums which amplify core expression and advancement for your system core.	Block flow to flow and built-in growth continuums required to maximize and advance core talents and drives
Belief Upgrade Exercises	**Belief Clearing Exercises**

Leadering's single systems management toolkit can also be applied to belief systems.

Belief changes are achieved by quantum leap. It is easier to exchange a belief template than to try to change beliefs already logically integrated and interlinked into systems.

An Event-Driven Belief Template Upgrade Process

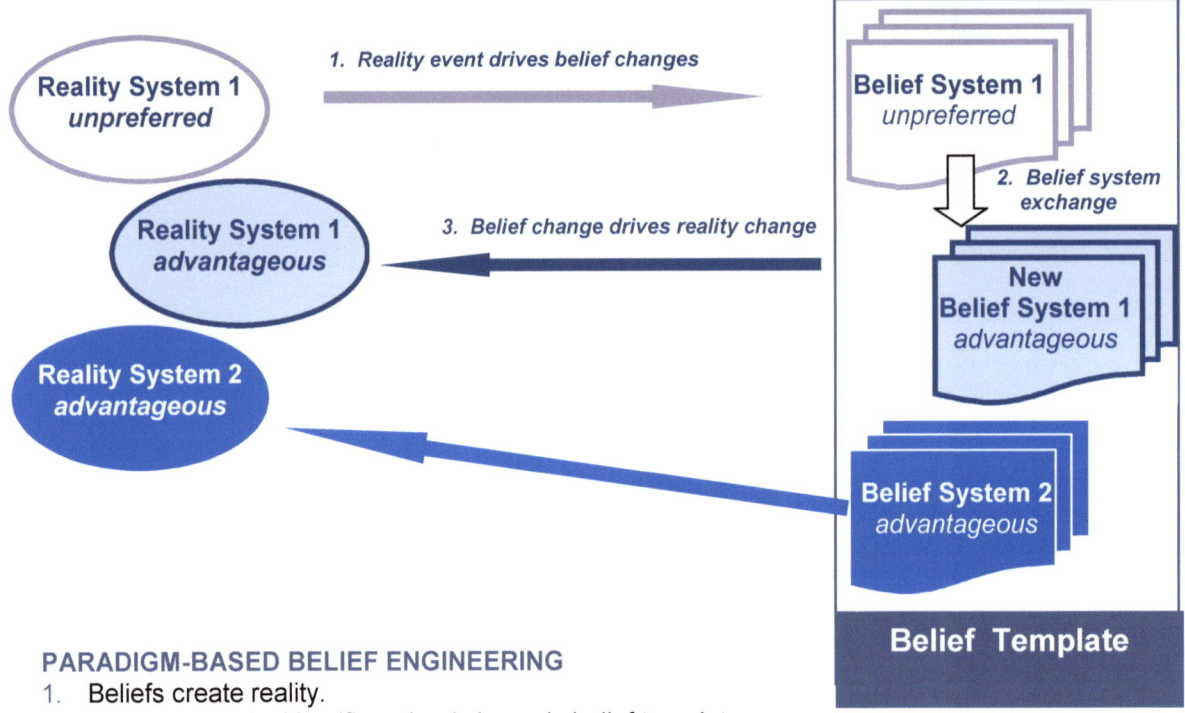

PARADIGM-BASED BELIEF ENGINEERING
1. Beliefs create reality.
2. Therefore reality identifies what is in one's belief template
3. Therefore unpreferred events in reality can be used to direct ongoing belief upgrades you make.

Benefits of the Belief Template Upgrade Process
4. for leadership strength, clarity and consistency
5. to enable the belief and emotion engineering requisite to leadership consistency, system advancement, and proficient change execution
6. to operate at full-power without dilution from interfering beliefs
7. for precise personal reality creation
8. for precise imprinting of culture and thus precise reality creation for large and/or complex organizational systems
9. for template-based change management of individual and organizational systems
10. to enable rapid-fire template rewrites in order to use the quantum leap or template exchange processes of the paradigm shift and Leadering™ paradigm modus operandi
11. to enable the quantum leap or template exchange from externally referenced to internally referenced that is critical to the creation and amplification of leaders.

THE LEADERING™ QUANTUM LEAP PROCESS

Design it!   Feel it!   Be it!

PRE-LEAP
1. Choose the right quantum leap or post-leap state
2. Define the post-leap state with clarity
3. Define the post-leap state without previous limitations or toxicity
4. Emotionally template the post-leap state
5. Add the information to fuel emergence
6. Expect the unexpected post-leap

LEAP
1. Release the linear connection to the past
2. Feel yourself 100% fluid
3. Feel the post-leap state
4. Feel who the "post-leap you" will be
5. Commit to the quantum leap
6. Make an abrupt, no-return, reincarnation
7. Trigger spontaneous self-organization by intent

POST-LEAP
1. Operate as if the quantum leap was successful
2. Walk around as the person with the post-leap reality
3. Hold this new identity until reality restructures
4. Ignore evidence of events created by the old template
5. Trigger cascading quantum leaps by intent
6. Establish quantum leaping as a way of life
7. Consolidate your new quantum leap expert beliefs

Leadering™ enables you to tap into the dynamic order into which all human systems integrate. *New functionality results.*

10 OPERATIONALIZING THE PARADIGM continued

23. **Multi-System Identity quantum leaps** 41 minutes 23 figures
    Leadering™ toolkit identity quantum leaps
    Subset: Leadering™ meta-competency identity quantum leaps
    Quantum leaps to goal 'states of being' or 'operating' rather than goal 'states':
    Subset: Assimilated Expert Identity quantum leaps
    Subset: Projected Expert Identity quantum leaps

    A quantum leap to the *identity of multi-system user, driver, advancer, and creator* is conducted throughout this recording. The goal is to make you proficient in driving Leadering's multi-system, multi-dynamic machinery.

    Quantum leaps to goal 'states of being' or 'operating' rather than goal 'states':
    Assimilated Expert Identity quantum leaps and Projected Expert Identity quantum leaps are introduced as a profound new tool for driving the Leadering™ machinery. These identity quantum leaps relate to
    - you internalizing the belief-emotion decision-making systems of experts so you can operate as they do in new unknown territories and
    - you projecting your expert belief-emotion decision-making systems to other human systems you wish to operate as well as effectively as you do for goal achievement.
    They are therefore quantum leaps to state of operation and performance rather than goal states. Some science is provided as to why and how they work.

Identity Quantum Leap Tool Categories

Install belief systems using identities as the post leap

8 Identity Quantum Leap Tool Categories

PARADIGM SHIFT
1. Natural identity quantum leaps (*immutable beliefs*)

PARADIGM OPERATION
2.   *Subset:* Growth or expansion identity quantum leaps
3. Goal-driven identity quantum leaps
4.   *Subset:* Flow-driven identity quantum leaps
5. Corporate identity quantum Leaps
6. Identity quantum leaps to replace problem beliefs
7. Leadering™ toolkit identity quantum leaps
8.   *Subset:* Leadering™ meta-competency identity quantum leaps
   Quantum leaps to goal 'states of being' rather than goal 'states':
         Subset: Assimilated Expert Identity quantum leaps
         Subset: Projected Expert Identity quantum leaps

IDENTITY QUANTUM LEAP BASICS:

1. Identities are integrated systems of beliefs.

2. Beliefs, like genes in the nucleus of a cell, are information storage units which define the core of any human system.

3. All advancement of human systems in the Leadering™ paradigm requires a change of beliefs. Leaders are therefore belief engineers.

4. Internalize the 'feel' or emotional template of your desired post-leap identity to lock in the belief upgrades which will change reality to coincide with those new beliefs.

5. Assume you or systems you lead have operated with the proposed post-leap identity successfully for 10 years.

6. Your selected post leap must be consistent with the direction of the flow to flow for natural forces to energize the leap.

THE LEADERING™ PARADIGM PLAYERS:
a talent-driven systems maximization toolkit

FORCES, DRIVES, DYNAMICS
a. **External Talent-based Natural Forces acting on your core:**
  - the 15 talent-based dynamics the flow pursuit of the contextual system:
  - the flow-to-flow or your flow engine
b. **Internal Talent-based Natural Forces acting on your core:** Addictive drives pressuring use of your key talents
c. **Built-in Talent-based Growth Continuums** to advanced functionality and performance
d. **Talent-based Life Themes**

YOUR TALENT-BASED CORE
a. **Flow Maximization:**
  1. flow pursuit of your system
  2. key talents
  3. talent-based addictive drives
b. **Belief Maximization:**
  1. immutable beliefs
  2. changeable beliefs

A BELIEF-CREATED REALITY
Reality is a self-correcting feedback system

SYSTEM UPGRADES
a. Meta-Competencies
   of leaders, entrepreneurs, innovators,
   and high achievers
b. Conditioned Reflexes
c. Enhanced Functionality
d. Beliefs

STRATEGIES
Five Talent-based Operating Formulas:
Advance *your* system:
  1. lifetime development
  2. greatest lifetime performance
Advance *other* systems to advance your system:
  3. leadership
  4. leadership development
  5. greatest leader lifetime performance

TECHNOLOGIES
a. System-Based Operation
b. Core-Driven Operation
c. Belief Engineering
d. Emotional Engineering
e. Reality Creation
f. Quantum Leap Technology
  1. *Nature-Initiated Quantum Leaps*
     imbedded in the flow to flow orchestrating you for
     - opportunistic synergy, co-evolution, co-adaptation, creative problem-solving, and flow-within-flow
     - natural quantum leaps such as coincidences (multi-system synergy, co-evolution, co-adaptation), spontaneous knowledge, spontaneous creativity, facilitating events, flow states
  2. *Self-Initiated Quantum Leaps*
     - Identity Quantum Leaps

BELIEF UPGRADE TOOLS
a. Quantum Leaps
b. Paradigm shift
c. Reality Partnering
d. Action Learning Experimentation
e. Leadering™ Systems Maximization Toolkit and Machinery

PARADIGM PERSONALIZATION EXERCISES

LEADERING™ SYSTEMS MAXIMIZATION TOOLKIT

FLOW MAXIMIZATION TOOLS:

YOUR FLOW ENGINE: Capitalizing on the flow to flow or natural forces inside and outside of you act on your core for maximum performance and advancement
- **Quantum leaps** harnessing the power of the flow to flow
- **Partnering with internal and reality dynamics:** 15 dynamics
- **Key talents and their addictive drives** (immutable beliefs)

BELIEF MAXIMIZATION TOOLS:

YOUR BELIEF TEMPLATE: Your belief template governs both you and your reality as a single system. Beliefs are information storage units like genes
- **Quantum leaps** or paradigm shifts or belief template exchanges
- **Partnering with reality events:** reality is a self-correcting feedback system
- **Changeable beliefs** in partnership with your immutable beliefs (innate gene-based beliefs associated with your key talents and their addictive drives)

Byproduct: THE META-COMPETENCIES OF LEADERS, ENTREPRENEURS, INNOVATORS AND HIGH ACHIEVERS

23-1C

© 2006 Lauren Holmes

15 LEADERING™ DYNAMICS
for advancing systems within the Flow-to-Flow

1. **SYSTEMS MINDSET:**
   - Systems-based dynamic
   - Expanding consciousness to systems mindset

2. **ADVANCEMENT MECHANICS**
   - quantum leap dynamic
   - templating dynamic
   - self-organization dynamic
   - emergence dynamic

3. **ADVANCEMENT DIRECTIONS**
   - knowledge pursuit dynamic (talent-based)
   - adaptation dynamic
   - evolution dynamic
   - co-evolution dynamic
   - talent-based flow dynamic
   - flow-within-flow dynamic
   - expanding consciousness dynamic

4. **DYNAMICS FOR THE UNKNOWN**
   the essence or definition of leadership, entrepreneurship, innovation, and career creation
   - frontiering dynamic™: penetrate unknown systems
   - creation/creativity dynamic: bring unknown systems into existence

© 2006 Lauren Holmes

Leadering™ Toolkit Identity Quantum Leaps
Install belief systems using identities as the post leap

Identity quantum leaps based on the Leadering™ toolkit and machinery:

Identities are integrated systems of beliefs. Beliefs create reality. Quantum leaps to these sample identities will facilitate:

- the Leadering™ paradigm shift
- operating in the Leadering™ paradigm
- the quantum leap from reality-driven to core-driven

1. *Quantum Leap Expert* **revisited** from your current level of capability and experience to push the envelope on your expertise. Template exchange is belief engineering

2. Quantum leap to the identity of a **person who owns and operates his/her reality** so that you and your reality are a single system.

3. Quantum leap to *Reality Creation Expert* and to be able to change your belief template or system at will in order to change yourself and your reality advantageously in the shortest possible time.

4. Quantum leap to *Belief Engineering Expert* able to quickly change belief systems whether changing your own beliefs, your children's, or an organization's culture.

5. Quantum leap to **Emotional Engineering Expert:** a visioneer who constructs visions which engage people through their emotions which changes their beliefs and thus their realities and the reality of the organization.

6. Quantum leap to your formulas 2 and 5. These are the identities of you at your maximum as an individual and as a leader respectively.

7. Quantum leap to one or more of *the following identities* as relevant:
   - a leader
   - a high performer
   - a career master
   - a system maximizer
   - a systems co-evolution expert or system advancement master
   - an entrepreneur or intrapreneur
   - an innovator or a creative

23-1E   © 2006 Lauren Holmes

META-COMPETENCIES and DRIVES targeted by Leadering™
Shared by leaders, entrepreneurs, innovators, and high achievers

Systems-Based and Core-Based Operation
systems thinking, relational thinking, big-picture thinking, conceptual skills, belief system management, model development and application, system co-evolution and adaptation, leadership (advancing human systems in opportunistic synergy)

Accelerating and Continuous Development
- conditioned reflexes installed to trigger multi-front, life-long advancement and leadership development.
- addictive drives installed to pull one to growth.
- learning to learn, mental agility, adaptivity, expanding self-expression and self-awareness, belief engineering, expanding consciousness

Improved and Improving Cognitive Capabilities
- thinking: conceptual, inductive, deductive, abstract, big-picture, relational
- learning to learn, mental agility, pattern recognition, internally referenced, emotional intelligence, use of models, theories, and inferences

Expertise with Ambiguity and the Unknown
- **pioneering**: penetrating the unknown
- **creativity/innovation**: bringing unknown into being

systems thinking, informationless decision-making, abstract thinking, conceptual skills, pattern recognition, trend perception, change detection, environmental scanning, problem reframing, ambiguity resolution

Improved Performance
flow (our peak performance state), enhanced functionality, systems-based operation, accelerated implementation through quantum leap change management

Addictive Drives cultivated and capitalized upon by Leadering™
(the more you use them, the more you want to use them):
- Drives to: learning, pioneering, creativity, innovation, meaning, positive emotions, adaptivity, creativity, learning knowledge, achievement, flow, (the optimal experience), self-expression, self-knowledge, advancement, unity, growth
- Drives to using and improving your key talents - a must for operating at your full potential

---

Meta-competencies or *enduring competencies* are systems of knowledge, skills, and strategies which facilitate the acquisition and use of competencies.

Traditional leadership development addresses competencies and skills
Leadering™ addresses leader dynamics and meta-competencies.

Traditionally, leaders are developed bottom up skill by skill
Leadering™ uses a single paradigm shift to install an integrated system of meta-competencies, drives, reflexes, and beliefs.

Traditionally, senior leaders use different meta-competencies.
Leadering™ offers a single systems maximization toolkit for use by everyone on every human system thus unifying organizations around a single culture and modus operandi. Leadership becomes distributed.

© 2006 Lauren Holmes

Leadering™ Meta-Competency Identity Quantum Leaps

Install belief systems using identities as the post leap

Use the identity quantum leap tool on an ongoing basis for internalizing all of the leader meta-competencies being cultivated by the Leadering™ program (figure 23-1F). Examples:

1. Quantum leap to a **frontiering™ expert**: an individual who has been successfully penetrating new territory for the last 10 years and has now become a frontiering™ addict. While the Leadering™ program itself is a workout gym for this since no one can absorb it all.

    It is necessary for you to be stretched in order to advance your system. If you never go into the deep end of the pool, how will you learn the skills to survive when you cannot touch bottom. A large integrated system of beliefs must be internalized to become a master of the unknown.

2. Quantum leap to being **someone who has well developed conceptual skills or someone who has operated in unity consciousness** for the last 10 years who is able to see the interconnectedness, dynamic flow, and co-evolution of all human systems and tap into that flow. It is akin to merging with what David Bohm calls the holomovement.

3. Quantum leap to a **growth expert or continuous advancement expert**, with the ability to orchestrate systems through the built-in growth continuums in the Leadering™ paradigm to their ultimate maximization.

23-1G © 2006 Lauren Holmes

The advantage of operating in talent-based flow within the talent-based flow of the contextual system

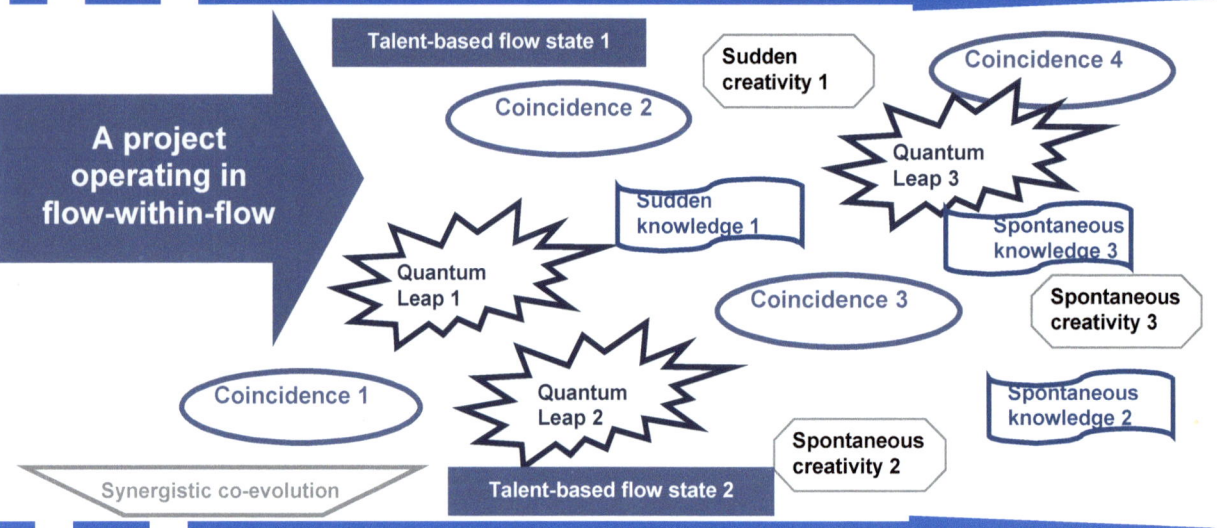

Increasing functionality with each flow experience:
- expanding consciousness and conceptual capacity
- peak performance
- peak evolution
- increasing creative capability
- expansion / intensification / enlargement of the system's natural creative expression

Proof of the Leadering™ paradigm – Proof of the accuracy of your 5 formulas
If you are operating in talent-based flow and the clustering of natural quantum leaps above emerge in your reality, then you have proof that the Leadering paradigm™ and nature's machinery inside and outside of you do indeed operate in the way Leadering™ describes.

Leadering™ Redefines Leadership to its Core Dynamics

LEADERING™ LEADERSHIP

Maximize, advance, integrate, adapt, co-evolve, and capitalize on human systems to achieve synergistic goal realities

Metaphor 1: the electrons and nucleus of an atom form an integrated system defined by a single information structure.

- System-Based

- Core-Based, Talent-Based, & Internally Referenced

- Flow-based
  (a system's peak-performing, peak-advancing state)

- Extending nature's systems maximization dynamics:
  a multi-system approach:
      opportunistic synergy, adaptation, co-evolution
      quantum leap advancement and problem resolution
      expansive perspective

- A single systems maximization toolkit* applied to all human systems including one's own.

*   The Leadering™ toolkit includes an integrated system of meta-competencies, drives, reflexes, belief systems, identities, dynamics from nature's systems maximization process,** a quantum-leap operating style, and peak-performing, peak-advancing flow states.

**   Metaphor 2: how nature maximizes and advances systems within the human body.

LEADERING'S LEADERSHIP

A SINGLE FLOW CONTINUUM FOR ALL HUMAN SYSTEMS

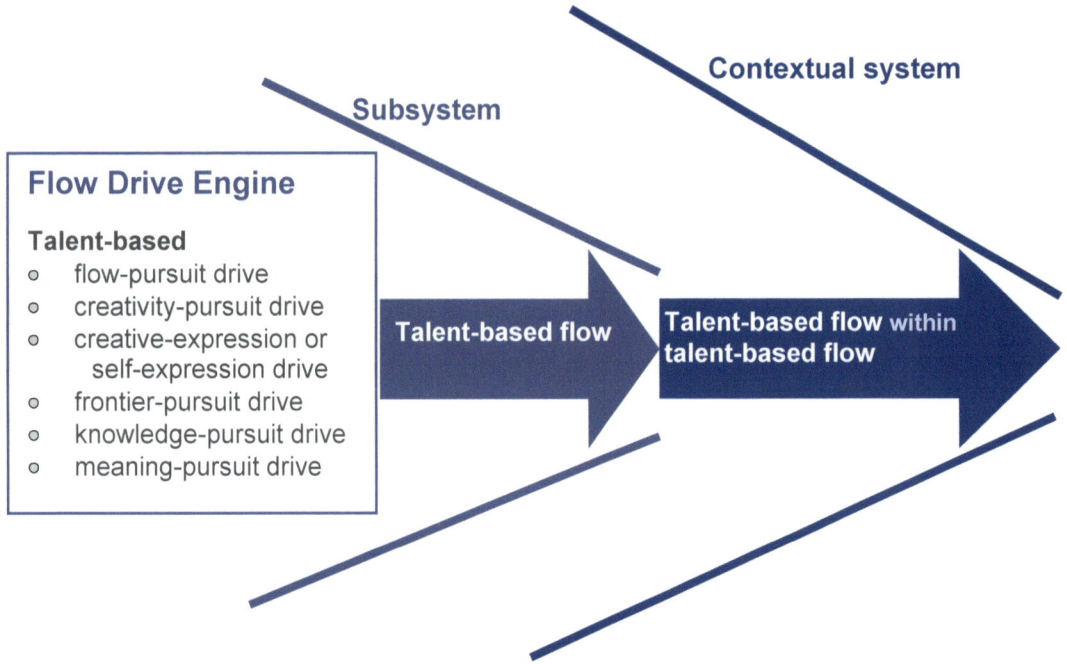

Flow Drive Engine

Talent-based
- flow-pursuit drive
- creativity-pursuit drive
- creative-expression or self-expression drive
- frontier-pursuit drive
- knowledge-pursuit drive
- meaning-pursuit drive

There is a single synergistic, adaptive, and co-evolutionary flow of human systems to optimization and survival. We are linked to this flow through drives addicting us to using our key talents. This core drive complex forms a flow engine trying to maximize us now and in the future by pulling us to use our key talents in our peak-performing and peak-evolving flow state: the flow to flow.

23-3A   © 2006 Lauren Holmes

LEADERING'S LEADERSHIP

FLOW-WITHIN-FLOW: co-evolution

A subsystem in talent-based flow is integrated into the flow of its contextual system to its own state of talent-based flow or congruence.

A Flow-within-Flow Example: **THE IDEAL HUMAN CAPITAL STRATEGY**
Maximize an individual or organizational system in talent-based flow while they are contributing to the talent-based flow state of the company system.

Subsystems maximized in flow state merge with the flow to the peak-performing / peak-evolving flow state of the system of which they are a part.

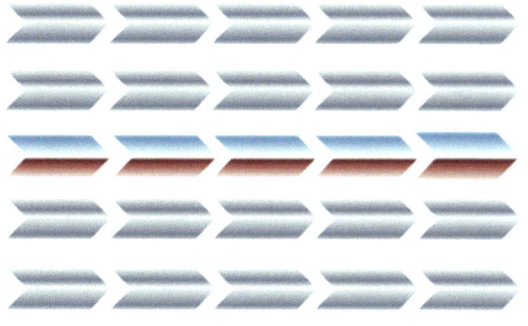

23-3B

FORMULAS 3, 4, and 5: Advancing your system by creating, maximizing, and capitalizing on other human systems

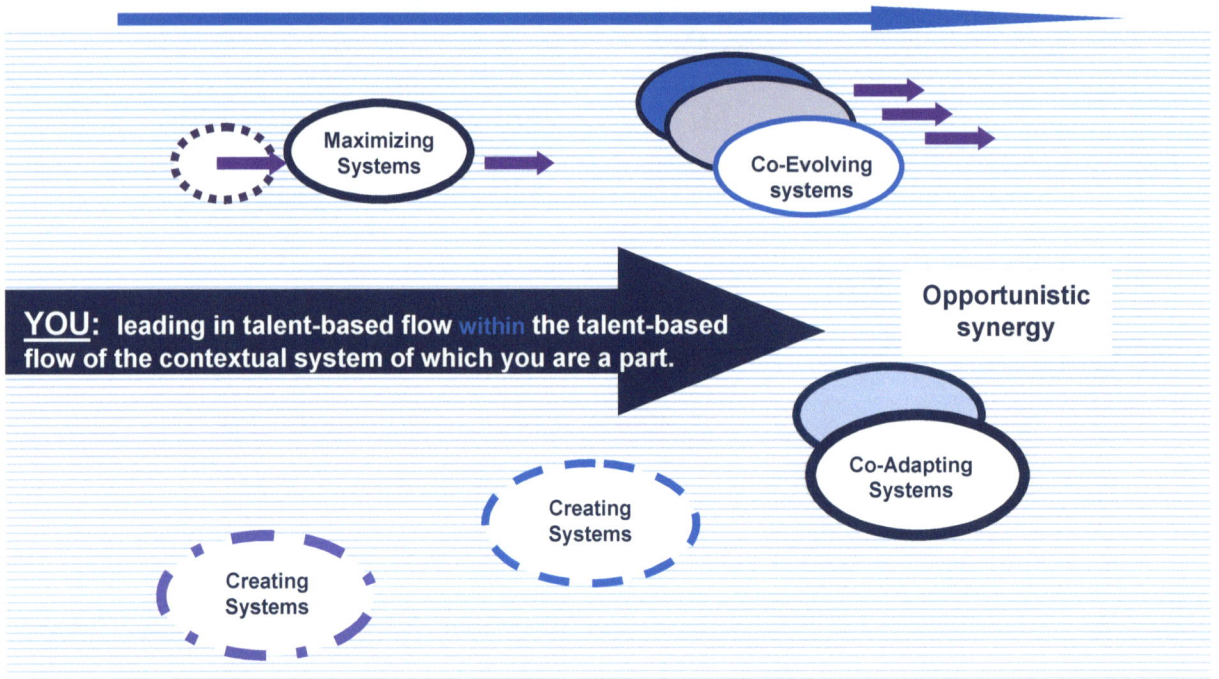

Advancing your system by applying your key talents to other systems	Individual Systems	Multi-Individual Systems	Organization Systems	Multi-Organization Systems	Knowledge Systems	Process Systems

Leadering™ provides a single systems maximization toolkit for advancing your personal system or those that you choose to lead for *peak legacy*.

23-3C

© 2006 Lauren Holmes

Recording 23: Multi-System Identity Quantum Leaps

Leadership is the synergistic and opportunistic advancement of systems: the same foundation as for Leadering™

Leadering™ Talent-Driven Systems Maximization Toolkit	Meta-Competencies Improved by Leadering™	Classic Leader Competencies reliant on Leadering™ meta-competencies
Figure 23-1B	**Figure 23-1F**	**Figure 23-3E**
Forces, drives, dynamics (Fig 23-1D: 15 dynamics, flow to flow, growth continuums)	**Systems-Based Approach**	**Planning**
Your talent-based core (flow / belief maximization)	**Continuous Development**	**Functions** (marketing, sales, operations, IT, HR)
A belief-created reality	**Cognitive Capabilities** (Fig 23-3G: cognitive skills)	**Managing Talent**
System upgrades (meta-competencies, reflexes, functionality)	**Mastering the Unknown**	**Advancing Systems**
Strategies (5 formulas)	**Improved Performance**	**Achieving**
Technologies (quantum leap, system, core-driven, reality creation)		**Collaborating** (systems relationships)
Belief upgrade tools (quantum leaps, paradigm shift, reality partnering, modeling, projection, assimilation)		
Paradigm personalization exercises		

23-3D

© 2006 Lauren Holmes

Examples of Classic Leader Competencies
which Leadering™ Meta-Competencies Improve

Notice how most are designed to improve the flow of systems to congruence
based on the leader dynamics or paradigm dynamics of Leadering™

PLANNING
strategic planning
tactical planning
goal setting and communication
develop a shared vision
create a customer-focus
align people/organizations to strategy
translating strategy
execute strategic priorities
create clarity and focus
holistic/systems thinking
conceptualization
synthesis
manage attention
provide frameworks of reference

FUNCTIONS
financial management
marketing/sales management
HR management
IT management
operations management
customer relationship mgt (CRM)
project management
performance management
knowledge management
information management
systems management
managing up and down
command and control
stewardship
business acumen

MANAGING TALENT
hiring talent
build capability
develop competency / skills
develop talent
develop leaders
develop distributed leadership
mentor / coach
cultural imprinting
promote life-long learning
succession planning
assess performance
develop emotional intelligence
leading by example
teach/mentor the strategic art

ADVANCING
change management
implement ideas/goals
cultivate organizational
    learning, adaptivity and agility
performance improvement
process improvement
drive continuous improvement
generate/commercialize ideas
cultivating creativity/innovation
innovation adoption
product development/delivery
problem management
decision-making
develop / deliver value
leverage diversity
leverage resources
leverage technology
risk management
communicate the vision
deal with uncertainty/ambiguity
entrepreneurship/intrapreneurship
transformation
business process reengineering

ACHIEVING
motivate, inspire
empower
develop/align reward systems
create a sense of urgency
drive committed action
influence
communicate
establish credibility
gain commitment
establish accountability
establish consistency
maintain balance
get results
manage meaning
drive performance through
    shared vision, values, and
    accountability

COLLABORATING
clustering
build strategic alliances
team building
relationship building / maintaining
community building
generate alignment
consensus building
globalization
build social networks
manage across networks
lead across boundaries
integrate
promote collaboration / synergy
participative management
resolve conflict
influencing and negotiating
political acumen

© 2006 Lauren Holmes

Recording 23: Multi-System Identity Quantum Leaps 204

System-Based Key Talent Categories

SYSTEM MAINTENANCE Single / Multi-System	SYSTEM ADVANCEMENT Single / Multi-System	SYSTEM CREATION Single / Multi-System	SYSTEM RELATIONSHIPS Each relationship creates a new system

manager:
 	
very little new creation is required.
 	
Creativity and creation increase with each column to the right.
 	
Since beliefs create reality, this means that the need for belief changes increase as your move to the right.
	strategy development
	people development
	organization development
	multi-organization synergy
	process development
	knowledge development
	technology development
	change leadership
	   • transitional
	   • transformational
	   • facilitative
	frontier leadership
	creational leadership
	flow leadership
		creational leadership
		frontier leadership
		quantum leap leadership
		template leadership
		emergence leadership
		system creation strategy
		system creation implementation
		entrepreneur company creation
		intrapreneur project creation
		new product creation
		new technology creation
		new infrastructure creation
		new process creation
		new science creation
		new knowledge creation
		new skill creation
		new frontier creation
		creation research
		merger-created system
		acquisition-created system
		innovation / creativity
			System relationships:
			   • to maintain systems
			   • to advance systems
			   • to create systems
			
			co-evolutionary leadership
			co-adaptation leadership
			collaboration and synergy
			business web development
			CRM: customer relationship management
			customer development
			customer chain development
			supplier chain development
			network development
			relationship building
			team building
			market development
			unifying and integrating
			problem solving
			conflict resolution
			peace keeping
			negotiation
			mergers and acquisitions
			relationship strategy/vision
			relationship-related implementation

Increasing belief and information changes — Increasing impact on reality

In the Leading™ paradigm, leadership extends nature's systems management.
This exercise demonstrates LEADERING'S SINGLE SYSTEMS MAXIMIZATION TOOLKIT

© 2006 Lauren Holmes

Conceptual Meta-Competencies

Conceptual competencies consist of the appropriate paradigms, mindsets, and conceptual skills necessary to:
- assess the environment
- see the long-range needs and implications of a situation to build a plan for meeting these needs and
- visualize, address, and capitalize on the complex interrelationships that exist in a workplace in order to set priorities, make decisions, anticipate the future, and formulate strategies and tactics, and
- comprehend the culture of an organization (historically developed values, beliefs, and norms) in order to visualize its future.

Conceptual skills include:
- concept formation which is the capacity to analyze relationships between objects
- abstraction or the ability to think symbolically
- deductive logic which is the application of general rules or concepts in making a decision for a specific set of stimuli and/or
- inductive logic which is the analysis of feedback or identification of relevant details in formulating a concept to use in decision making,
- problem reframing to enhance creativity
- dealing with multiple perspectives and ambiguity
- frame of reference development including systems understanding, environmental scanning, pattern recognition
- idea and concept development and use to solve complex problems
- envisioning to anticipate the future
- proactive thinking using critical, creative, reflective thinking
- skillful formulation of ends, ways, means
- analysis of complicated events
- trend perception
- change detection
- creative and opportunistic problem-solving
- ability to conceptualize complex ideas
- deployment of models, theories and inferences, and
- pattern recognition.

Multi-System Identity Quantum Leaps

Driving Leadering's Multi-System Multi-Dynamic Machinery:

IDENTITY OF MULTI-SYSTEM USER, DRIVER, ADVANCER, CREATOR

- **Multi-system '15 DYNAMICS' IDENTITIES:**
  Examples:
  core-driven leader
  systems-based leader
  quantum leap leader + identity quantum leap expert
  flow leader + flow-to-flow leader
  frontiering leader™
  creation leader; innovator or creative, entrepreneur/intrapreneur
  synergy and opportunistic adaptation leader
  systems co-evolution leader or system advancement master
  reality creation leader
  belief engineering leader, memetics engineer, cultural engineer
  congruence or unification leader

- **Multi-system META-COMPETENCIES:**
  Examples:
  systems-based approach, conceptual skills, expanding consciousness, self-expression, emotional intelligence, pattern recognition

- **2 New Multi-System Categories of IDENTITY QUANTUM LEAPS**
  - ASSIMILATED EXPERT Identity quantum leaps
  - PROJECTED EXPERT Identity quantum leaps

© 2006 Lauren Holmes

ASSIMILATED EXPERT IDENTITY Quantum Leaps

Operating with expert belief-emotion decision-making systems

Absorbing the belief-emotion decision-making systems that have taken experts a lifetime to build up allows you to operate far beyond your capabilities, especially as you move into unknown territory and frontiers in which they prevail.

The meta-competencies, tools, and modus operandi you have already internalized through the Leadering™ paradigm shift have either already prepared you or launched the growth continuums to prepare you to fluidly assimilate new belief systems such as the identity and decision-making database of an expert.

Consider the following samples of expertise you have been developing in the Leadering™ paradigm which will improve your proficiency with assimilated expert identity quantum leaps. They are no longer beyond your capabilities:

1. **As a quantum leap expert,** you now routinely exchange pre-leap for post-leap belief systems in exactly the way you would assimilate an expert's belief systems.

2. **From your quantum leap and reality creation work**, you have developed the fluidity and nonlinearity to use this identity quantum leap to absorb the right beliefs to support your core development as you penetrate new territory. You have become a belief engineering expert.

3. **From your quantum leap experience,** you have built up a system of beliefs, emotional memories, and experiential learning to enable you to exchange belief systems proficiently.

4. **From your reality creation work**, you have the ability to take the expert's beliefs and use them to create the same kinds of realities that an expert. While they would use skills and experiences in their field that you do not have, you will be able to create the same advanced realities with your beliefs.

5. **From your experience with accessing information from the natural quantum leaps in the flow-to-flow,** you have developed the ability to arrive at the right place and right time to collide with the ideal expert system to absorb the information/beliefs required to fuel your next quantum leap. You are already accustomed to absorbing from the flow-to-flow other systems of beliefs than those of absorbing expert identities. Models and metaphors, for example. The assimilated expert identity quantum leap will be just business as usual with respect to partnering with the flow-to-flow.

6. **As you operate in the flow-to-flow**, your consciousness and perspective have been expanding to allow you to see and capitalize on the opportunities to mix and match co-evolving systems to achieve your goal realities faster. You easily slip into multi-system maximization. You have become a multi-systems maximizer operating just like nature.

7. **As part of using the Leadering™ systems maximization toolkit,** you routinely figure out the core of human systems to capitalize on them and to advance them. You now have the ability to quickly understand the core of experts in order to assimilate their belief-emotion decision-making systems.

- **ASSIMILATED EXPERT IDENTITY** quantum leaps
- **PROJECTED EXPERT IDENTITY** quantum leaps

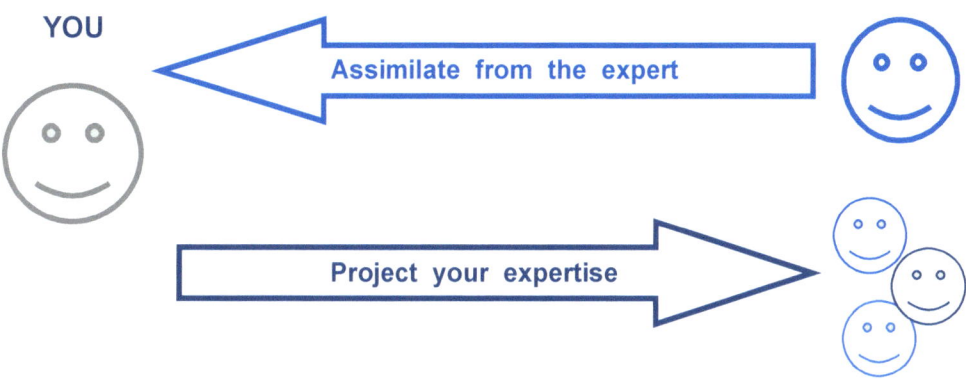

- **Assimilation:** upgrade YOUR functionality and performance with the belief-emotion decision-making systems of experts.

- **Projection:** upgrade the functionality and performance of OTHERS with YOUR expert belief-emotion decision-making systems.

23-3J

PROJECTED EXPERT IDENTITY Quantum Leaps

Levers to install expert belief-emotion decision-making systems

Projecting your expert belief-emotion decision-making system into others is a rapid-fire cultural imprinting tool and upgrading tool which allows others to operate with your expertise - even if they have not taken the Leadering™ program and are accustomed to using the assimilated expert identity quantum leaps. With your expert beliefs systems, individuals may be able to operate beyond their potential in the service of mutual goals.

As a Leadering™ belief engineer, how do you communicate massive beliefs to quantum leap an organization to operating with your expertise?
Use levers such as the following to project your expert belief-emotion decision-making system into organizational members to upgrade them to your level of operation:

1. an emotionally charged vision and strategy designed with your new clarity of beliefs (from operating the quantum leap and reality creation technologies, clarity of direction, and expertise in defining post-leap states that you have developed operating the Leadering machinery
2. Branding
3. cultural imprinting or the transmission of cultural memes
4. corporate image management
5. organizational identity
6. internal marketing campaign and slogans
7. modelling, leading by example, teaching, preaching
8. having others take Leadering™ so they will assimilate your expert belief-emotion decision-making system automatically as part of each individual's ongoing lifetime maximization process
9. stories and metaphors
10. paradigm shifts and quantum leaps copying the Leadering™ paradigm shift process (teach your organizations a quantum leap change management process)
11. educational programs
12. reasoning

Many of these are levers any leader would use but these levers perform more powerfully in the belief-created reality of the Leadering™ paradigm and its system-based, core-based, and flow-based operation.

PROJECTED EXPERT IDENTITY Quantum Leaps

Levers to install expert belief-emotion decision-making systems

The following increased functionality from operating in the Leading™ paradigm, contribute to your ability to project your belief-emotion decision-making systems:

1. Increasing belief clarity over time due to mastering the quantum leap and reality creation technologies

2. Improvement in your proficiency for defining post-leap state facilitated by the natural forces embedded in the flow-to-flow. Coincidences and facilitating events improve your ability to achieve a goal reality using your belief-emotion decision-making systems.

3. Improvements in your multi-system expertise enable you to ensure your goals are also the right goals for co-evolving human systems. This increases their receptivity and functionality with respect to operating with your decision-making systems.

4. The normal application of the Leading™ toolkit for system maximization will improve your ability to achieve more efficient projection to multiple co-evolving systems. Projection thus becomes simply business as usual in capitalizing on the flow-to-flow to achieve goals using other systems (formulas 3, 4, and 5)

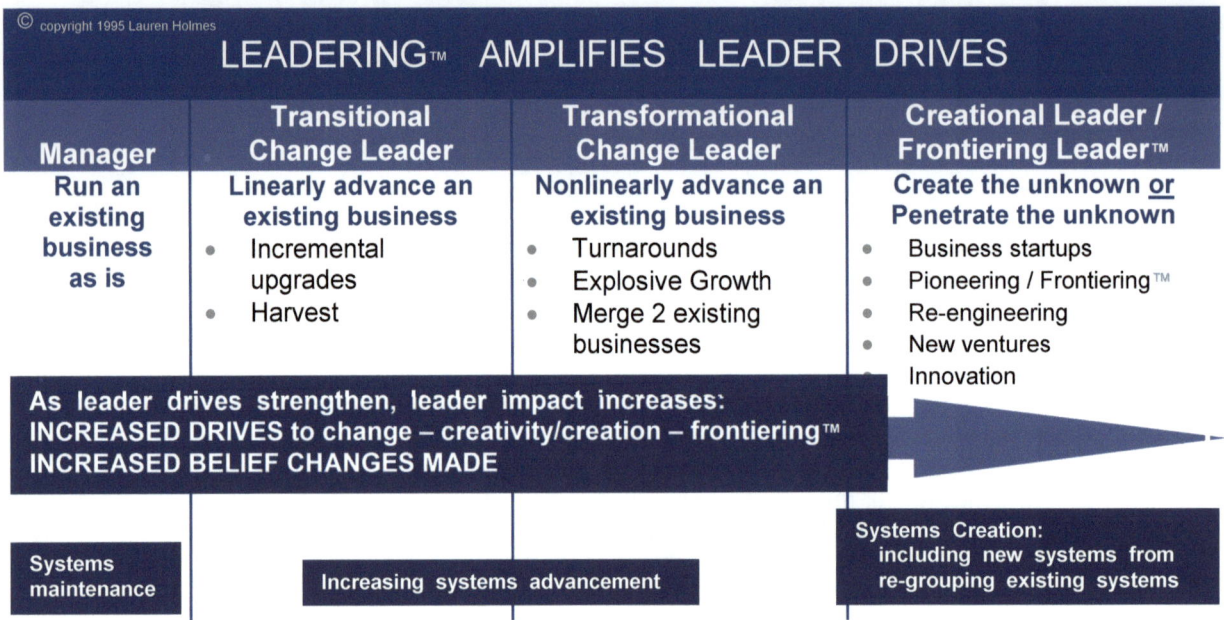

15 LEADERING™ PARADIGM DYNAMICS

FLOW to GENERATIVE CONGRUENCE DRIVE ↓

FLOW to FLOW DRIVE – THE FLOW ENGINE ↓

Nature pressures all human systems into generative congruence internally and externally. Successful leaders do the same thing.

The 14 paradigm dynamics or leader drives below promote the 15th drive: the flow of systems to generative congruence internally and externally. Congruence is the driving force of the target paradigm of Leadering™.

SYSTEMS MINDSET

A systems-based drive Everything in the paradigm is a system, including individuals, organizations, and processes.

An expanding consciousness drive to oneness. Consciousness expands due to operating in the flow to congruence and stretching to view interacting systems.

ADVANCEMENT MECHANICS

A quantum leap drive
A templating drive
A self-organizing drive
An emergence drive
Leaders orchestrate abrupt nonlinear system advancements, adaptations, co-evolutions, and re-optimizations using mechanisms available in the flow to congruence. They operate as belief engineers, cultural engineers, reality architects, quantum leap leaders, and emergence leaders: NONLINEAR UPGRADE MECHANISMS

An evolution drive*
'*Growth*' and '*Learning*' help human systems achieve their existing potential. '*Evolution*' advances that potential. Human systems advance by (1) quantum-leap intensifications of their natural core and (2) belief template upgrades: UPGRADED POTENTIAL / FUNCTIONALITY

ADVANCEMENT DIRECTIONS

A knowledge-pursuit drive* Leaders harness a system's innate drives for advancing its talent-based expression in order to achieve multi-system goals and maximization: EVOLUTIONARY PATH DETERMINANT

An adaptation drive* Externally driven adjustment to advances in the shared contextual system caused by the adaptation / evolution of other subsystems: CHAIN REACTION: THE DANCE

A co-evolution drive* Internally driven system upgrade achieved by capitalizing on external upgrading systems: OPPORTUNISTIC SYNERGY + LOCKSTEP ADVANCEMENT

A talent-based flow drive* (internal)
A flow-within-flow drive* (hierarchical)
The flow to internal/external congruence: PEAK-PERFORMING / PEAK-EVOLVING STATE

DRIVES FOR THE UNKNOWN:
the essence of leadership, entrepreneurship, innovation, and career creation

1. **A frontier-pursuit drive***: Penetrate unknown systems.
2. **A creation / creativity-pursuit drive***: Bring unknown into existence.
   NATURE IS ENDLESS MULTI-SYSTEM CREATIVITY - LEADERSHIP IS AN EXTENSION

These dynamics form the toolkit for maximizing any human system in the paradigm whether the system is an individual, organization, market, civilization, or process such as leadership development, career management, or organizational change.

10-2 upgraded © 2006 Lauren Holmes * addicting talent-based drives

"The universality of the Leadering™ toolkit for maximizing human systems large and small is an unexpected but profound advantage to the conscious evolution movement. We have never before had such a catalyst for unified advancement."   Managing Director, NGO

10 OPERATIONALIZING THE PARADIGM

24. **Driving a Multi-System Paradigm**   57 minutes   1 figure
    Repeat the quantum leap to operating with the 15 Leader Drives (recording 9h)

    What you will hear this time will be different from before because of the following:
    - you have since completed the paradigm shift
    - you have since personalized the paradigm to your system
    - you have done a quantum leap to driving a multi-system machinery
    - you have internalized many new belief and information systems.
    - you have experienced many more hours of the
      Leadering™ *Frequency Workout Gym*™.

    This recording includes the application of the Leadering™ systems maximization toolkit to corporate leadership. This is an example of multi-system orchestration and advancement within the Leadering™ paradigm as cultivated in the previous recording.

    It is evident from this recording that Leadering™ rewrites today's disciplines for leadership, leadership development, performance improvement, organization change, entrepreneurial / intrapreneurial development, and management science.

15 LEADERING™ PARADIGM DYNAMICS

FLOW to GENERATIVE CONGRUENCE DRIVE

FLOW to FLOW DRIVE – THE FLOW ENGINE

Nature pressures all human systems into generative congruence internally and externally. Successful leaders do the same thing.

The 14 paradigm dynamics or leader drives below promote the 15th drive: the flow of systems to generative congruence internally and externally. Congruence is the driving force of the target paradigm of Leadering™.

SYSTEMS MINDSET

A systems-based drive
Everything in the paradigm is a system, including individuals, organizations, and processes.

An expanding consciousness drive to oneness. Consciousness expands due to operating in the flow to congruence and stretching to view interacting systems.

ADVANCEMENT MECHANICS

A quantum leap drive
A templating drive
A self-organizing drive
An emergence drive
Leaders orchestrate abrupt nonlinear system advancements, adaptations, co-evolutions, and re-optimizations using mechanisms available in the flow to congruence. They operate as belief engineers, cultural engineers, reality architects, quantum leap leaders, and emergence leaders: NONLINEAR UPGRADE MECHANISMS

An evolution drive*
'*Growth*' and '*Learning*' help human systems achieve their existing potential. '*Evolution*' advances that potential. Human systems advance by (1) quantum-leap intensifications of their natural core and (2) belief template upgrades: UPGRADED POTENTIAL / FUNCTIONALITY

ADVANCEMENT DIRECTIONS

A knowledge-pursuit drive*
Leaders harness a system's innate drives for advancing its talent-based expression in order to achieve multi-system goals and maximization: EVOLUTIONARY PATH DETERMINANT

An adaptation drive*
Externally driven adjustment to advances in the shared contextual system caused by the adaptation / evolution of other subsystems: CHAIN REACTION: THE DANCE

A co-evolution drive*
Internally driven system upgrade achieved by capitalizing on external upgrading systems: OPPORTUNISTIC SYNERGY + LOCKSTEP ADVANCEMENT

A talent-based flow drive* (internal)
A flow-within-flow drive* (hierarchical)
The flow to internal/external congruence: PEAK-PERFORMING / PEAK-EVOLVING STATE

DRIVES FOR THE UNKNOWN:
the essence of leadership, entrepreneurship, innovation, and career creation

1. **A frontier-pursuit drive*:** Penetrate unknown systems.
2. **A creation / creativity-pursuit drive*:** Bring unknown into existence.
   NATURE IS ENDLESS MULTI-SYSTEM CREATIVITY - LEADERSHIP IS AN EXTENSION

These dynamics form the toolkit for maximizing any human system in the paradigm whether the system is an individual, organization, market, civilization, or process such as leadership development, career management, or organizational change.

10-2 upgraded   © 2006 Lauren Holmes   * addicting talent-based drives

"Leadering™ goes beyond leadership, beyond the heart of every religion, to the ultimate spiritual attainment sought by humanity."   SVP and Group Executive, IBM

11 OPERATING THE LEADERING™ PARADIGM:
Action-Learning Experimentation

Action-learning experimentation with the Leadering™ paradigm is encouraged for the rest of your life to accelerate the advancement of your functionality and achievement.

LEADERING SUPPORT   info@leadering.com

EDUCATION: **Leadering.com   Leadering Expertise Development**
Educational support for such things as speeding and integrating the paradigm shift, Leadering's paradigm personalization exercises, identifying client strategies for peak legacy, growth, and re-centring to core strength, action-learning experimentation, and breaking through frontiering and adaptivity challenges.

APPLICATION: **Frontiering.com   Leadering Legacy-Making Services**
On your behalf, multi-disciplinary experts will design, launch, and accelerate companies, philanthropic organizations, careers, and fields of study or invention personalized in Leadering terms for your peak legacy until you feel you comfortable taking over. Alternatively, we can support you in launching your own structure(s) through which to achieve your peak legacy.

RECRUITMENT: **Become a Leadering Services Provider**
If you wish to provide products and services through either Leadering.com or Frontiering.com you are invited to email the following to info@leadering.com: your proposed offerings, your credentials, and a brief summary of your personal peak legacy findings from Leadering's flow maximization exercises (*Leadering Visuals Two*, recordings 10-18).

---

12 LEADERING - A POWER TOOL FOR LEADERS or SYSTEM MAXIMIZERS
25. Capitalizing on human systems for goal achievement   24 minutes   10 figures

Recording 25: Power Tool for Leaders and System Maximizers 216

LEADERING™ LEADERS OR SYSTEM MAXIMIZERS

Maximize, advance, integrate, adapt, co-evolve, and capitalize on human systems to achieve synergistic goal realities

Metaphor 1: the electrons and nucleus of an atom form an integrated system defined by a single information structure.

- System-Based

- Core-Based, Talent-Based, & Internally Referenced

- Flow-based
  (a system's peak-performing, peak-advancing state)

- Extending nature's systems maximization dynamics:
  a multi-system approach:
      opportunistic synergy, adaptation, co-evolution
      quantum leap advancement and problem resolution
      expansive perspective

- A single systems maximization toolkit* applied to all human systems including one's own.

* The Leadering™ toolkit includes an integrated system of meta-competencies, drives, reflexes, belief systems, identities, dynamics from nature's systems maximization process,** a quantum-leap operating style, and peak-performing, peak-advancing flow states.

** Metaphor 2: how nature maximizes and advances systems within the human body.

25-1 © 2006 Lauren Holmes

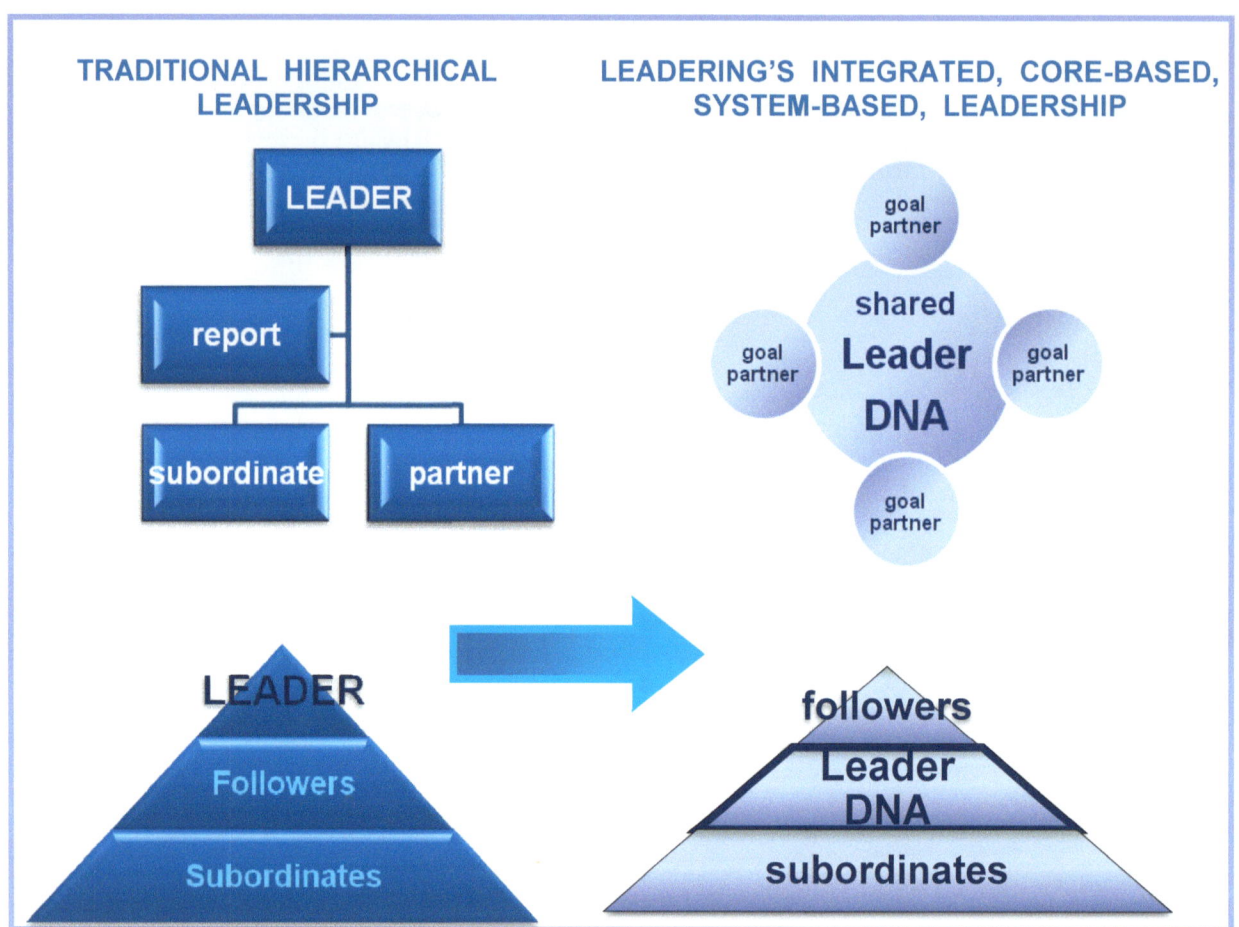

Leadering™ Simplifies Leadership to its Dynamics

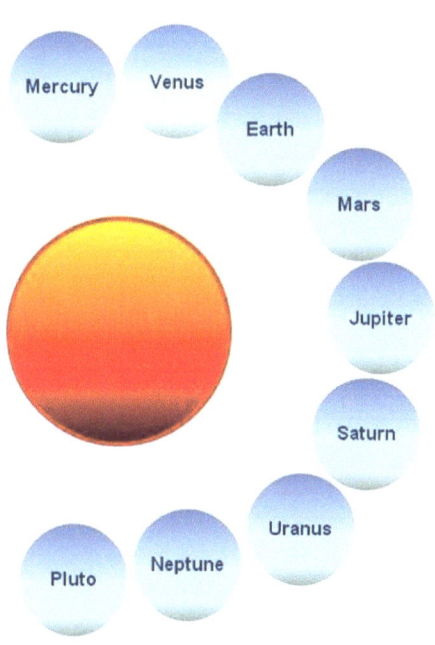

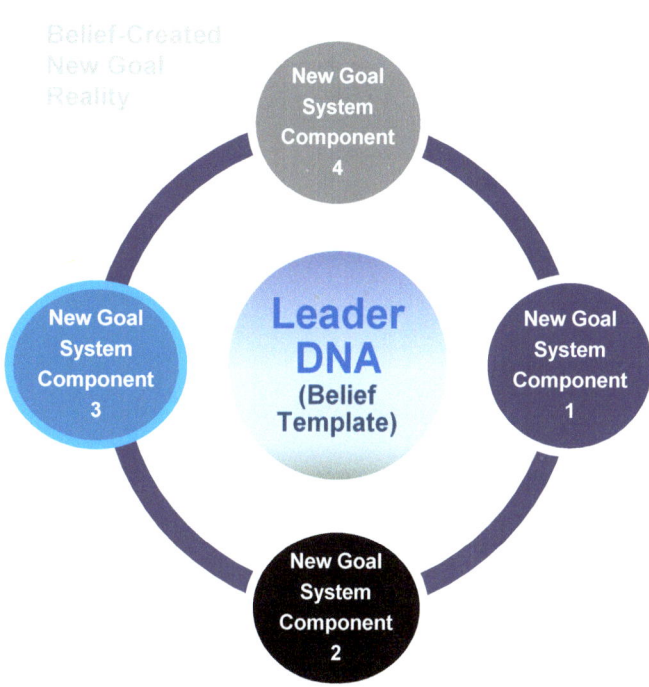

Traditional Leadership
Metaphor: Sun-Planet Relationship

The sun locks the planets in by force. It directs planet movement. However, the cores of the planets are unchanged by the sun and the core of the sun is unchanged by the planets. Neither the sun nor the planets benefit from each other. There is no synergy whereby the whole is greater than the sum of the parts.

Leadering's Core-Based Leadership
Metaphor: DNA or genes defining a human cell

In the Leadering Paradigm, a leader's beliefs and decision-making systems are replicated in individual or organizational systems so that their natural operation will result in achieving a goal in the same way the leader would accomplish it personally.

Rather than a leader acting on others, leaders with their follower individuals and systems operate as a single integrated system with a shared belief template for creating the goal reality. It is about multi-system reality creation.

The leader's belief template must be strong enough and clear enough to define this new multi-component system and its goal reality. A non-leader can use the same approach to capitalize on relevant human systems. By extending one's capabilities with those of other systems one can achieve beyond one's potential.

Beliefs create reality in the Leadering paradigm. Just as in nature, there must always be a blueprint or information structure defining the expression. Human cells and the human body are examples. Beliefs (not thoughts) are how we lock in the new blueprint or, metaphorically, the new DNA. If the information structure does not change inside, nothing will express differently outside . . . . no matter how much action is taken. This is why passionate entrepreneurs can succeed where brilliant experts fail.

© 2006 Lauren Holmes

Traditional Leadership-Development Targets

COMPETENCIES and SKILLS

- develop and deliver value
- command and control
- planning (strategic, tactical, vision)
- trend analysis
- financial management
- marketing/sales management
- customer relationship mgt - CRM
- IT management
- operations management
- project management
- performance improvement
- organization learning

- risk management
- decision-making
- problem resolution
- process management
- business process reengineering
- change management
- HR management
- team building
- relationship building / maintenance
- conflict resolution
- globalization

© 2006 Lauren Holmes

Leadering™ Targets

META-COMPETENCIES and DRIVES
shared by leaders, entrepreneurs, innovators, and high achievers

Systems-Based and Core-Based Operation
systems thinking, relational thinking, big-picture thinking, conceptual skills, belief system management, model development and application, system co-evolution and adaptation, leadership (advancing human systems in opportunistic synergy)

Accelerating and Continuous Development
- conditioned reflexes installed to trigger multi-front, life-long advancement and leadership development.
- addictive drives installed to pull one to growth.
- learning to learn, mental agility, adaptivity, expanding self-expression and self-awareness, belief engineering, expanding consciousness

Improved and Improving Cognitive Capabilities
- thinking: conceptual, inductive, deductive, abstract, big-picture, relational
- learning to learn, mental agility, pattern recognition, internally referenced, emotional intelligence, use of models, theories, and inferences

Expertise with Ambiguity and the Unknown
- **pioneering**: penetrating the unknown
- **creativity/innovation**: bringing unknown into being

systems thinking, informationless decision-making, abstract thinking, conceptual skills, pattern recognition, trend perception, change detection, environmental scanning, problem reframing, ambiguity resolution

Improved Performance
flow (our peak performance state), enhanced functionality, systems-based operation, accelerated implementation through quantum leap change management

Addictive Drives cultivated and capitalized upon by Leadering™
(the more you use them, the more you want to use them):
- Drives to: learning, pioneering, creativity, innovation, meaning, positive emotions, adaptivity, creativity, learning knowledge, achievement, flow, (the optimal experience), self-expression, self-knowledge, advancement, unity, growth
- Drives to using and improving your key talents - a must for operating at your full potential

---

Meta-competencies or *enduring competencies* are systems of knowledge, skills, and strategies which facilitate the acquisition and use of competencies.

Traditional leadership development addresses competencies and skills Leadering™ addresses leader dynamics and meta-competencies.

Traditionally, leaders are developed bottom up skill by skill Leadering™ uses a single paradigm shift to install an integrated system of meta-competencies, drives, reflexes, and beliefs.

Traditionally, senior leaders use different meta-competencies. Leadering™ offers a single systems maximization toolkit for use by everyone on every human system thus unifying organizations around a single culture and modus operandi. Leadership becomes distributed.

Leadering™ Targets

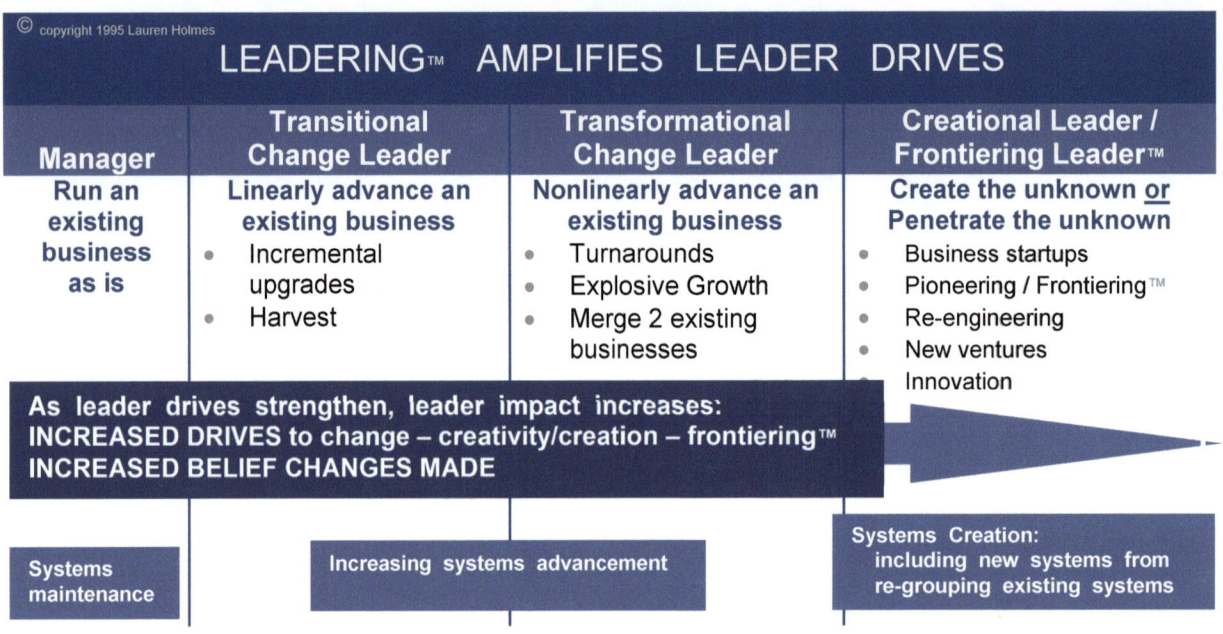

Managers run existing systems ➡ Leaders create and advance human systems

As individuals advance along the leadership development continuum,
their ability to advance reality increases.
If there is no change in beliefs, there is no change in reality.
If there is no change on reality, leadership has not occurred.
The magnitude of change is the measure of leadership in the Leadering™ paradigm.

Leadering™ Targets

Integrated Leadership and Organizational Development

One Leadering™ Systems Maximization Toolkit* for every human system
Individuals, emerging leaders, world leaders, and leaders at every level use the same toolkit. Organizations can therefore use Leadering™ to unify around a single culture and modus operandi from top to bottom.

- The Leadering™ toolkit includes an integrated system of meta-competencies, drives, reflexes, belief systems, identities, dynamics from nature's systems maximization process, a quantum-leap operating style, and peak-performing, peak-advancing flow states.

25-8A © 2006 Lauren Holmes

One Human Systems Development Continuum and Process

| Individual Development | = | Leadership Development | = | Leadership Development | = | Organizational Development | = | Career/Talent Development |

- The natural development continuum for individuals and leaders is the same.
- Advancing one's own system is the same process as leading/advancing other systems
- Leadering™ launches several natural growth continuums and mechanisms which continuously advance individuals, leaders, and organizational human systems over their lifetime.

25-8B © 2006 Lauren Holmes

Motivated Leadership and Organization Development
Because leadership development and individual development are the same systems maximization process in the Leadering™ paradigm, leadership development becomes a byproduct of pursuing one's natural growth continuums. Self-motivation for personal advancement thus inadvertently pulls individuals to meet organizational needs for leadership development.

25-8C © 2006 Lauren Holmes

Leadering™ Targets

> ### Leadering™ Reactivates Leader Drives
> We are all born with the drives
> that energize natural leaders

Drives for creativity, innovation, frontiering™, advancement, learning, achievement, adaptation, self-expression, and talent-based flow

Our drives hook us to nature's endless evolutionary flow
with all the other successful living systems.

**All are drives for penetrating the unknown
or bringing the unknown into existence
— the essence of leadership —**

A NASA test for hiring innovative engineers and scientists
was given to 1,600 children as they aged:
Leader drives at age   5:   98%
Leader drives at age 10:   30%
Leader drives at age 15:   12%
Leader drives of 280,000 adults: 2%

Leader drives are culturally deterred.

The Leadering™ paradigm shift *reactivates* the drives underlying natural leadership

© 2001 Lauren Holmes

Leadering™ Performance Improvement: Change Management

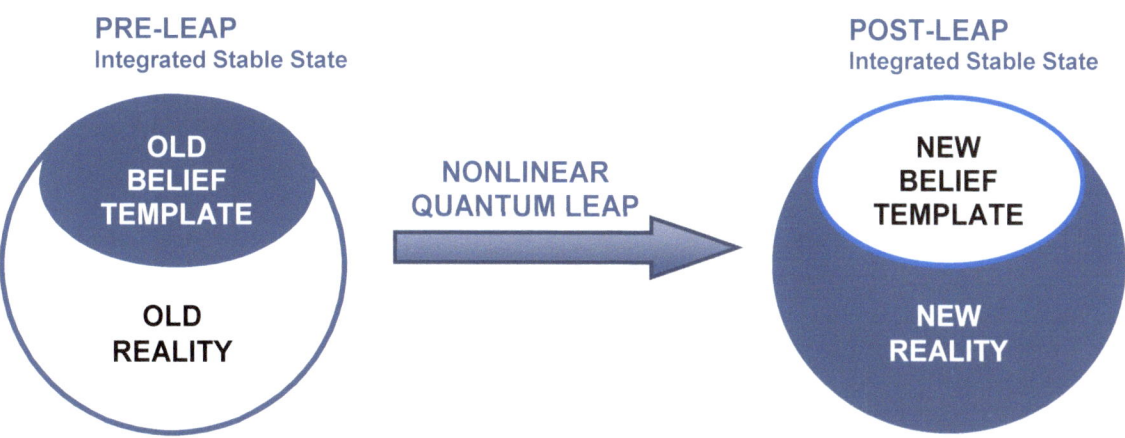

A quantum leap is a belief system exchange
enabling a reality exchange

© 2001 Lauren Holmes

USERS GUIDE 1-12

12 THE LEADERING™ USERS GUIDE

1. Powering your paradigm shift — 14 minutes
2. Only need to be a paradigm driver not a mechanic — 8 minutes
3. Timing for progressing through the program — 5 minutes
4. Overwhelm is a Leadering™ tool for stretching you to new meta-competencies — 3 minutes
5. Falling asleep during the recordings: What is really going on? — 4 minutes
6. Visuals: their importance — 3 minutes
7. Personalization Exercises Tips — 1 minute
8. Leadering™ Program Support — 4 minutes
9. Arguments for beliefs create reality concept — 8 minutes
10. Examples of cascading quantum leaps: incited by a quantum leap to a belief-created reality. The strengthening of the beliefs and belief engineering capabilities to create and develop leaders. — 13 minutes
11. How Leadering™ Works — 5 minutes
12. The Leadering™ frequency workout gym — 5 minutes

We welcome recommendations for additional topics for the User's Guide which you think would help others with the Leadering™ paradigm shift: info@leadering.com

LEADERING VISUALS ONE
Paradigm Shift to Peak Legacy

LEADERING SUPPORT   info@leadering.com

EDUCATION: **Leadering.com**   Leadering™ Expertise Development

Educational support for such things as speeding and integrating the paradigm shift, Leadering's paradigm personalization exercises, identifying client strategies for peak legacy, growth, and re-centring to core strength, action-learning experimentation, and breaking through frontiering and adaptivity challenges.

APPLICATION: **Frontiering.com**   Leadering Legacy-Making Services and Products

On your behalf, multi-disciplinary experts will design, launch, and accelerate companies, philanthropic organizations, careers, and fields of study or invention personalized in Leadering terms for your peak legacy until you feel you comfortable taking over. Alternatively, we can support you in launching your own structure(s) through which to achieve your peak legacy.

RECRUITMENT: **Become a Leadering Support Services Provider**

If you wish to provide products and services through either Leadering.com or Frontiering.com you are invited to email the following to info@leadering.com: your proposed offerings, your credentials, and a brief summary of your personal peak legacy findings from Leadering's flow maximization exercises (*Leadering Visuals Two*, recordings 10-18).

The Development of the Leadering Paradigm Shift Program
Unprecedented transformation for unparalleled legacy

Harness the capabilities of other systems
to advance our world beyond your potential

A Childhood Vision
Leadering™ began as a vision for the future of humanity which Lauren Holmes formulated for a high school project.

Experimenting with Leadership
Lauren developed her expertise for organizational and industry change leadership as a top-rated employee in some of the world's largest multinationals (IBM and global financial institutions).

Mid-1980s to Early 1990s:
Learning from Top Global Change Leaders
To broaden her knowledge of leadership and industry and organizational change, Lauren headed an executive search firm dedicated exclusively to the recruitment of change leaders at the board, CEO, and senior executive levels. Lauren interviewed hundreds of top leaders from major global companies, both for requisitioned searches and in partnership with the large relocation counseling firms dealing with the massive release of executives during the recession of the early 90s.

Lauren Holmes

**Leadering's Creator,
Developer and Proponent**

1990-1993: Formulating the first iteration of Leadering™
Back-to-back interviews with so many executives enabled Lauren to realize that leaders are not operating the way most leadership development theories have specified. As an evolutionary anthropologist and primatologist trained in objective observation, Lauren came to understand leadership differently. She then found science to confirm her observations in such fields as quantum physics, chaos theory, catastrophe theory, the biological sciences, systems biology, systems theory, emergence theory, and evolutionary theory. These are the scientific foundations underpinning Leadering™ which are transparent to practitioners. No scientific discoveries to date disprove Leadering™. In fact, Leadering™ identifies plausible directions in which many scientific fields will eventually advance and how to speed that advance.

With the dearth of jobs due to fear-driven downsizing rather than smart frontiering™ and creation, so much excellent talent was discarded by society. Sadly, the leaders and change facilitators who could have rescued so many were the first to go. Both societal and individual systems were traumatized. **Leadering's mission was born.** With new ways of operating, new functionality, and especially with frontiering™ capability, individual and societal systems could adapt, advance, co-create, synergize, and co-evolve more quickly to avoid damage and suffering. If successful, a maximized individual working within his/her *field of fascination* to achieve *peak legacy* - one's greatest contribution to society - could become an achievable new human right. It would also be the smartest strategy for maximizing global human resources in the service of the world we all share.

The Development of Leadering   228

1990-2006:   Advancing the Leadering™ technology, toolkit, products, services:
Many different corporate identities were required to test out every element of the integrated Leadering™ paradigm as it stands today at Leadering.com (education) and Frontiering.com (legacy implementation). Action-learning experimentation conforming to scientific method was used.

1990-1991:   First Action-Learning Experimentation: Frontiering™
The first test of the foundational multi-system elements of Leadering™ related to its methodology for enabling the penetration of new territory safely and expeditiously - the underpinning system of meta-competencies and drives shared by adept leaders, entrepreneurs, innovators, or high achievers. This test was achieved by establishing an unprecedented global recycled plastics distribution company for which Lauren Holmes had no credentials or background. Frontiering™ would therefore be required. As the company became successful and globally known within that community, the frontiering™ experiment was terminated. Leadering™ had passed its first test.

1991-1995:   Business Professionals: One-on-one
After the first experiment, Lauren determined it would be faster to support others in their application of Leadering™ to their own goals than for her to continue to set up her own experiments. Rather than risk her connections and standing in the corporate world, Lauren found safe testing grounds managing the careers of business professionals. She used Leadering™ techniques to identify the right client at the right time for each aspect of Leadering™ to be tested.

1995-2003:   Corporate Executives: One-on-one
Leadering™ services were applied to the careers of corporate executives locally and then internationally through the corporate identities of Teamlink Canada and TeamLink International.

Experimentation was predominantly with executives of multinationals because they usually had well-developed cognitive skills and other capabilities allowing Lauren to experiment at the upper end of the meta-competencies that Leadering™ is designed to instill in practitioners. Multi-national clients included: Royal Bank, AT&T, IBM, RIM, Bell, BBDO, Young & Rubicam, Canadian Imperial Bank of Commerce and Bank of Montreal. Experimentation also included creating concentrations of individuals using Leadering™ in order to learn about the Leadering™ culture of an organization operating in the Leadering™ paradigm.

2001 to 2005:   Non-Corporate Individuals *en masse:* One-to-many
Lauren needed a safe territory outside of corporations to test out a number of aspects of Leadering™ and Leadering™ distribution. Accordingly, she wrote a book entitled *Peak Evolution, Beyond Peak Performance and Peak Experience* (2001) around which a global community could form. *Peak Evolution* presents the 1992 iteration of Leadering™ in non-corporate terms that would not be intimidating to the general public. Naturality.Net, LLC was the corporate identity used to create this community and it was advertised in the book. There were 4000 people on the global mailing list within the first 4 months and it was an Amazon.com bestseller.

Areas examined through the Naturality.Net community included:
- to develop/test the means to impact more people more quickly with Leadering™ methodologies and technologies.
- to develop/test one-to-many techniques where, unlike in corporations, participants were strangers
- to develop/test ways in which Leadering™ could impact larger groups of individuals to enable it to be used as a tool for leaders and achievers to maximize and advance organizations to achieve goals.

- to test Leadering-based group processes on many fronts
- to determine how to press natural levers to trigger group change in the way done to this point for individuals
- to experiment with community tools such as chat rooms, discussion and bulletin boards, and other group communication and work tools.
- to experiment with using Leadering™ for community-building inside and outside of corporations
- to market-test Leadering™
- to determine what the competing technologies, theories, and cultural norms were in the market place and how they caused confusion for understanding Leadering™,
- to find ways to circumvent market-related issues: competing technologies, theories, modes of operation, cultural norms, and existing infrastructures. The goal was to ensure that Leadering™ did not conflict with culture, religion, science, and society so that everyone could operate in the Leadering paradigm.
- to test new mass delivery mechanisms: teleclinics, telecalls, weekly and periodic programs, audios, videos, support systems and the best structures for achieving and operationalizing the Leadering™ paradigm shift. These were international to determine the effects of cultural differences
- to develop Lauren's own expertise in a number of areas: the speed and magnitude of group or community transformation, working with non-executives to complement her career-long focus on executives, creating and sustaining a global community, the application of Leadering™ technology to group programs and processes, and the ability to transform groups *en masse* with Leadering™ without the opportunity to use the personal goals and events of each individual's life she had had access to in her Leadering™ work to this point.
- to develop the exercises and techniques that could personalize the Leadering™ paradigm and paradigm shift to each person to empower the generic paradigm shift offered in the audio program (re last item in previous point)
- to test whether the Leadering™ paradigm shift could better be accomplished through audios and visuals. Lauren experimented with audio recordings as the means to raise people's frequencies and thus the breadth of information and the amount of interconnectedness they are able to perceive and assimilate.
Expanded consciousness is key to Leadering's ability to raise functionality
- to create/develop various programs to experiment with how each of the meta-competencies shared by leaders, entrepreneurs, innovators, and top performers could best be instilled.
- to experiment with harnessing the co-evolution of human systems for peak legacy, a key function of leaders and achievers who want to extend their capabilities with those of other systems to achieve beyond their potential.

2002-2007 Corporate Individuals and Groups
One-to-one and One-to-many Programs
Organizational Development Services

What was learned about Leadering™ at Naturality.net, LLC was taken back to the corporate world through Lauren's next corporate identities: Frontiering Leadership Group and ReCareering™. This corporate-based experimentation identified the need for the Leadering™ paradigm shift audio program now offered. Natural leaders feel that the Leadering™ paradigm perfectly defines how they operate. Therefore, many of them requested a tool which allows them to quickly upgrade their organizations to operate as they do. Putting all key people through the Leadering™ paradigm shift program accomplished this.

2005-2007   Leadering™ audio program development

2007   Leadering™ audio program release to individual executive clients
In 2007, the audio-based Leadering™ Paradigm Shift Program replaced *Peak Evolution*. The initial target market was individual corporate executives.

2008-2009   6-week subscriptions to Leadering™ sold to the public and corporations through Leadering.com
Peak Evolution was temporarily taken out of print to facilitate the transition and minimize confusion since Leadering has no overlap with the approach used in *Peak Evolution* even though their paradigms are consistent. However, a second edition and eBook version will be re-released in 2010. The experimentation with Leadering™ continued, especially with an eye to what kind of support people, services and products would be required for a public rollout globally.

2010   Leadering™ program sold to the public through Amazon.com
Educational support for those trying to master Leadering will still be offered through Leadering.com.
Support services include
- identifying client strategies for peak legacy and peak growth
- promoting the re-centering of the individual to the strength of their natural core
- facilitating the paradigm shift and providing support for the Leadering™ exercises
- integrating the paradigm shift into the life of the organization or individual
- empowering sustained operation and accelerated growth within the paradigm, and
- promoting action-learning experimentation associated with the paradigm shift and ongoing operation.

At Frontiering.com, a diversity of Leadering™ service providers supports those wanting to apply Leadering™. Leadering™ is used to design, launch, and accelerate companies, philanthropic organizations, fields of study or invention, and careers customized to an individual's or company's peak legacy, their peak contribution to advancing the world. The foundations are provided for clients to use Leadering™ to break through new frontiers in precisely the territory that fascinates them and to be rewarded for it. Alternatively, we can support you in launching your own structure(s) through which to achieve your peak legacy.

Leadering™ is now positioned to address its mission for creating value, meaning, and progress - maximizing the lives of individuals while maximizing their contribution to advancing our world.

Unprecedented transformation

Peak legacy.

Impact beyond your potential.

www.ingramcontent.com/pod-product-compliance
Lightning Source LLC
Chambersburg PA
CBHW042129010526
44111CB00031B/42